How the French Invented Love

ALSO BY MARILYN YALOM

The American Resting Place: Four Hundred Years of History Through Our
Cemeteries and Burial Grounds, with photographs by Reid S. Yalom

Birth of the Chess Queen

A History of the Wife

A History of the Breast

Blood Sisters: The French Revolution in Women's Memory

Maternity, Mortality, and the Literature of Madness

Le temps des orages: Aristocrates, bourgeoises, et paysannes racontent

How the French Invented Love

Nine Hundred Years
of Passion and Romance

MARILYN YALOM

HARPER PERENNIAL

NEW YORK • LONDON • TORONTO • SYDNEY • NEW DELHI • AUCKLAND

HARPER ⬤ PERENNIAL

HOW THE FRENCH INVENTED LOVE. Copyright © 2012 by Marilyn Yalom. All rights reserved. Printed in the United States of America. No part of this book may be used or reproduced in any manner whatsoever without written permission except in the case of brief quotations embodied in critical articles and reviews. For information address HarperCollins Publishers, 10 East 53rd Street, New York, NY 10022.

HarperCollins books may be purchased for educational, business, or sales promotional use. For information please write: Special Markets Department, Harper-Collins Publishers, 10 East 53rd Street, New York, NY 10022.

FIRST EDITION

Designed by Michael P. Correy

Library of Congress Cataloging-in-Publication Data is available upon request.

ISBN 978-0-06-204831-8

12 13 14 15 16   OV/RRD   10 9 8 7 6 5 4 3 2 1

NEITHER YOU WITHOUT ME, NOR I WITHOUT YOU

Ni vous sans moi, ni moi sans vous

Le lai du chèvrefeuille, Marie de France, twelfth century

Contents

A NOTE TO THE READER

Contents

A NOTE TO THE READER

How THE FRENCH LOVE LOVE! It OCCUPIES a privileged place in their national identity, on a par with fashion, food, and human rights. A French man or woman without desire is considered defective, like someone missing the sense of taste or smell. For hundreds of years, the French have championed themselves as guides to the art of love through their literature, paintings, songs, and cinema.

We English speakers often turn to French expressions for the vocabulary of love. We refer to tongue-locked embraces as "French kissing." We have adopted the words "rendezvous," "tête-à-tête," and "ménage à trois" to suggest intimacy with a French flavor. Our words "courtesy" and "gallantry" come directly from the French, and "amour" doesn't need to be translated. Americans, like much of the world, continue to be fascinated with anything French that promises to improve our physical appearance or our love lives.

ONE DEFINING FEATURE OF LOVE À LA *française* is its forthright insistence on sexual pleasure. Even older French men and women today cling to a vision of love grounded in the flesh, as indicated by a recent poll of American and French citizens aged fifty to sixty-four. According to a study published in the January–February 2010 issue of *AARP The Magazine*, only 34 percent of the French group agreed with the statement that "true love can exist without a radiant sex life," as compared to 83 percent of American respondents. A 49 percent difference in opinion on the need for sex in love is a startling statistic! This French emphasis on carnal satisfaction strikes tighter-laced Americans as deliciously naughty.

Moreover, the French idea of love includes the darker elements that Americans are reluctant to admit as normal: jealousy, suffering, extramarital sex, multiple lovers, crimes of passion, disillusion, even violence. Perhaps more than anything, the French accept the premise that sexual passion has its own justification. Love simply doesn't have the same moral overlay that we Americans expect it to have.

From the medieval tale of Tristan and Iseult to modern films like *Mississippi Mermaid*, *The Woman Next Door*, and *Leaving*, love is represented as a *fatum*—an irresistible fate against which it is useless to rebel. Morality proves to be a weak opponent when confronted with erotic love.

In this book I trace *l'amour à la française*—love French-style—from the emergence of romance in the twelfth century until our own era. What the French invented nine hundred years ago, and have been reinventing through the ages, has traveled far beyond the borders of France. Americans of my generation thought of the French as purveyors of love. From their books, songs, magazines, and movies, we concocted a picture of sexy romance that was at odds with the airbrushed 1950s American model. How did the French get that way? This book was written to answer that question.

How the French Invented Love

TOMBEAU D'HELOÏSE ET D'ABEILLARD

Abélard and Héloïse, Patron Saints of French Lovers

THROUGHOUT MY LIFE, GOD KNOWS, IT HAS BEEN YOU,
RATHER THAN GOD, WHOM I FEARED OFFENDING,
YOU, RATHER THAN HIM, I WANTED TO PLEASE.

Héloïse to Abélard, circa 1133

A BÉLARD AND HÉLOÏSE ARE AS FAMILIAR TO the French as Romeo and Juliet are to Americans and Brits. This pair of lovers, living in the early twelfth century, left behind a story so bizarre that it reads like a gothic novel. The astonishing letters they wrote each other in Latin and Abélard's autobiography, *Historia calamitatum* (The Story of My Misfortunes), have become charter texts in the history of French love.

Abélard was an itinerant cleric, scholar, philosopher, and the most popular teacher of his age. He became famous in his twenties and thirties for his speeches on dialectics (logic) and theology. And his good looks didn't hurt. Like rock stars today, he brought out adoring crowds in his appearances as a public speaker. Before the establishment of universities in France, there were urban schools that rose up around celebrated scholars, and the one Abélard created in Paris brought together students from every part of Christendom.

Héloïse, the niece and ward of a church canon living in Paris, was already renowned in her teens for her brilliant mind and advanced learning. By then, she had already mastered Latin and would go on to become conversant in Greek and Hebrew. Attracted by her singular talents, Abélard devised a surefire method to seduce her: he would lodge in the canon's house and give her private lessons. It did not take long for them to fall into each other's arms and develop a mutual, searing passion.

During the winter of 1115–1116, when they first became lovers, Héloïse would have been barely fifteen and Abélard around thirty-seven. Yet he claimed to have been celibate before their encounter and was totally unprepared for the overpowering force of their shared entrancement: "With our books open before us, more words of love than of our reading passed between us, and more kissing than teaching. My hands strayed oftener to her bosom than to the pages; love drew our eyes to look on each other more than reading kept them on our texts."[1]

For Héloïse, their love was a rapturous paradise she could never erase from her mind: "The pleasures of lovers which we shared have been too sweet—they can never displease me, and can scarcely be banished from my thoughts."

But there was a downside to erotic love. Abélard's work began to suffer, and his students began to complain of his absentmindedness. More occupied with composing love songs for Héloïse than with making theological pronouncements, he became deaf to the rumors that rose up around them. Finally, Héloïse's uncle could no longer remain blind to the affair, and the lovers were obliged to separate, but not before Héloïse had become pregnant. Abélard sent her away to his family in Brittany, where she remained throughout her pregnancy, while he stayed in Paris and faced her uncle's wrath. The men agreed that the lovers should marry so as to repair her dishonor. No one paid any attention to Héloïse's objections: she would have preferred to remain Abélard's mistress rather than become his wife, since she knew that matrimony would be disastrous for his career, and she shared the general view that love could not thrive within marriage.

Nevertheless, soon after the birth of their son, named Astrolabe, Abélard and Héloïse were secretly wed in church in the presence of her uncle and a few witnesses. They wanted the marriage to remain secret so that Abélard's reputation would not be ruined. But this covert situation did not satisfy Héloïse's uncle, with whom she was still living. When he began to abuse her with vicious words and unrestrained blows, Abélard decided to place her temporarily in Argenteuil Abbey, the same convent where she had been educated as a girl. Believing that Abélard had sent Héloïse to the abbey to be rid of her, her uncle had him punished by a monstrous act: at night while Abélard was sleeping, servants stole into his room and castrated him. Castrated! Even our worst-taste horror movies are reluctant to portray such a gory crime.

I PROBABLY FIRST HEARD THE NAMES OF Abélard and Héloïse in the Cole Porter song "It Was Just One of Those Things" from the 1935 musical *Jubilee*: "As Abélard said to Héloïse, / Don't forget to drop me a line, please."

That song was popular throughout the mid-twentieth century when sophisticated theatergoers were expected to recognize such references. But the names meant nothing to me until I studied medieval French literature at Wellesley College in the 1950s and read the well-known "Ballade of the Ladies of Bygone Times" written by the fifteenth-century poet François Villon:

> *Where is the learned Héloïse*
> *For whom Abélard was gelded*
> *And made a monk at Saint Denis?*
> *For her true love he bore those trials.*[2]

I looked up the word *châtré*, translated here as "gelded," though "castrated" is closer to the original, and then I got up the nerve to ask my professor for further explanation. Professor Andrée Bruel, a hulking female who had no problem demonstrating the gestures used by knights in battle, awkwardly explained that Pierre Abélard had indeed lost his testicles at the hands of thugs engaged by Héloïse's uncle. Then she cut the matter short and referred me to the letters exchanged by the two lovers and to Abélard's autobiography.

I somehow managed to read these texts (in a French translation from the Latin) between my regular class assignments and was dumbfounded. How could this teenager—younger than I was—have surrendered so completely to a man more than twice her age, and a cleric to boot! How could they have defied the strictures of the Roman Catholic Church with its known contempt for human passion and its belief that making love, unless performed by a married couple for the purpose of procreation, was sinful fornication? How could they have endured societal and family pressures that penalized unwed mothers and married clerics? How did they survive the pain and ignominy of Abélard's emasculation?

I now know that Abélard's gruesome mutilation would not have prevented him from living with Héloïse as her husband. Having been married within the church, they were legal spouses in every sense of the word, and the church granted annulment only when a marriage had not been consummated. Yet this domestic scenario was not to be. Abélard instructed Héloïse to enter the convent permanently and to take religious vows, which he would also take as a monk. Why did he make this decision and why did she follow his command?

Long after their separation, Abélard tried to justify his actions in his *Historia calamitatum*, written in the form of a consolation letter to a friend. He explained:

> I admit that it was shame and confusion in my remorse and misery rather than any devout wish for conversion which brought me to seek shelter in a monastery cloister. Héloïse had already agreed to take the veil in obedience to my wishes and entered a convent. So we both put on the religious habit, I in the Abbey of St Denis and she in the Convent of Argenteuil.

His letter to a supposed friend was circulated among those who could read Latin and eventually came to the attention of Héloïse. By that time, she was past thirty and had been living apart from Abélard for about fifteen years, first at Argenteuil where she had become its prioress, and later as the abbess of the Oratory of the Paraclete, founded by none other than her erstwhile husband Abélard. Still, her passion had lost none of its ferocity, and she reproached him for having made no effort to contact or comfort her, as he had done for his anonymous friend.

"Tell me one thing, if you can," she cried out. "Why after our entry into religion, which was your decision alone, have I been so neglected and forgotten by you? . . . I will tell you what I think and indeed the world suspects. It was desire, not affection which bound you to me, the flame of lust rather than love."

Héloïse zeroes in on a distinction that will be made over and over again as we consider variations on the theme of love. Are men motivated mainly by physical desire and women more by their emotions? Or put more grossly, are men led by their penises and women by their hearts? A combination of physical desire and emotional attachment is what Héloïse felt for Abélard, whereas she thought he had experienced only lust. This sounds like a difference between females and males that is still much debated today. (I'm thinking in particular of the books by neuropsychiatrist Louann Brizendine, *The Female Brain* and *The Male Brain*, which point out that a man has two and a half times as much brain space devoted to sexual pursuit as a woman, while the female brain's empathy system is considerably more active than the male's.[3]) Certainly, Héloïse had held onto her "love beyond all bounds" for Abélard long after he had withdrawn from her.

Fifteen years earlier, she had taken the veil for his sake, without any inclination of her own, and her absolute allegiance to him rather than to God had not changed over time. Even as the abbess of the Paraclete, she still cast him in the role of "master," "father," and "husband," with complete power over her fate. Being a woman in those days meant being subservient to men. This was true in both personal and religious life, though some female religious orders managed to establish considerable autonomy for themselves and some forceful women were able to reign over their husbands. The one place no one could control, not even Héloïse herself, was her unconscious.

In her letters to Abélard, she confessed to erotic desires that had not disappeared with the years, whereas he had accepted his castration as a form of divine punishment. Fifty-four at the time of the letters and lacking the body parts that contribute to virility, Abélard looked back on their love affair and marriage as past history, which had been entirely replaced by the love of God. He counseled Héloïse to try to follow his example. But Héloïse was then only thirty-two and still pined for lost pleasures. While she fulfilled her role as abbess with outward distinction, she remained in her imagination Abélard's wife and lover, consumed by lubricious memories:

Wherever I turn they are always there before my eyes, bringing with them awakened longings and fantasies which will not even let me sleep. Even during the celebration of the Mass, when our prayers should be purer, lewd visions of those pleasures take such a hold upon my unhappy soul that my thoughts are on their wantonness instead of on prayers. I should be groaning over the sins I have committed, but I can only sigh for what I have lost. Everything we did and also the times and places are stamped on my heart along with your image, so that I live through it all again with you.

Héloïse's impassioned cry has echoed through the ages. She speaks for all women who have loved without reserve and then found themselves deprived of the one they loved. Death, divorce, abandonment, physical impairment have reduced countless women, and men, to lives of unquiet desperation. Separated so abruptly and so grotesquely, Héloïse and Abélard lived out their remaining years as members of the religious orders that had taken them in, even if Abélard was constantly at war with fellow theologians and Héloïse was ceaselessly tormented by longings of the flesh. Already, during their lifetime, they were regarded with awe by their contemporaries, and in later centuries they acquired a devoted following who treated them like patron saints. Undoubtedly, Abélard's castration contributed to their sacred aura, since bodily mutilation of some sort—think of Saint Sebastian's arrow-pierced chest or Saint Agatha's amputated breasts—is often associated with sainthood. It was not difficult to consider the famous pair, Abélard with his debilitating wound and Héloïse with her mental anguish, as martyrs to love.

Following Abélard's request, he was buried at the Paraclete in 1144, to be joined by Héloïse two decades later, on May 16, 1164. Later, at the time of the French Revolution, when the convent was sold and the buildings demolished, their bones were taken to the nearby Church of Saint-Laurent in Nogent-sur-Seine. In 1817, their remains were transferred to the Père-Lachaise Cemetery in Paris, where they now lie under a soaring Gothic-style tomb. In time, lovers began to make pilgrimages to their grave. The last time I visited it, I saw a bouquet of daffodils and a small card asking the long-dead couple for their blessings.

CHAPTER ONE

Courtly Love

How the French Invented Romance

IN MY OPINION, A PERSON IS NOT WORTH ANYTHING
IF HE OR SHE DOES NOT DESIRE LOVE.
Bernart de Ventadorn, activity circa 1147–1170

M Y FRENCH FRIEND MARIANNE MARRIED PIERRE IN 1977, soon after a divorce that gave her sole custody of her twin daughters. She was twenty-nine at the time, and Pierre was forty-nine. Pierre's sister, Jeanne, warned him that with such an age difference, he was likely to become a cuckold. Pierre responded that if that time were to come, he would survey the field of available men and choose a lover for his wife. Marianne did not wait for Pierre to find her a lover. Some fifteen years into their marriage, she fell in love with Stéphane, a Frenchman of her own age. Stéphane and Marianne did their best to keep their affair secret, but she was seen once too often exiting his apartment, and word got back to Pierre, who was at first incredulous and then enraged. He confronted his wife, asking her to choose between him and her lover. Deeply attached to Pierre, who had helped raise her daughters, but madly in love with Stéphane, she was torn between the two men and could not leave one or the other. Eventually she turned to Pierre's sister, Jeanne, begging her to negotiate an arrangement.

She would stay in the marriage until death, if she were allowed to be out of the house with no questions asked, from four to seven o'clock, every day except Sunday. After many hours of painfully frank talk, Pierre swallowed his pride and accepted her terms. They stayed married for another twelve years, until Pierre became terminally ill, whereupon Marianne nursed him faithfully until he died. She grieved him sincerely and then moved in with Stéphane.

It is, I believe, a quintessentially French story. Since I knew all the parties concerned, I can say that they carried it off with great dignity. Marianne never spoke to me, or to anyone else, about the arrangement: I heard it from Jeanne. Although most of the people in their circle knew that Marianne and Stéphane were lovers, no one ever mentioned it. Everyone kept up appearances following the etiquette of their upper-bourgeois social class.

How is it that Marianne, Pierre, and Stéphane were able to live out this unconventional scenario? Where in French history do we find the origins of such behavior? My mind immediately jumps back to the Middle Ages, to the fervent love stories of Lancelot and Guinevere, and Tristan and Iseult, and other tales of women halved between their husbands and their lovers. If this topos is by now a stock theme, incarnated in such world-famous novels as *Madame Bovary* and *Anna Karenina*, we should not forget that adultery as a literary subject first became fashionable in twelfth-century France.

Yes, we are talking about the same century that encompassed the real-life history of Abélard and Héloïse.

In real life, medieval women were subject to male authority, be it the rule of the father, the husband, or the priest. Remember how Héloïse submitted to absolute decisions made by her uncle and her teacher-lover-husband. Under Abélard's tutelage, she was initiated into sex and love. At his insistence, she went to Brittany to have her baby and gave him up to the care of Abélard's family. She married Abélard in secret despite her reservations about marriage, and she complied with his order to hide out in the convent where she had been raised. She even took the veil at his behest, though she had no sense of a religious vocation. Even such a remarkable woman as Héloïse bowed to the dictates of men. This was undoubtedly the case for almost all medieval women, be they peasants or princesses.

Unlike the marriage of Abélard and Héloïse, most marriages among the nobility and upper bourgeoisie had nothing to do with love. In fact, the very suspicion of love between the unmarried was heavily censured, given the belief that love (*amor* in old French) was an irrational, destructive force. Marriages among the privileged classes were arranged by families in the interest of property and desired kinship, rather than by the future spouses themselves. Girls as young as thirteen or fourteen, but usually fifteen to seventeen, were married off to men of their same social condition, who were generally five to fifteen years older.

But in literature and song things could be different. Twelfth-century lyric poetry and verse narratives responded to the fantasies of women as well as men, especially when women were patrons of the arts—a role they acquired increasingly in regional courts.

Within a few generations, epic poems centering on battles, among them the heroic *Song of Roland* inspired by the First Crusade (1096–1099), gave way to chivalric romances featuring courageous knights and the gracious ladies they adored. If the lady happened to be someone else's wife, well, that just added spice to the story. Indeed, more often than not, the beloved female *was* someone else's wife. It didn't take long for the lady and her lover to assume star billing in the cult of *fin'amor*—a term we usually translate as courtly love. This new vision of amorous relations between the sexes, which first emerged in song and on the page, would ultimately evolve into a model for all Western men and women, with or without the adulterous component. Today we call it romantic love.

Let me pause for an objection. Surely men and women experienced something akin to romantic love before the twelfth century. The Bible tells us that King David lusted after Bathsheba, and that Isaac loved his new wife Rebekah. Ancient Greek tragedy gave us Phaedra, who burned with desire for her stepson Hippolytus, and Medea, whose jealous rage against her husband Jason caused her to murder their children. The Greek poet Sappho petitioned Aphrodite to transform her unrequited ardor for a young woman into reciprocal love, and the philosopher Plato extolled the love of boys as a natural phenomenon for older men. And who can forget Dido's impassioned suicide after Aeneas abandoned her in Virgil's great Latin epic, *The Aeneid*? Or Ovid's rollicking *Art of Love*, which gave advice to randy suitors? It is easy to assume that love, such as we understand it today, has always existed.

Yet something new in the history of love did emerge in France during the 1100s, a cultural explosion that proclaimed the rights of lovers to live out their passion despite all the objections mustered by society and religion. Even the history of Abélard and Héloïse, however rooted in submission to the church and traditional male dominance, was marked by this fledgling spirit that championed love for its own sake.

In medieval stories, ardent lovers find themselves caught in a web of uncontrollable desire, placing them on a collision course with priests, parents, neighbors, and the ever-present husband. We see husbands enraged by wives attracted to other men. We see women making false accusations against the men who reject them. Reasonable men become bewitched by women, who are invariably young, beautiful, and blond. Foolish older women bemoan the loss of their charms and cling to younger men whose eyes search elsewhere. Money, social position, and age weigh in favor of some prospective mates over those who are less endowed. However great the differences between a twelfth-century castle and a contemporary ranch house, all these concerns are still with us. In matters of the heart, we are still kin to the storybook inhabitants of medieval France.

This chapter describes how the French invented and propagated the ideals of courtly love. We start, as we must, in southern France, where troubadours introduced a new kind of song-poem in praise of an honored lady. Next we move to northern France, where minstrels took up troubadour themes and added their own refinements. In the north, at the court of Marie de Champagne, chivalric romances written in verse became the rage, most notably those of Chrétien de Troyes, whose tale of Lancelot and Guinevere would be read and imitated for centuries to come. Marie de Champagne's chaplain, Andreas Capellanus, merits our attention for his *Art of Courtly Love*, which spread the precepts of courtly love throughout medieval Europe. We shall also look at a nasty interaction between a minstrel and a lady in an unusual verse story written by Conon de Béthune. Then we shall move to England, where a mysterious woman, Marie de France, gave poetic voice to many of the trials faced by lovers. To complete this collection of songs, poems, and stories destined for noble audiences, we shall consider laments of the "unhappy wife," popular among the peasantry. This tour of twelfth-century culture will allow me to venture several generalizations that are open to debate.

ONE MEDIEVAL INHABITANT OF SOUTHERN FRANCE HAS been credited with sowing the seeds for the flowering of romantic love in the Western world. In the early twelfth century, William IX, Duke of Aquitaine, created the first troubadour love lyrics. These song-poems written in his native Provençal language focused exclusively on love and especially on the beloved woman, the *domna*. In a dramatic disavowal of traditional practice, William reversed masculine and feminine roles, granting the woman power over the man. Some of his early poems, it is true, reeked of gross misogyny and treated women as little more than "horses" to be ridden for male satisfaction, but other poems introduced the vision of the beloved as a mistress to be served and obeyed. It is this second model that would take root in high culture and spread its tendrils all over Europe.

Before his death in 1127, Duke William was the most powerful nobleman in France. He possessed more land than the king and even refused to pay him homage, as was required by the feudal system. William was known as a rapacious warrior in battles against his neighbors and as the leader of a failed Crusade to the Holy Land. But he was, at the same time, a ladies' man who carried his exploits to the bedchamber. All women were fair game, and he probably took some of them by force, as he took his neighbors' lands. When he tired of his second wife, he simply replaced her with the Vicomtesse de Châtellerault. It didn't matter to him (or to her?) that she was already married to one of his vassals. Not surprisingly, William was excommunicated. It is one of the ironies of history that such a brutal man was the founding father of romantic love.

This example from one of William's eleven extant poems reveals the newly exalted status of the female.

> *By granting joy, my Lady can heal,*
> *By her anger she can kill.*
> . . .
> *If my Lady is willing to give me her love,*
> *I am ready to receive it and be grateful,*
> *Either to hide or proclaim it, and speak and act according to her*
> *pleasure . . .* [1]

The William of this poem is respectful, submissive, attentive to his lady's requests, willing to suffer her unpredictable whims—a far cry from the earlier brute who tyrannized men and women alike. Where did this new personality come from? Could it have been the influence of one woman, the Vicomtesse de Châtellerault? Does it echo strains of Christianity from the nascent cult of the Virgin Mary? Could it have sprung from Arab literature, which had already introduced love songs both in far-off Baghdad and nearby Spain? These questions continue to be debated by scholars, but all agree that William's changed persona gave birth to a dramatically different vision of how women should be treated by men.

The word "joy" employed by William became a key term in troubadour poetry. It represents the mystical fusion of two bodies and two souls in mutual ecstasy. In the words of the troubadour Bernart de Ventadorn, who sang the praise of William IX's granddaughter, the renowned Eleanor of Aquitaine: "Joy, myself. Joy, my lady above all else."[2] Eleanor was married to the French king Louis VII from 1137 to 1152. By all accounts, she was a lively, beautiful, headstrong queen who may have strayed from the marital bed, while her earnest husband followed the straight and narrow. When their marriage was annulled, she left her two daughters in France and took as her second husband Henry II of England. At the court of England, Eleanor gave birth to three more daughters and five sons and continued to patronize the troubadours and minstrels who spoke her two native tongues—*la langue d'oc*, or Occitan, the language of southern France; and *la langue d'oïl*, the language of northern France, which we now call Old French.

TROUBADOURS INCLUDED MEN OF HIGH RANK AND men of humble origins, and occasionally the troubadour was a *trobairitz*—that is, a woman. The Comtesse de Die, writing between 1150 and 1160, boldly presented herself as the director of erotic joy.

> *My good friend, so pleasing, so handsome,*
> *When I hold you in my power,*
> *Sleeping with you at night,*
> *And give you a kiss of love,*

Know that my great desire
Is to take you instead of my husband,
But only if you will promise
To do everything according to my will.[3]

Rarely has a woman articulated her role as dominatrix with such clarity! She suggests that any man wanting a place in her bed would have to follow her sexual whims and fantasies. Still, legend tells us that the Comtesse de Die, married to Guilhem de Poitiers, fell unhappily in love with the poet and *grand seigneur* Raimbaut d'Orange, for whom she wrote poems of a very different nature.

I have to sing, but I don't want to sing,
I am so full of rancor against the one I love
I love him more than anything in the world.
But neither kindness, nor courtesy, find favor with him
Neither my beauty, nor my worth, nor my wit.
I find myself cheated and betrayed
As if I were ugly to behold.[4]

Like her spiritual ancestor William IX of Aquitaine, the Comtesse de Die made no pretense that love existed without voluptuous intimacy. (Fortunately for posterity, the music to one of the Comtesse de Die's song-poems has been preserved and can be heard today on a disc by the remarkable interpreter of medieval music, Elisabeth Lesnes.)

IN THE NORTH, MINSTRELS KNOWN AS *TROUVÁRES* took up troubadour themes, though the music itself was heavily influenced by the Parisian school of Notre Dame, which was devoted to the cult of the Virgin Mary. When you listen to this music from the late twelfth and thirteenth centuries, you discover that sacred and profane songs sound much alike, even if the words are different. Enough manuscripts still exist to give us a sense of the music, which was sung to the accompaniment of a small harp. Love in the north of France appears to have become more and more idealized, and the beloved lady more and more inaccessible, with the poet-minstrel downplaying his expectation of a physical reward. Unlike their southern counterparts, northern minstrels emphasized a love of longing rather than fulfillment.

Suffering was a given for the lover-poet, such as Gace Brulé around the turn of the thirteenth century, who proudly proclaimed:

> *I want my heart to suffer from Good Love*
> *Because no one has a heart as loyal as mine.*

Or again:

> *Love makes me love the one who does not love me*
> *Thus I shall know nothing but pain and suffering.*

And:

> *I am willing to suffer these sorrows*
> *So that I can augment my worth.*[5]

Suffering became a character test that would make the lover worthy of his lady's affection. But whatever her feelings toward him, he was expected to be submissive and unswerving in his devotion, despite malevolent adversaries resolved to undo him. Those adversaries, called *vilains* or *vileins* in Old French (which originally meant of low birth and ultimately developed into our English word "villain"), might reveal the lover's secret to a jealous husband or slander the lover or even injure him bodily.

From the second half of the twelfth century onward, traveling minstrels celebrating the love of high-born women were ubiquitous in all French-speaking courts, not only on French soil but also in England at the court of Eleanor of Aquitaine and Henry II. Women were becoming a force to be reckoned with in noble society. While their men were often away at war or on Crusades or at the hunt, the women directed everyday life inside the château with their children, parents, servants, household knights, clerks, visiting friends, sycophants, and traveling entertainers. In numerous miniatures, they are portrayed dining at banquets, sharing the delights of music, food, and dance, and enjoying the pleasures of *fin'amor*. In romance texts, the number of female characters increased dramatically during this period, as if to reflect the growing importance of women in aristocratic life. Suddenly, more women were depicted in the song-poems recited before illiterate audiences gathering at castle doors and indoors among an aristocracy eager to hear the latest love story. What had previously been a poetic enterprise devoted primarily to male exploits now became truly co-ed. Alongside men warring against men in fierce battles, women and men became noble adversaries in the courtly game of love.

I would like to have lived through that shift in sensibility, when it became no longer possible for a knight to rely exclusively on his horse and sword. Male courtiers schooled in the new model of chivalry were required to learn dancing, verse writing, sweet talking, and chess. I would like to have seen the puzzled face of an old-time warrior as he listened to tales recounting the temptations of love or the earnest face of a mother as she encouraged her daughter to become not only a fine spinner and embroiderer but also an accomplished musician and an expert chess player. As I have elaborated in my book *Birth of the Chess Queen*, the board game that became de rigueur for aristocratic men and women provided a space where they could spar with their feelings as well as their chess pieces. And unlike games of dice, which were associated with license and disorder, chess provided a perfect metaphor for the ceremony of love among the nobility.

By definition, that ceremony of love was intended primarily for the upper-class clique that frequented a court. Indeed, the French word *courtoisie* and its English cognate "courtesy" derive from the medieval *cort*, spelled *cours* in modern French and "court" in modern English. In the courts of French kings and queens, dukes and duchesses, counts and countesses, and lesser nobility, practitioners of *courtoisie* followed a prescribed set of rules designed to ensure polite commerce between the sexes and promote the idealized love created by southern troubadours and northern minstrels.

The most famous court where this fashionable new love was celebrated belonged to Marie of Champagne, the eldest daughter of Eleanor of Aquitaine and Louis VII. Through her marriage to Comte Henri of Champagne in 1164, Marie took possession of the court of Troyes, where she would reign until her death in 1198. It was under her auspices that some of the reputed "love trials" took place, she herself handing down seven judgments on the proper etiquette for lovers. For example, what gifts could lovers give each other? The Comtesse de Champagne answered: "a handkerchief, hair ribbons, a gold or silver crown, a clothes fastener, a mirror, a belt, a purse, a clothes tie, a comb, a muff, gloves, a ring, perfume, vases, trays, etc."[6] Asked in another case about the choice of a lover when a woman had two possibilities who were exactly equal except in fortune, the countess replied that the first man who had presented himself should be preferred. In a commentary that strikes us as unusual for its time, she added: "Indeed, a woman overflowing with material goods is more praiseworthy if she becomes devoted to a poor man rather than a very rich one."

One case with wide-ranging implications for romantic love asked whether true love could exist between spouses. In 1176, at the age of thirty-one, the countess answered in no uncertain terms: "Love cannot establish its claims between spouses." She based this decision on the belief that marriage was based on mutual obligation, and thus precluded the spontaneous attraction required for true love. Other grand ladies echoed her position when they handed down their own judgments. Ermengarde, the Vicomtesse of Narbonne, insisted that affection between spouses and love between lovers were completely different sentiments. The reigning queen of France, Adèle of Champagne, the third wife of Louis VII, added: "We would not dare contradict the decision of the Comtesse de Champagne: true love cannot extend its claims to spouses."

The question was thus settled by the grandest of ladies. Or was it? Around 1177, Marie de Champagne became the patron of Chrétien de Troyes, the most eminent French writer of his age. His narrative poems dealing with chivalric romance would be recited in all French-speaking courts and would quickly spread throughout Europe. Some of these *romans* (the term has evolved to mean "novel" in modern French) run counter to the notion that true love is impossible within marriage. Indeed, one of Chrétien's first works, *Erec et Enide*, shows nuptial bliss so consuming that the hero must be sent back into the world of errant knighthood in order to regain his stature. Oddly enough, his wife insists on accompanying him, and she is allowed to do so with the provision that she never speak to him. That makes for a suspenseful tale amid monster giants and magical gardens and other fairy-tale elements. In the end, the spouses make their way to the court of King Arthur, where they are finally allowed to settle down.

Similarly concerned with marital love, *Yvain*, written toward the end of Chrétien's life, tells the tale of a knight who wins the wife of the lord he has slain in combat. But then, instead of settling permanently into wedded bliss, he asks his wife's permission to join his fellow Arthurian knights in another round of combat and jousts. She gives him leave to be absent for a year, after which time she will no longer take him back. Yvain becomes so embroiled in chivalric adventures that he forgets his wife and his promised date of return. Then, when she forbids him to reappear in her presence, he goes mad and must undergo Herculean ordeals to regain his sanity and win his wife once more. *Yvain* is something of a morality tale, suggesting that family life requires men to give up the warlike practices of youth. As an author, Chrétien de Troyes had no difficulty imagining love between spouses and tried to reconcile romantic love with the demands of domesticity; yet when he entered the service of Marie de Champagne, whose opinionated pronouncements on true love excluded marriage, he was persuaded to write the story of Lancelot and Guinevere, which he turned into a foundation tale of death-defying adultery.

• • •

WHO HAS NOT HEARD OF THE LOVE between Sir Lancelot and Queen Guinevere, the wife of the legendary King Arthur? Even before the twelfth century, Guinevere was a familiar character to English and French audiences, who had come to know that elegant and capricious lady from oral Celtic tales. But no one before Chrétien de Troyes had imagined Sir Lancelot as her lover. Chrétien's *Lancelot: The Knight of the Cart* gives us a hero who is both a perfect knight and a perfect lover. His extraordinary strength in battle stems from his intense love for Queen Guinevere. Nothing can stop Lancelot in his quest to save her from the evil prince who holds her in captivity, and when the time comes to reward him, she does so in the flesh.

If we consider the story in detail, it is possible to see how Chrétien refashioned Celtic myth and troubadour poetry into a novel of love. For, without doubt, this is a novel, albeit a novel in verse. It is the ancestor of all the romance novels we devour today.

Chrétien's first words set the tone of complete submission to a woman above his station, in this case Marie de Champagne: "Because my lady of Champagne / Wants me to start a new / Romance, I'll gladly begin one, / For I'm completely her servant / In whatever she wants me to do."[7] Then the narrator jumps immediately into a scene at the court of King Arthur, with his barons, the queen, and many "beautiful high-born / Ladies, exchanging elegant / Words in the finest French." Right from the start, the qualities admired in a woman are stated explicitly: she must be beautiful and articulate. The tyranny of good looks and the requirement for lively speech set standards for desirable Frenchwomen up to our own time.

Into this convivial scene a prince appears with an unsettling announcement: he holds in captivity many of Arthur's people—knights, ladies, and girls. He does not intend to release them, but if there is a knight from Arthur's court who is bold enough to bring him Queen Guinevere as a hostage, and if this knight can defeat him in battle, he promises to return all the prisoners along with the queen.

Against his will, King Arthur is forced to send Queen Guinevere to the court of this evil prince. But hard on her heels is a band of men, including Arthur's nephew, Sir Gauvain. Another knight arrives covered with sweat and out of breath; this is Lancelot. Of course, true to the dictates of mystery and suspense, the reader is not told immediately the name of this extraordinary knight. In fact, he is not named until halfway through the story! Nor are we told explicitly that he and Guinevere have exchanged oaths of love, though there is a guarded allusion to her lover when she is first sent away: "Oh, my love, if only / You knew . . ."

The first half of the narrative is constructed around Lancelot's adventures as he goes in search of Guinevere. These lead him into supernatural terrains and meetings with uncanny women, reminiscent of Celtic myth. He undergoes life-threatening trials and engages in fierce combats, all enacted according to the chivalric code expected of a faultless knight. But Chrétien introduces an odd element that departs from this idealized picture and gives the story its subtitle, *The Knight of the Cart*. Early in his quest, Lancelot, having lost his horse, is obliged to get into a cart driven by a dwarf in order to discover the whereabouts of the queen. Lancelot hesitates before entering the cart, which generally carries brigands, criminals, and people of the worst repute. The author tells us that the cart is a traveling pillory, inspiring ridicule and fear in the general populace, who never fail to cross themselves as they see it go by. It is understandable that Lancelot is reluctant to be seen in such an ill-famed vehicle; yet we are told he was wrong to be ashamed because Love ordered him to move as quickly as possible in pursuit of the queen. "He listened / To Love, and quickly jumped in, / Putting all sense of shame / Aside, as Love had commanded." Despite the burden of ridicule he must bear because of the ignoble cart, Lancelot conducts himself nobly. He always wins the battle, even when his opponents outnumber him, and he always treats women with courtesy, even when they make outrageous demands.

One of the most delightful is an encounter with a bold young woman who offers him lodgings in her castle on the condition that he share her bed. Although he tries to abstain, he ends up accepting her proposal, resolved in his heart to do nothing more than sleep at her side. Here we see not only the skill of Chrétien as a storyteller, his use of irony and humor, but also details that reveal the refinements that had been adopted by the wealthy nobility. The table is set with a large tablecloth, candlesticks and candles, goblets made of gold-encrusted silver, and two jugs—one filled with blackberry wine, the other with a heady white wine—all creating a suitable aesthetic atmosphere. One doesn't just throw oneself into sleep or sex in a medieval romance. The height of refinement appears in the two bowls of hot water provided for washing one's hands and the finely worked towel used for drying them. These are amenities that Chrétien had become accustomed to at the court of Marie de Champagne and that he proudly shares with his readers.

The scenes that follow are masterful presentations of chivalry in action. After eating and drinking together, Lancelot goes to join the young lady in her bed, as he had promised. But he finds to his horror that she is being attacked by another knight intent upon raping her! "Help me! Help me!" she cries out. "Unless you get him off me / He'll dishonor me while you watch!" Although there are other knights armed with swords and four henchmen with axes, Lancelot summons the courage to confront the lady's assailant. "My God, what / Can I do? I began this great / Quest for Guinevere's sake. / I can't proceed if my heart / Is only as brave as a rabbit's."

With Guinevere's image spurring him on, Lancelot succeeds in overcoming all his enemies. We are not spared the gory details of heads split open "down to the teeth." It's a scene familiar to us from a hundred movies featuring sword fights between swashbuckling actors, the hero always overcoming his evil adversaries despite their numerical advantages. And always there is a lady to be fought over and won.

The comic originality of this episode lies in the role Lancelot must play as bedmate to a woman for whom he feels no desire. His desire is firmly fixed on Guinevere and remains attached to her even when he finds himself lying on clean white sheets next to the unnamed lady. Still, he can't help noticing the niceties of upper-class hanky-panky. The lady has not set out a common straw mattress, nor a rough blanket, but a "coverlet of flowered / silk." He keeps his chemise on and makes sure that "no part / Of his body was touching hers." Staring at the ceiling (the image of Billy Crystal after he had made love to Meg Ryan in *When Harry Met Sally* comes to mind), Lancelot cannot remove from his heart the imprint of his one true love. "Love, which rules / All hearts, allows them only / One home." Mindful of his deepest feelings, he rejects the sexual advances of a charming young lady, and she, having sensed his disinclination, goes off to sleep in another room. Now, what woman, other than Guinevere, could expect comparable abstinence from her partner? However unrealistic, romance literature fulfills the aspirations of idealized love.

Keeping a promise—either to sleep alongside a woman or show up at a tournament or return to captivity when released for a limited period—is the mark of a true knight. Lancelot has many occasions to demonstrate that he is a man of his word, often at his risk and peril. But above all, it is his promise to be a faithful servant to Guinevere that overrides all other considerations. Over and over again, Lancelot must obey her commands, however arbitrary they appear. She orders him to stop in the middle of a combat he is winning against the evil prince; he stops. She sends a message for him to fight badly in a tournament; he behaves like a poltroon and incurs the contempt of all assembled. She sends another message for him to fight as well as he can; he defeats all his opponents and distributes his booty to the multitude who had ridiculed him the day before.

Lancelot serves his lady as others serve God—an analogy that is brought home in several telling incidents. When, after numerous adventures, he finally finds Guinevere and steals into her bedchamber at her request, "He approached the queen's bed, / Bowing in adoration / Before the holiest relic / He knew." And when he reluctantly leaves in the morning, "He bowed and crossed himself, / As if Acknowledging / An altar." Courtly love borrowed from religion some of its most sacred rituals, and would continue to do so as the cult of love and the cult of the Virgin Mary developed side by side and grew in strength during the twelfth and thirteenth centuries.

The bedchamber scene leaves no doubt as to the corporeal pleasures both lovers enjoyed.

> *It was so exceedingly sweet*
> *And good—the kisses, the embraces—*
> *That Lancelot knew a delight*
> *So fine, so wondrous, that no one*
> *In the world had ever before*
> *Known anything like it, so help me*
> *God! And that's all I'm allowed*
> *To tell you; I can say no more.*

The art of Chrétien is not prurient. It stops short of describing the physical details of lovemaking because such descriptions were considered too coarse for noble sensibilities. A chivalric story respects silence and leaves much to our imagination.

Chrétien set the gold standard for love stories during the late twelfth century. His numerous imitators spread the vision of the young hero doggedly pursuing a sentimental education alongside his escapades as a warrior. There could be various twists in the plot, but if the story did not portray romantic love, it would not have found an enthusiastic audience.

ANOTHER COMMANDING FIGURE AT THE COURT OF Marie de Champagne was the chaplain Andreas Capellanus. Like Chrétien, he wrote and prospered under Marie's generous patronage. His book *The Art of Courtly Love* (*De arte honeste amandi*), written in 1185, became the official guide for practitioners of *fin'amor*, not only in the provincial city of Troyes but throughout medieval Europe. Circulated both in the original Latin and in the vernacular of each country, its admonitions were cited endlessly to demonstrate how lovers should behave.

Capellanus presented love as an all-consuming attraction between two noble participants who were equal in every way. The man had to treat the lady as if she were of higher status, however. He had to address her as if he were her feudal subject and he always had to submit to her will. In the first part of his treatise, he lays out thirteen precepts for an ideal lover.

Flee avarice like the plague and embrace its opposite.

Remain chaste for the one you love.

Don't try to destroy the love of a lady who is happily bound to another.

Don't look for love with a woman you would not marry.

Remember to avoid lying.

Avoid revealing the secrets of your love.

By obeying in every way the commands of the ladies, try to belong to the chivalry of love at all times.

When giving and receiving the pleasures of love, try to respect modesty at all times.

Don't bad-mouth others.

Don't divulge lovers' secrets.

In every circumstance, be polite and courteous.

In giving yourself to the pleasures of love, do not exceed the desire of your lover.

Be worthy of the chivalry of love.[8]

The lover was expected to show respect for his beloved, demonstrate extravagant marks of adoration, perform exploits in her honor, and remain true to her even if he received nothing in recompense. It was up to the lady to decide if she would reward him with the gift of her person. For the most part, Capellanus focused on extramarital love and repeated Marie de Champagne's declaration that love could exert its power between two married people because they were bound by duty. Married people could not even experience jealousy in regard to one another, according to Marie and Capellanus, since marriage was a contractual arrangement that had nothing to do with spontaneous attraction. Only nonmarried lovers could experience jealousy, which was considered intrinsic to "true love." Marie's reasoning suited her personal situation, first as a married woman whose husband was away for long periods during the Crusades, and then as an unmarried widow. Just as she had persuaded Chrétien to privilege adultery in his *Lancelot*, so too she leaned upon Capellanus to write about nonmarital love as if it were a lofty ideal.

But by the time Capellanus had finished his opus, he made a complete about-face and no longer condoned extramarital affairs. Suddenly, in the third and final section of his work, he condemned adulterous love and made a good case for love in marriage, but the damage had already been done. Adultery had already become the major model for romance in medieval France.

Courtly love was predicated on desire so intense that it could not be bound by the conventional rules of society. Passion took precedence over everything, including ties to husbands, family, overlords, and the dictates of the Catholic Church. Not surprisingly, the church reacted vigorously to the adulation of profane love; at the beginning of the thirteenth century, it even tried to suppress it through the arm of the Inquisition. But before that time, the cult of courtly love openly defied religious prohibitions, and in so doing, created the trio of familiar stock characters: the husband, the wife, and her lover.

Another adulterous couple, Tristan and Iseult, rivaled Lancelot and Guinevere as the most popular French model of star-crossed lovers. Later audiences throughout the world would come to know them through Wagner's incomparable opera, *Tristan and Isolde*. In the earliest Tristan saga based on oral Celtic sourses, the hero is sent to Ireland by King Mark to fetch his bride, Iseult. On the return voyage, Tristan and Iseult accidentally drink the love potion intended for Iseult and Mark. Henceforth, the lovers are eternally bound to each other by a fatal passion, despite Iseult's subsequent marriage to King Mark. In centuries to come, the love potion became a robust metaphor for the mystery of passion that starts at first sight and endures in spite of everything designed to annihilate it.

WHILE THE WORKS OF CHRÉTIEN AND CAPELLANUS and various versions of *Tristan and Iseult* were creating a groundswell in favor of courtly love, the poet Conon de Béthune revealed its underside in a long poem derived from an unpleasant incident at the French court at the time of the marriage of the young king Philippe Auguste to Isabelle de Hainaut. Philippe Auguste was the son of the widowed Adèle de Champagne, the third wife of Louis VII. Her two brothers, Henri and Théobald de Champagne, married the two daughters of Louis VII and Eleanor d'Aquitaine, thus making Adèle the wife of her brothers' father-in-law! More pertinent to our concern, it also made her the sister-in-law of Marie de Champagne. When the minstrel Conon de Béthune came to the royal court, both Adèle and Marie ridiculed him because of his Flanders accent.

Conon got his revenge on these contemptuous ladies in the following savage piece, which I have translated at length, since you are unlikely to find it elsewhere.

> *Once upon a time, in another country,*
> *There was a knight who had loved a lady*
> *While she was in her prime.*
> *She refused him her love and drove him away*
> *And then one day, she said: "Dear friend,*
> *I have given you a very hard time,*
> *Now, I recognize and grant you my love."*

The knight responded:

> *"By God, my lady, I'm sick to death*
> *Not to have known your favor in the past.*
> *Your face that was once like a lily*
> *Has so changed from bad to worse,*
> *That it seems to have been stolen from me."*
> *When the lady heard herself so mocked,*
> *She became very angry and treacherously said:*
> . . .
> *"You would probably prefer*
> *The hugs and kisses of a beautiful young boy."*

Stop for a moment to consider this amazing turn of events. The aging lady scorned by the knight accuses him of homosexuality, which was a crime punishable by death. She continues:

"Seigneur, knight, you have spoken badly
When you called my age into question.
Even if I've used up all my allotted youth
I am still beautiful and of such high estate
That one would love me now with only partial beauty."

The knight ends up telling her that she is mistaken:

"One does not love a lady for her parentage,
But because she is beautiful, courteous, and wise.
You will have to learn that truth once more."[9]

The bitterness carousing through this poem betrays the tensions that covertly existed between minstrels and their superiors, between suitors and supercilious ladies, between ideal love and base reality. The ideal lady, "beautiful, courteous, and wise," is turned on her head in this picture of a proud aristocrat, who is vain, unsightly, and foolish. There is also a hint of the misogyny that was a given in medieval society, always ready to spring forth in vituperative denunciations of women. From the early days of Christianity, the church fathers presented women not only as inferior to men in every way but also as temptresses responsible for bringing evil into the world. Men were cautioned to beware of the Eve lurking in every woman. Still, though women were constantly devalued in religious discourse, as well as in the coarsely humorous, secular tales known as fabliaux, one didn't expect to hear such sentiments on the tongue of a court minstrel.

ANOTHER FIGURE WHO CONTRIBUTED SIGNIFICANTLY TO THE flowering of chivalric romance in the late twelfth century was a mysterious woman called Marie de France. We know virtually nothing about her except that she lived in England and wrote twelve delightful lays and a number of fables. Presumably performed before the Anglo-Norman nobility that had ruled England since 1066, these "stories in verse," as Marie called them, were undoubtedly instrumental in spreading the gospel of *fin'amor* to the other side of the English Channel.

All of Marie's lays dealt with love and presented the trials of lovers roiled by unfavorable forces: husbands, of course, but also the lovers themselves. Lovers were judged according to their generosity of spirit, their willingness to suffer, and, above all, their unending loyalty. There was no more noble goal in life than love, but only if the lovers were up to its measure. True love could even dissolve differences in rank, making a man or woman of low estate the equal of a prince or princess. Other song-poets, like Gace Brulé, would elaborate on this theme: "Love looks at neither birth nor riches. . . . It conquers all creatures . . . counts, dukes, kings of France."

When the king in Marie de France's story "Equitan" offers himself to the wife of his seneschal, he woos her in the language of equality:

> *Dearest lady, I give myself to you!*
> *Don't think of me as your king,*
> *But as your vassal and your lover!*[10]

With such honey-tongued speech, the king has little difficulty winning his suit. But these two lovers have internal flaws that lead to their doom. They plot the murder of the lady's husband in a boiling bath and end up bringing this very same catastrophe upon themselves. The story ends with an explicit moral: "Whoever wishes evil on someone else will see misfortune fall back on himself."

As in "Equitan," most of Marie de France's lays concern women married to men they do not love; eight of the twelve center on adultery. Consider the story "Guigemar," in which the leading lady has a jealous husband who keeps her permanently imprisoned in a room facing the sea. Her entire company consists of a sympathetic female servant and a priest-guardian. This unfortunate lady's story is destined to intersect with that of the young knight Guigemar.

In the beginning of the tale, Guigemar has all the attributes of the perfect knight except one: he is not susceptible to love. We are told, "Nature had committed an error by making him indifferent to love. . . . He acted as if he did not want to experience love. His friends as well as strangers saw this as a defect."[11] One day when he is at the hunt—his favorite activity—he spies a white hind and her fawn. Without hesitating, he aims an arrow that wounds the mother but also ricochets back upon him. In an instant, both knight and hind are lying on the ground, with Guigemar close enough to hear her expiring words: he will find no remedy to his wound until a lady suffers for the love of him and he for the love of her. As in Celtic legend, the supernatural erupts in the midst of a realistic scene and causes little surprise to the characters.

Guigemar sets out on a journey that will bring him to the lady in question. He finds a boat conveniently moored without trace of an owner and settles in among luxurious furnishings, such as fine blankets, precious candlesticks, and a pillow that keeps you eternally young. (What a lovely idea!) As in Chrétien's *Lancelot*, the narrator delights in the fabulous riches found within an enchanted realm. The magic boat carries Guigemar across the sea to his fated destination, to meet the lady sequestered by her jealous husband.

Once the lady and her servant find Guigemar, more dead than alive, they carry him inside and tend to his needs. It is there that Guigemar is cured of his injury, only to fall into a kind of lovesickness that is equally painful. While he no longer feels the wound inflicted by the arrow, he discovers that "Love is a wound in his body." Marie de France's language, like that of Shakespeare and Proust, calls upon the vocabulary of sickness and injury to evoke the fierce turmoil that romantic love can generate. Of course, the lady is similarly wounded by love and shares with Guigemar the discovery of a mutual passion that will endure for a year and a half.

Where is the husband during all this time? We don't need to know. Inevitably he returns and discovers his wife's adultery, putting an end to the lovers' happiness. Guigemar is sent away in the same boat that took him to the land of love, and he returns, dejected, to his homeland. This last part of the story is replete with many more marvelous adventures that entail further use of the magic boat—this time by the lady—and the eventual reunion of the lovers.

All these tales of female adultery probably sprang from the fact that medieval marriages among the nobility were rarely affairs of the heart. As we have seen, it was common for a nubile woman—as young as fifteen—to be wed to a much older man for reasons of property and rank. Small wonder that she dreamed of an attractive knight her own age with whom she could share transports unknown to conjugal life. Marie's lays offered amorous fantasies as a counterreality to lived experience. If husbands had to put up with stories about wives in adulterous triangles, they could comfort themselves with the hope that such women appeared only in fiction.

It is impossible to know to what extent female adultery was enacted in real life. Wives caught in the act might be turned out of the home by an irate husband, but the adulteress was not burned alive, as she might have been in earlier days, say, in ancient Rome, which condoned the slaying of both the woman and her lover. By the twelfth century, canon law regulated marriage in France, and its stance on adultery had considerably softened since antiquity. It specifically stated: "No man may kill his adulterous wife."[12] In fact, if a husband did not want to cast off his adulterous wife, it was he who had to do penance for two years.

As for male adultery, it was never considered sufficient cause for a wife to forsake her husband. There had to be aggravating circumstances, such as the presence of the husband's mistress under the marital roof. While medieval literature reflected a widespread obsession with female adultery, it paid scant attention to adulterous husbands, who were undoubtedly more common.

WAS THE MODEL OF COURTLY LOVE RESTRICTED to the nobility? In all probability, yes. Members of the lower classes had more elemental concerns, such as providing shelter and food for themselves and their families. Peasants and serfs in the country and artisans and merchants in the cities were as far removed from the tales of chivalric romance as jobless Americans were from the drawing-room characters of 1930s cinema. And yet there is evidence that even the lower strata of medieval society were not uninfluenced by the adulterous fantasies of their "betters." A type of medieval song known as the "lament of the unhappy wife" (*la mal mariée*) was popular among peasants; it repeatedly explored the triangle of wife, husband, and lover. Here is one example drawn from a group collected by Ria Lemaire at the University of Poitiers:

> *Fat lot I care, husband, about your love*
> *Now that I have a friend!*
> *He looks handsome and noble*
> *Fat lot I care, husband, about your love.*
> *He serves me day and night*
> *That is why I love him so.*[13]

The unhappily married wives of these popular songs, unaffected by feelings of guilt, sing out defiantly: "My husband cannot satisfy me / As a compensation I will take a lover." In one ballad, the speaker complains of being beaten by her husband because he saw her kissing her *ami*. Now she plans her revenge: "I'll make a cuckold of him. . . . I'll go and sleep completely naked with my friend."[14]

In another ballad, the unhappy wife cries out repeatedly: "Don't beat me, miserable husband!" But she also warns him:

> *Because you mistreat me so,*
> *I shall choose a new lover.*
> *. . .*
> *He and I shall love each other*
> *And our pleasure will be double.*[15]

These songs suggest a trickle-down theory of culture, from high nobility to the popular classes. And since they are in the voice of the wife rather than her lover, they also reveal how cultural roles can cross gender boundaries. Some of the earliest troubadour poets were women, and some of the earliest popular French songs were sung by women "blues singers" bemoaning their marital fates and lauding their lovers.

ALTHOUGH IT IS DIFFICULT TO KNOW HOW much these songs and stories related to actual practice, it is safe to say that they did affect the way people began to think about love. The invention of romantic love represents what we today call a paradigm shift, one that offered a radically new set of relations between the sexes and one that has had surprisingly long-lasting consequences.

First, love became feminized. The lady took center stage and has, I believe, commanded the spotlight ever since. Both as the object of man's desire and as the subject of her own desire, Frenchwomen have enjoyed unrivaled erotic prestige. In life as in literature, the descendants of Iseult and Guinevere are expected to be sexy. The French have never believed that women are any less passionate than men.

Moreover, the twelfth century inaugurated a tradition of French women writers, who took up the theme of love from their own perspective. To name a few of the best known during the past nine hundred years: Marie de France, Christine de Pizan, Louise Labé, Madame de La Fayette, Madame de Staël, Marceline Desbordes-Valmore, George Sand, Colette, Simone de Beauvoir, Violette Leduc, Marguerite Duras, Françoise Sagan, Hélène Cixous, and Annie Ernaux. Many of these women openly expressed sexual longing, as in Labé's cry that she was "burning" from love.

Second, men and women had to meet certain standards appropriate for lovers. Looks counted, and still count, especially the woman's looks. Falling in love was often occasioned by a lady's sublime beauty. Love entered through the eyes and went directly to the heart. While the French speak of *un coup de foudre* (a stroke of lightning), the English expression is even more visually explicit: love at first sight. The man, too, was expected to be attractive, though his major attributes might lie elsewhere: he was judged primarily through his courage and loyalty.

Third, it was generally agreed that romantic love was predicated on obstacles, there to intensify the experience, as any steamy novel worthy of the word "romance" will demonstrate today. Denis de Rougemont's highly influential analysis argued that romantic love, as invented in the twelfth century and practiced since then, thrives by confronting obstacles.[16] Yet, however perilous the journey and despite the opposition of family, religion, and society, medieval stories of extramarital love did not usually end in permanent ostracism or suicide. Their heroines were not likely to kill themselves, like Dido in Virgil's *Aeneid*, and they weren't constrained to wear an A for adultery as in Hawthorne's *Scarlet Letter*.

To this day, adultery just doesn't have the same moral stigma in France that it has in the United States. My French friends could not understand the hullabaloo around Bill Clinton and Monica Lewinsky and criticized him only because they thought he should have chosen someone thinner with more class. Even a woman deputy in Parliament and leader of the religious right—anti-abortion and anti-gay—congratulated Clinton on his libido: "He loves women, this man! . . . It's a sign of good health!"[17]

The French are used to presidents who scarcely bother to conceal their extramarital affairs. Giscard d'Estaing, president from 1974 to 1981, even wrote about them in his memoirs and in two novels, the last one written when he was in his eighties. The adulterous secrets of Jacques Chirac, president from 1995 to 2007, were revealed by his former chauffeur, Jean-Claude Laumond, in a 2001 publication, and that same year, Chirac's wife, Bernadette, admitted that she put up with his roving libido for the sake of the children, without letting him forget that he would be lost without her.[18]

The late François Mitterrand, when asked by a journalist during his presidency whether it was true that he had a daughter outside his marriage, replied: "Yes, it's true. And so what? It's none of the public's business." When he died, the children from both of his unions attended his funeral in the company of their mothers, Danielle Mitterrand and Anne Pingeot.

American wives of political husbands who have strayed from the marital bed and embarrassed the family—for example, the wives of Governors Mark Sanford and Arnold Schwarzenegger—no longer put up with such behavior; they head for the divorce courts and try to protect their children as best they can.

It is noteworthy that all of these examples concern male adulterers. No woman has been president of France, and relatively few have been ministers, senators, or deputies. But Nicolas Sarkozy's wife, Carla Bruni, has a past that would undoubtedly bar her from becoming an American first lady. An incredibly successful singer, songwriter, and former model (whose nude photos have circulated on the Internet), she made no secret of her thirty-some lovers, including singer Mick Jagger and former French prime minister Laurent Fabius. Her eight-year liaison with radio personality Raphaël

Enthoven, which began when he was still married, produced a son out of wedlock. Enthoven's ex-wife, Justine Lévy, got her revenge by writing about the affair in her 2004 novel, *Rien de grave* (*Nothing Serious*). Bruni's surprising 2008 marriage to Nicolas Sarkozy, soon after his divorce, helped him regain some of the popularity he had enjoyed when he was first elected president.

Sarkozy lost the presidency to François Hollande in 2012. Both men had unconventional marital lives behind them: Sarkozy's three marriages and Hollande's common-law union with Ségolène Royal, the mother of their four children. Having split with Ségolène following her unsuccessful bid for the presidency in 2007, Hollande could openly admit to the affair he was having with a journalist ten years younger. Any single one of these indiscretions would have doomed the candidacy of an American president.

Fourth, though medieval literature privileged extramarital love, it also produced several remarkable works portraying spouses, like Erec and Enide, who remain passionately attached to one another. These tales suggest that marital love requires the same qualities of ingenuity, playfulness, and forbearance commonly associated with unmarried lovers.

In the French circles familiar to me for the past fifty years, I have been struck over and over again by the efforts many men and women make to maintain the aura of romance in their marriages. Frenchwomen tend to privilege their roles as wives, whether they have children or not, whether they have jobs or not. Remember that the French word for woman—*femme*—is identical with the word for wife. In her best-selling book *Le conflit: La femme et la mère* (literally "The Conflict: Woman and Mother"), Elisabeth Badinter argues that women should not let the pressures of motherhood undermine their roles as wives.[19]

I wonder if American women, especially if they have children and careers, privilege their position as wives in quite the same way. They would be unlikely to practice the kind of artifice I saw on the part of a woman in her eighties who made extreme efforts to keep her somewhat younger husband in her thrall. One day, returning from a shopping trip, she dramatically recounted how she had tripped and fallen in the street. Her husband, alternately distressed and angry, said she shouldn't be gadding about in high heels. Later, when she told me that it wasn't much of a fall, I asked why she bothered to mention it. "To keep Paul interested. If that hadn't happened, I would have made up something else."

I RECALL A CONVERSATION WITH ELISABETH BADINTER that was another eye-opener in my understanding of French romance. When her husband Robert Badinter was elected to the French Senate after a very long government career at the highest level, I thoughtlessly inquired, "I don't know how old he is . . ." She cut me short with a smiling response: "He's sixty-eight and handsome as a god." I was amazed at her open expression of sensual love and could only babble: "An American woman would not have said what you just said."

"Why not?"

"I don't know."

"What would she have said?"

"More likely, he's sixty-eight and a pain in the ass."

We broke into laughter, and then I tried to correct myself.

"I'm probably exaggerating. Maybe an American woman would say, 'He's still in good shape,' but I don't think she would use the English equivalent of what you said. 'He's sixty-eight and looks like a movie star.' We Americans just don't say such things about our husbands."

I'm still wondering why not.

Diane Ackerman, in her lyrical book, *A Natural History of Love*, claims that American society is embarrassed by love. She writes: "We reluctantly admit to it. Even saying the word makes us stumble and blush."[20] That verbal diffidence becomes even greater when we compare ourselves to the French.

HERE'S A VIGNETTE OF ANOTHER VERY ATTRACTIVE Parisian couple, where the man is more openly affectionate than his wife. Carl is a charming lawyer in his midfifties. His beautiful, strong-willed wife, also a lawyer, is not always easy. Simone sets the bar very high for everything from clothes and food to education and repartee, and comes down hard on Carl if he misses the mark. After one of her put-downs, Carl turned to me and said wistfully: *"J'ai le malheur d'aimer ma femme."* ("I have the misfortune of loving my wife.")

This man—handsome, gallant, well-spoken, a connoisseur of art, and clearly still in love with his wife after some thirty years—comes right off the pages of a medieval romance. He is willing to put up with her imperious behavior because he loves her. Like a faithful knight, he honors love, despite its torments. And she, in turn, reciprocates that love, in her fashion.

My youngest son once commented on Simone's difference from the American women he knew. "Not just beautiful," he said, "but more mysterious." Indeed!

Frenchwomen cultivate mystery. I was not surprised to read in a recent magazine dedicated to the subject of monogamy that French psychotherapists have very different views from their American counterparts as to whether couples should discuss with each other all aspects of their lives. A Parisian family therapist expressed horror at the thought, even in a counselor's office. He is quoted as saying: "Mystery is an essential ingredient in maintaining interest in our partner over time. To keep my marriage enlivened, I must feel there's always more to my wife than what I already know."[21] He portrayed a good marital relation as two intersecting circles that do not entirely overlap. "In France," he said, "when we think about 'the relationship,' there's rarely more than one-third of each circle that overlaps. Married people here are not only entitled to their privacy, they *must* have private lives to remain interesting and alluring to each other."

Call it "mystery" or "subterfuge" or "dishonesty," but when it comes to love, French men and women have little regard for the tell-all ideal so popular among many Americans. They prefer to think of love as a game in which you do not show your hand.

I have pondered this difference for the better part of a lifetime and garnered a few enduring insights by considering our respective national histories. The American ideal of love, with its own transformations over four hundred years, developed in a strange new world where spouses had to depend on each other as "yoke partners." Far from settled communities, without parents or siblings to count on, husbands and wives were thrust together in a battle against the elements and other peoples. Romantic love did not become the major factor in American marriages until the early nineteenth century, and even then "the couple" quickly ceded primacy to "the family." For a long time, American women have lived in a culture of what one author has called "strong mothers, weak wives."[22] Today, the needs of the married couple frequently take second place to the needs of the children, with romance between husband and wife often difficult to maintain. My French daughter-in-law remembers being shocked when she first came to the United States and heard one of her coworkers dismiss her husband as "incidental" to the primary relationship she had with her children.

The French, on the other hand, with centuries of court culture behind them, have developed their ideas on love from the top downward. Kings and queens, lords and ladies, minstrels and writers eulogized, poeticized, and acted out love within a world of their peers. From the Middle Ages onward, erotic love was a privileged phenomenon, with standards and ideals that were shared by members of the same social circle. In time, what began in the enclosed atmosphere of provincial and royal courts would ripple out far beyond regional boundaries, and far beyond the age of the troubadours.

CHAPTER TWO

Gallant Love

La Princesse de Clèves

AMBITION AND LOVE AFFAIRS WERE THE LIFE-BLOOD OF THE
COURT, ABSORBING THE ATTENTION OF MEN AND WOMEN ALIKE.
Madame de La Fayette, *La Princesse de Clèves,* **1678**

FROM THE TWELFTH CENTURY ONWARD, FASHIONABLE COURTS
throughout France promoted all the arts, including the art of
love. Certainly Anglophiles, Italianophiles, and Germanophiles (or
Spanish, Dutch, Czech, Greek, Russian, and Scandinavian aficionados) can point to their own glories during the Middle Ages and
Renaissance, but it is safe to say that the French cultural beacon
illuminated the rest of Europe until the fall of the monarchy at the
end of the eighteenth century.

In matters of love, a new style called *galanterie* became the
rage. Broadly defined as a set of refined manners directed toward
the opposite sex, and narrowly defined as the art of pleasing the
ladies, it would dominate polite society for at least three hundred

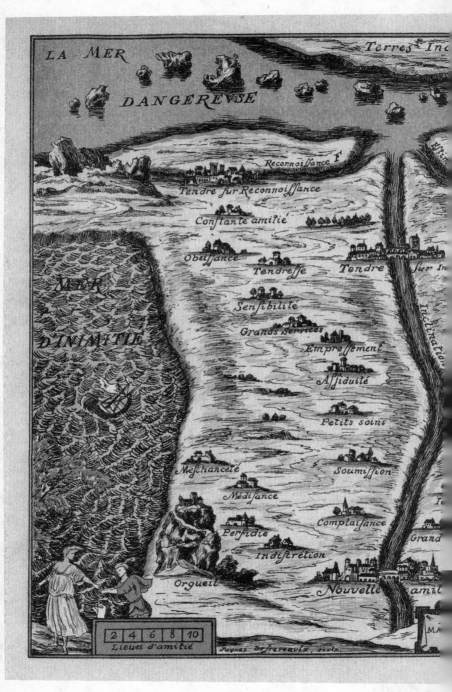

LA MER

DANGEREVSE

Terres Inc

Reconnoissance F.

Tendre sur Reconnoissance

Constante amitié

Obeissance

Tendresse

Tendre

sur In

MER

D'INIMITIE

Sensibilité

Grands Services

Empressement

Assiduité

Petits soins

Meschanceté

Soumission

Médisance

Perfidie

Complaisance

Grand

Indiscretion

Orgueil

Nouvelle

amit

Inclination

| 2 | 4 | 6 | 8 | 10 |

Lieues d'amitié

Jacques de Fraveaulx sculp.

CARTE
DU
PAYS
DE
TENDRE

ndre sur Estime

LAC
D'INDIFERENCE

Oubli

Légereté

Tiedeur

Esgalité

Comme on peut avoir de la tendresse par trois causes, ainsi on va de NOUVELLE AMITIÉ au bas de la carte, à TENDRE par la route de Grande Estime, ou par celle de Reconnoissance ou encore par celle d'Inclination.

la
LLET

years. Though its meaning would change over time, we still apply the word "gallant" to men when they demonstrate courtesy and charm.

Galanterie, galant, galante, Le Vert Galant, fêtes galantes, Le Mercure Galant, les Indes galantes, annales galantes, lettres galantes, les muses galantes—these terms proliferated among the upper classes. Men were expected to exercise gallantry with the same ease required of them in the saddle. To show no interest in the fair sex was as much a flaw among noblemen of the sixteenth, seventeenth, and eighteenth centuries as it had been among the troubadours of an earlier period, the main difference being that gallantry did not promise lifetime loyalty. Courtly love in the Middle Ages had required devotion to only one lady, who was usually married and of higher status than the knight. Gallantry could be spread around: men usually courted women of their own rank, but could also reach out to women above and beneath them, as long as everyone understood that lovers of unequal status were not likely to marry.

Gallantry started at the highest level, at the level of kingship. Unlike the cuckold depicted in medieval literature, the king, rather than the queen, was entitled to bedmates beyond the royal spouse. While she ostensibly devoted her intimate parts solely to the purpose of producing heirs, he could receive other women in his bedchamber or find his way to numerous assignations where receptive women would meet him with open limbs. In time, royal mistresses rivaled legitimate queens in their opulence and influence.

The great Renaissance king François I (1494–1547) installed his official mistress (*maîtresse en titre*), Anne, Duchesse d'Étampes, in the royal castle of Fontainebleau. He pursued his love affairs—with her and with others—not only at Fontainebleau but also at the

Palais du Louvre and châteaux in the Loire Valley, which became gardens of pleasure for the king and his courtiers.

His successors, most notably Henri II, Henri IV, Louis XIV, and Louis XV, were famous for their amatory exploits with numerous women, starting with their official mistresses. You could say that French kings enjoyed a form of regal polygamy. Even if a woman was reluctant to grant sexual favors, as was the case of the teen-aged Gabrielle d'Estrées when approached by the "old" Henri IV (he was thirty-seven), it took little to persuade her that it was in her interest, and the interest of her family, to submit to the king's desires. Here's how he addressed her on April 19, 1593, in one of his many love letters: "Sleep well, my sweet love, so you'll be fresh and fleshy when you arrive."[1]

Among the more than fifty mistresses attributed to Henri IV, Henriette d'Entragues, who replaced Gabrielle after she died in childbirth, was arguably the most impertinent. She seems to have been able to do and say pretty much what she pleased with the king, including telling him to his face that he smelled like carrion. Henri IV kept Henriette on as his leading mistress even after he brought Marie de Médicis to Paris as his queen. During the ten years of their marriage (1600–1610), which produced six royal children, the queen had to put up with the king's voracious extramarital appetite. He came to be known as Le Vert Galant (the dashing gallant), a name that appears to this day on the marquee of a famous restaurant in Paris, not far from the statue of Henry IV on the Pont Neuf.

Right till the end of his life, Henri IV was in and out of bed with a wide assortment of women—those he professed to love and others he simply wanted to seduce. His very last love was a teen-ager stolen away from his friend, the soldier and diplomat François de Bassompierre. Here is how Bassompierre recounted the affair in his memoirs.

Bassompierre could boast of several mistresses. In October 1608, when he was twenty-nine, he was offered the possibility of marriage with the fifteen-year-old daughter of the Connétable de Montmorency. It would be an advantageous union for Bassompierre, and besides, the young woman was extremely beautiful. But in January 1609, the king saw her and, as he confessed to Bassompierre, fell "not only in love with Mademoiselle de Montmorency, but furiously and outrageously so. If you marry her and she loves you, I shall hate you."[2]

The king conceived another scenario: she would be the "consolation" of his old age. (He was fifty-six at the time and destined to die in little more than a year.) He would marry her off to his nephew, the Prince de Condé—a man who "loves hunting a hundred thousand times more than the ladies." The prince would receive 100,000 francs a year "to pass the time" while the young woman was in attendance on the king. He tried to make Bassompierre believe that he wanted nothing more from her than her affection. As a reward to Bassompierre for his loss, the king offered to arrange his marriage with another highly ranked woman and to make him a duke and peer of the realm. For Mademoiselle de Montmorency and Bassompierre, there was no choice but to acquiesce. However, the story did not end as Henri IV had planned. The marriage with the Prince de Condé took place on May 17, 1609, but shortly thereafter the couple stole off to Brussels, much to the king's chagrin.

It is clear from this example that sexual intrigue was as much a part of court life as political stratagem. Whom you slept with and whom you married were not just private affairs. They concerned relatives, friends, priests, even the king and queen, as members of the nobility jockeyed with each other for royal favor. In a society where whole families could be made or undone by a felicitous marriage or an ill-advised liaison, love was the least of many considerations to be taken into account by a young person experiencing his or her first pangs of passion.

No one has better described the amatory hotbed of the French court than Madame de La Fayette in her novel *La Princesse de Clèves*. She writes: "There were countless interests at stake, countless different factions, and women played such a central part in them that love was always entangled with politics and politics with love."[3]

Published anonymously in 1678, *La Princesse de Clèves* became an instant best-seller in France, to be followed the next year by a popular translation into English. Controversy over the book erupted in both countries. Who was this person—who were these "wits of France"—responsible for revealing the erotic commerce of the French court?[4]

While Madame de La Fayette never confessed to having written this work (or others that were subsequently attributed to her), there is little doubt today that she was the author. Perhaps she did collaborate with some of the men in her intellectual circle, most notably her intimate friend, the Duc de La Rochefoucauld, whose cynical *Maximes* had already attracted a wide readership. Anonymous publication, in and of itself, points to a woman's hand, since it was not considered seemly in the seventeenth century (as in the eighteenth and nineteenth) for a woman to publish under her own name.

La Princesse de Clèves is one of the first "psychological" novels ever written, and, in my opinion, it has no equal among seventeenth-century works of fiction. As I explain later, it played a significant role in my life, so much so that I felt personally offended when President Sarkozy, in 2009, dismissed the book as irrelevant to the education of French students. Had I not been five thousand miles away, I would have joined the French protesters who took turns reading it in public as an act of political opposition. As President Sarkozy's popularity declined among the French, sales of *La Princesse de Clèves* soared.

This relatively short work has had a multitude of fans worldwide for good reasons. It is a love story, albeit a thwarted one, between a young married noblewoman and her equally noble suitor. It is a marital drama quite unlike any other that had been written until then. It is a story that sometimes strains the reader's credulity, with overheard conversations and lost letters, but redeems itself as a convincing portrayal of the sentiments felt by women and men as they fall heedlessly in and out of love.

Madame de La Fayette set her novel in the sixteenth century during the reign of Henri II, specifically during the years 1558 and 1559. In this respect, it is a "historical" novel based on real personages and events. Only the Princess de Clèves herself is entirely fictitious and her story, as it intertwines with the lives of others, is a *roman* in every sense of the word. The seventeenth-century novel still bore the hallmarks of medieval romance in its central preoccupation with the efforts of valorous men to win the hearts of high-born ladies, usually married to someone else. Looking back a hundred years to the time when Diane de Poitiers, the renowned mistress of King Henri II, overshadowed his queen, Catherine de Médicis, the author had found the perfect setting for her tale of nascent love within a web of court intrigue. Yet the shift backward in time fooled no one: *La Princesse de Clèves* held a mirror to the court of Madame de La Fayette's own king, Louis XIV. Behind the formal hierarchy and stiff etiquette of court events, there lay a hidden world of secret assignations where men and women abandoned their social roles along with their clothes and wigs. There, the young and the old expressed their inner longing for reciprocal love and reciprocal pleasure.

Even Louis XIV had been known to follow his heart in his youthful love for Mademoiselle de Mancini, jeopardizing his projected marriage with Maria Theresa of Spain. Though he was persuaded to make the political marriage, his subsequent libidinous history included a long list of royal favorites, including his first official mistress, Louise de La Vallière, with whom he had two surviving children. Even more influential were Madame de Montespan, who bore him no less than seven children, and Madame de Maintenon, the governess of these illegitimate children, whom he secretly married during the winter of 1684–1685 after his relations with Madame de Montespan had come to an end and after Maria Theresa had died. Maria Theresa had been a loving wife for more than two decades, accepting her husband's mistresses with astonishing grace. Louis is known to have said upon her death: "This is the first chagrin she has ever caused me."

As we have seen, there was a long tradition in France that allowed, even expected, French kings to take sexual partners in addition to their wives. The king was allowed "two bodies"—one considered "divine" that extended in an unbroken line from king to king; the other "human," all too human. No one but censorious priests objected to the king's sexual exploits. The number of his liaisons attested to his virility. This attitude has persisted in

France long after the demise of the monarchy, spilling over onto presidents, whose extramarital involvements were publicly known and never detrimental to their careers.

The future Madame de La Fayette became well versed in the bedroom ploys of the French elite when she was maid of honor to Louis XIV's mother, Anne of Austria. Then, through her marriage to the Comte de La Fayette in 1655, she had continued familiarity with court life, although she and he also lived at his far-distant estate in Auvergne. At the time of her marriage, she was twenty-one and no longer a "young" bride, since it was common for noblewomen to be married off in their late teens, before they had any chance of becoming corrupted by would-be seducers. And like most women of her class, she was married to an older man. Arranged marriages among the nobility, like those of Madame de La Fayette in real life and the Princess de Clèves in fiction, were the norm well into the early twentieth century. Parents sought unions for their sons and daughters in the interest of fortune, title, and family connections. One did not expect to marry for love.

So, in the novel, when the future Princess de Clèves, barely sixteen, is offered the Prince de Clèves as a suitable match, she does not find him unacceptable, even though she does not love him. For one thing, she has never felt those delicious internal stirrings that the French aptly call *troubles*. She has lived a protected life under the guidance of her widowed mother, Madame de Chartres, a woman of known distinction and virtue. Madame de Chartres had not only sought to cultivate her daughter's wit and beauty—the two qualities considered necessary for a marriageable woman—she had also tried to make her "virtuous." Female virtue consisted mainly in shunning the practices that led to sexual entanglements. Madame de Chartres warned her daughter of love's dangers, however attractive they were made to appear: she spoke to her of "men's insincerity, of their deceptions and infidelity, of the disastrous effects of love affairs on conjugal life," and she argued convincingly for "the only thing that can ensure a woman's happiness," namely, reciprocal love between husband and wife.

The young woman's first appearance at court produced a sensation. The Prince de Clèves was struck by her beauty and modest behavior, and fell in love with her on the spot. This was the classic *coup de foudre*, love at first sight, that enters through the eyes and travels immediately to the heart and other unmentioned organs.

Other love-struck rivals presented themselves, but events conspired to leave the field open to the Prince de Clèves. He managed to find an occasion to speak to her of his passion in a suitably respectful manner. "He begged her to let him know what her feelings were for him and told her that his own were of a kind that would make him eternally unhappy if she obeyed her mother's wishes only out of duty."

All this high-flown language centers on one question: "Do you love me?" It is still a question that causes anxiety on the part of the person who asks, as well as the person obliged to answer. "Loves me, loves me not" cannot be determined by plucking daisy petals. It is something one feels in a rush of hormones when one is very young, and even when one is supposedly mature. Mademoiselle de Chartres does not yet know what love feels like. She tells her mother that she would marry Monsieur de Clèves "with less reluctance than another man, but that she felt no particular attraction for his person."

Madame de Chartres accepted the prince's proposal for her daughter and had no reason to believe that she was giving her a husband she could not love. In this respect, the union was not unlike traditional marriages in India, where many parents still choose spouses for their children and hope that the bride and groom will come to love each other in time. Most young people today in the West assume they will choose their own mates on the basis of the shared love they have already known, whereas in arranged marriages you are given someone "to love" in the future. In *La Princesse de Clèves*, we are at a key point in Western history when romantic love was beginning to make inroads into marital choices, even at the highest level.

After a short engagement, Mademoiselle de Chartres and the Prince de Clèves are wed in a ceremony that takes place at the Palais du Louvre, followed by a nuptial supper attended by the king and queen. We are barely twenty pages into the novel and already the marriage has taken place. What would constitute the happy ending of an eighteenth- or nineteenth-century English novel occurs near the beginning of this quintessentially French story.

Unfortunately, marriage does not change the nature of the princess's feelings, and the prince is not satisfied with their union, though he has given her his name and has access to her bedchamber. (At this level of society, they would have had separate suites.) He wants her to love him with some measure of the passion he feels for her. But love and passion are still sentiments unknown to the princess. All she can feel for the prince is *amitié*, a form of affection closer to friendship than to sexual love. In this respect, the princess exemplifies the belief held by Marie de Champagne and her twelfth-century associates that true love cannot exist between spouses.

A twenty-first-century reader finding his or her way through *La Princesse de Clèves* will certainly notice its rich amatory vocabulary and the fine distinctions made between various shades of sentiment. *Amour, passion, amitié, tendresse, attachement, inclination, trouble, agitation, ardeur, flamme, embarras*—these are only some of the many terms that French characters use as they endlessly analyze their feelings. Let us not forget that Madame de La Fayette and other writers of her generation were influenced by the linguistic innovations introduced by a group of highly sophisticated ladies known as *précieuses*, who demanded purity in language, delicacy in thought, and a new psychological awareness. *Les précieuses* promoted an ultra-refined conversational tone that filtered into many important literary works. One of the first, Madeleine de Scudéry's novel *Clélie, histoire romaine* (Clelie: A Roman Story) offered an allegorical journey to the land of love. Its "Map of the Land of Tenderness" was to become the most celebrated graphic document of its day, and one that has been reproduced countless times. I still have a copy bought on the banks of the Seine, which is reproduced at the beginning of this chapter. Note how the lovers' path takes them through the many stages of love, from *Nouvelle amitié* (new friendship), *Billets doux* and *Petits soins* (love letters and minor attentions), upward toward the imaginary land of *Tendresse* (tenderness), with its surrounding communities of *Obéissance* (obedience), *Bonté* (goodness), and *Respect*. If the lovers wish to reach their goal, they must be especially careful to avoid the hamlets of *Perfidie* (perfidy), *Médisance* (slander), and *Méchanceté* (maliciousness), and not stray to the Lake of Indifference.

When we listen in on the conversations of the characters in *La Princesse de Clèves*, we hear echoes of *les précieuses* and their purified discourse. Gone are any blunt allusions to the flesh that often erupted in medieval and Renaissance literature. The prince speaks only of the greater privileges afforded him by the status of husband, without suggesting that they may have anything to do with the body. So too, Madame de Chartres speaks to her daughter about "love affairs" without any reference to their carnal nature. Does Mademoiselle de Chartres have any idea of what is in store for her on her wedding night? We shall never know. Whatever transpired that night does not seem to have affected her, for better or for worse. Her first experience of sexual intercourse (to revert to less elegant terminology) did not entail an assault upon her heart. Despite his best effort, the Prince de Clèves had not managed to lead his princess into the Land of Tenderness.

And now, of course, a third party enters the scene. The Duc de Nemours, the most handsome and attractive man at court, meets the princess in a thoroughly romantic manner: without ever having seen her before, he is ordered by the king to dance with her at a betrothal ball for the king's daughter, Claude de France. This fairy-tale meeting amid a crowd of awed admirers can lead in only one direction. Predictably, Monsieur de Nemours falls wildly in love with the princess, and the rest of the book describes his ill-fated attempts to claim her as his own. Or, in the language of the seventeenth century, Nemours plays the game of *galanterie* with a mastery unequaled by anyone else at court, and yet he fails to obtain the rewards he considers his due.

Why not? That is the essential question one asks after finishing the book. It is not because the princess is lacking in passion; the intense arousal sparked by the Duc de Nemours bears no resemblance to the sexless feelings she has for her husband. No, indeed.

Little by little, she comes to know the joys and torments of burning love for a man who is the darling of the French court and even a candidate for the hand of the queen of England, Elizabeth I. For the first time in her life, the princess conceals her feelings. But her mother is no fool, and she begins to suspect her daughter's budding love. Worry about her daughter precipitates her sudden illness and contributes to her decline, but before she dies, she makes sure that the princess becomes fully aware of the dangers before her. "You have an inclination for M. de Nemours; I do not ask you to confess it to me . . . you are on the edge of a precipice." Madame de Chartres counsels her daughter to withdraw from the court in order to avoid "the miseries of a love affair."

While the loss of her mother causes the princess great affliction, it also strengthens her will to resist the Duc de Nemours' advances. As a narrative strategy, the mother's death is a form of sacrifice for the good of her daughter, who retreats to the country and clings to her husband more than ever in the hope that her attachment to him will provide a defense against the duke. But in time, the prince and princess are obliged to return to the court, and she is once again confronted with the duke's winning ways.

He manages to declare his love to her in the oblique manner favored by *les précieuses*. "There are women to whom one dares give no sign of the passion one feels for them. . . . Since we dare not let them see we love them, we should at least like them to see that we have no desire to be loved by anyone else."

If anyone today were to declare his love in this manner, we would think of him as peculiar, if not downright zany. We would find such speech roundabout and devious. American men tend to be more laconic in their expressions of love, however sincere.

And what about Frenchmen today? Do they still practice an art of verbal gallantry meant to please the ladies? Some do, particularly older men of the educated classes, for whom *le bon mot*—the clever phrase—is still a must. It is still not uncommon for Frenchmen to make advances in a flowery style they learned from the classical texts they read in school. *"Madame s'amuse à Paris avec nos hommes galants?"* ("Madame is having a good time in Paris with our gallant men?") *"Cette robe a été faite exprès pour rehausser la couleur de vos yeux."* ("That dress was made specially to bring out the color of your eyes.") *"Votre passion pour la littérature française nous honore. Et le plaisir?"* ("Your passion for French literature honors us. And what about pleasure?") Pleasure? In French, the word for "pleasure" has a distinctly sexual connotation. I knew exactly what that gentleman had in mind, just as the princess knew exactly what the duke was saying.

Despite her good intentions, she is unable to hide the pleasurable stirrings she feels in the duke's presence. "A man less acute than he would perhaps not have noticed them; but so many women had already been in love with him that he could hardly fail to recognize the symptoms." Emboldened by this knowledge, the duke commits a shameless act: he steals a miniature portrait of the princess while they are both in the room of the Queen Dauphine. Even though the princess sees the theft, she cannot bring herself to denounce him or ask that he return the portrait.

At this point, the duke revels in the belief that he is "making her love him despite herself." When the theft is discovered, Monsieur de Clèves is pained by its disappearance and says, in jest, that his wife must have given it to a lover. The princess is filled with remorse, yet unable to quell the storm of emotions raging inside her. So the trio of husband, wife, and would-be lover continue their dance of deception and hurtle toward an inevitable confrontation.

From scene to scene, the princess descends the slope toward "the miseries of a love affair" against which her mother had assiduously warned her. She even discovers the torments of jealousy resulting from a far-fetched subplot: a letter from her uncle's mistress falls into her hands, and she mistakenly believes that it is addressed to the Duc de Nemours. Once she learns the truth, she is relieved of her jealousy, but the hurt still lingers and opens her eyes to questions she has not been willing to face before. She asks herself bluntly: "Am I ready to embark on a love affair? to be unfaithful to M. de Clèves? to be unfaithful to myself?" At this point, she is still able to answer no.

The plot becomes increasingly convoluted when the princess again retreats to the Clèves country home in a further effort to distance herself from her potential lover. And it is here that the most famous—and most incredible—scene of the book takes place. She confesses to Monsieur de Clèves that she loves someone else, a confession so remarkable that when the novel was published, the popular magazine, *Le Mercure Galant*, asked its readers this question: "Should wives confess to their husbands their passion for other men?" And if the confession wasn't difficult enough for a reader to swallow, the author would have us believe that the conversation between husband and wife is overheard by none other than the duke, silently hidden in the garden pavilion where the prince and princess are sitting. Do we believe? Judge for yourself when you read the book.

The Prince de Clèves is devastated. He asks his wife to try to resist her inclination, not only as her husband "but as a man whose happiness depends on you and who loves you more passionately, more tenderly, more violently than the man your heart prefers." The prince is a very decent man, a nobleman in every sense of the word, the very antithesis of a laughingstock cuckold. He clearly deserves to be loved, but in this story, that is not to be. Instead, aroused by further suspicions, he falls into despair and, "unable to resist the crushing sorrow" that overcomes him, he is struck down by a violent fever. As he sinks toward death, the prince musters his strength one last time to express his love and his fears for his wife. His death will turn out to be another sacrifice, like that of her mother, on behalf of the princess's character development.

For it is her story that gives the novel its title, and it is her story that grips us to the end. Now that she is free to follow her heart and marry the Duc de Nemours, she chooses another path. Despite the duke's continued attentions and her own rekindled passion at his sight, the princess turns down his offer of marriage. Why? The obvious answer is that she is filled with too much remorse at the thought of her husband's death, which she attributes directly to the duke's behavior and her own. The duke's attempt to discount her rejection of him as a "phantom of duty" does not work. She is adamant, and not only because she is consumed with guilt for the past. Another, deeper reason lies in her fears for the future with a husband such as Nemours. She presents this reason lucidly and eloquently in their spellbinding last meeting. Let us listen.

What I fear is the certainty that one day the love you feel for me now will die. . . . How long does men's passion last when the bond is eternal? . . . it seems to me, indeed, that your constancy has been sustained by the obstacles it has encountered.

There were enough of them to arouse in you the desire for victory. . . .

I confess . . . that my passions may govern me, but they cannot blind me. . . . You have already had a number of passionate attachments; you would have others. I should no longer be able to make you happy; I should see you behaving towards another woman as you had behaved towards me. I should be mortally wounded at the sight. . . . A woman may reproach a lover, but can she reproach a husband who has merely stopped loving her? . . .

I intend to remove myself from your sight, however violent the pain of separation. I implore you, by all the power I have over you, not to seek any opportunity to see me.

This long monologue plumbs the soul of an extraordinary lady, who has grown into her nobility through the course of two years and 150 pages. She has evolved from a naïve teenager into a mature woman who has learned from her own experience, including the experience of being in love. For how could she judge love's true worth without having undergone its delights and its torments? Anyone who has ever fallen in love, who has fantasized a meeting with a lover, who has woken up with the enhanced pleasure of knowing she will see him, who has put on a flattering dress and more makeup than usual—that person knows there is little in life so intense as being in love. Madame de Clèves knows all this and yet renounces a future with the man she loves.

Whether we agree with her decision or not, one thing is clear: henceforth love will have to bear the burden of trenchant psychological scrutiny. Henceforth love will be accompanied by a certain skepticism. Can it last? Is it worth it? Are men congenitally inconstant?

With *La Princesse de Clèves*, the medieval tradition of courtly love collides with seventeenth-century skepticism. Descartes and La Rochefoucauld, following on the heels of Montaigne, question the reliability of our most cherished beliefs. They bring critical thinking into the realm of human relationships, religion, philosophy, and what we now call psychology. Madame de La Fayette does not deny the power of love. She masterfully describes it, even inflates it, then analyzes and deflates it. She would have heard from her friend La Rochefoucauld some of his caustic maxims that warn against the folly of love: "All the passions make us commit faults; love makes us commit the most ridiculous ones." "The mind is always the dupe of the heart." "True love is like seeing ghosts: we all talk about it, but few of us have ever seen one."

Perhaps the Princess de Clèves had another quote attributed to La Rochefoucauld in mind when she mustered the strength to refuse the Duc de Nemours: "Before we set our hearts too much upon anything, let us examine how happy they are, who already possess it." Observing the fate of other women at court—wives and mistresses, women who had been loved, betrayed, and abandoned—she did not want to end up like them. She chose caution and renunciation over the hope of enduring love. We have come a long way from the reciprocal passion of Tristan and Iseult or Lancelot and Guinevere. Madame de La Fayette and many of her contemporaries regarded passion as a recipe for disaster.

La Princesse de Clèves marks a notable shift in the French erotic saga. While romantic love will return in various guises over and over and over again during the next three hundred years, it will never be the same. It will never be as free from suspicion as it was before Madame de La Fayette's masterpiece.

Reader, by now you have guessed that *La Princesse de Clèves* carries special meaning for me, as it did for the thousands of French men and women who were offended by President Sarkozy's dismissal of the book. I can even say that it changed my life. In fact, when Alain de Botton's lovely book *How Proust Can Change Your Life* appeared, I thought of how Madame de La Fayette had changed mine, for she was directly responsible for a major decision I made in 1976.

That winter, when I was still teaching French literature and Western civilization at a state university in California, I was asked to review the 1973 edition of the Norton *World Masterpieces Since the Renaissance*. It contained 1,859 pages of literature from France, England, Ireland, Germany, Italy, the United States, Russia, and Norway: 1,859 pages chosen and edited by seven men—1,859 pages that did not include a single selection from a woman! (You think the gender gap is bad now? Then it was undoubtedly much worse.) My mind jumped immediately to Madame de La Fayette. How could they have ignored *La Princesse de Clèves*? Yes, indeed, most of the authors included in the Norton anthology were men of great distinction, but I simply could not understand why there was a place for Solzhenitsyn and none for Madame de La Fayette, not to mention Jane Austen, Charlotte Brontë, Emily Dickinson, and Virginia Woolf. Rather than argue the respective merits of, say, Heinrich Heine and George Sand as representatives of European romanticism, or the need to include Simone de Beauvoir along with Sartre and Camus, I made my case to Norton on the basis of *La Princesse de Clèves*. Surely, this was a masterpiece in every sense of the word and deserved to be included in the next edition of *World Masterpieces*. I'm pleased to say that every subsequent edition of the Norton anthology has included selections written by women.

My experience in 1976 forced me to rethink what I was doing in a department of literature, a discipline that tended to ignore and often denigrate the contributions of women writers, however outstanding. In casting about for a different way of using my professional skills, I chanced upon the newly created Center for Research on Women at Stanford University. There I was able to find a home as a senior research scholar and, later, as one of its directors. Since that transition I have been engaged in writing about women's cultural history, with a special focus on women in France and the United States.

Thinking about women, I have never been far away from their relationships with men. I have tried to understand how men and women see themselves within a given culture and historical moment. I have read, with fascination, their accounts of how they acquired gender-specific traits and roles. While males and females in France and the United States pass through the same biological stages of infancy, childhood, adolescence, young adulthood, maturity, and old age, each of these stages is so shaped by a person's specific time and place that they often bear little resemblance to each other across the divide of language, region, and class, not to mention sex. The first great American poet, Anne Bradstreet (circa 1616–1672), who wrote amazing love poems for her husband, was born scarcely a generation earlier than Madame de La Fayette; yet in Puritan New England where Anne lived as an adult (after her earlier life in England), she conceptualized love in a manner so different from the courtiers of seventeenth-century France that we wonder if she and they are writing about the same thing. Love, too, we are forced to admit, is socially constructed.

For Madame de La Fayette, love was fabricated according to the rules of *galanterie* as dictated in the salons of the precious ladies and as practiced at the court of Louis XIV. While Louis XIV was alive—he did not die until 1715—gallantry remained an honored French attribute, a sophisticated game as in the title of Marivaux's famous comedy, *Le jeu de l'amour et du hasard* (*The Game of Love and Chance*), published in 1730.

In the seventeenth and eighteenth centuries, one learned how to please the opposite sex by reading novels and poetry, by attending plays, and by observing the conduct of one's elders and contemporaries. It was understood that a man should always make the first advance, never a woman. She, on the other hand, had the right to encourage or discourage a would-be suitor. This verbal play between man and woman was as essential to court life as music and dance. Let us not forget that in 1656, when Louis XIV was only eighteen, he danced in Lully's ballet entitled *La Galanterie du Temps* (Gallantry in Our Times). Following the example of their king, men were proud to be called *galants*. For women, however, the term *femme galante* was less flattering, implying "an easy woman" or even a courtesan.

By the time of Madame de La Fayette, in the last third of the seventeenth century, gallantry implied a certain emotional lightness. If you could manage it, it was even possible to juggle several affairs at the same time without sanction from one's peers—something that would have been denounced by Marie de Champagne in her twelfth-century verdicts.

The Duc de Nemours excelled at gallantry. His striking appearance, polite manners, and way with words lifted him far above the ordinary suitor. He was a star in a firmament of lovers, a catch for any woman, even for the Princess de Clèves. And yet . . . what woman would not fear that this very same man, with a string of love affairs behind him, would cast her off when the pleasures of love had become too familiar? Her all-engrossing fairy tale might eventually deteriorate into a demonic nightmare. She could not risk a catastrophic ending to her unparalleled story. Let it be one of emotion recollected in tranquility (*pace* Wordsworth) rather than in bitterness. Let it be a story that ennobles, without the negative side of gallantry.

Although the dissolute side of gallantry would become more pronounced in the eighteenth century, the French would continue to claim it with pride. Pierre Darblay, in his 1889 *Physiologie de l'amour*, would call it the "character of our nation."[5] In our own time, Alain Viala asks whether gallantry is a cultural category peculiar to the French. Indeed, when he mentioned his intended book title—*La France galante*—to British colleagues at Oxford, one called it a pleonasm.[6] He was right to associate gallantry with the French, not only for its privileged history within the *ancien régime* but also for its ongoing presence in postrevolutionary France, where it continues to inspire considerable admiration and a measure of mistrust from Anglo-Saxons.

The difference between English and French modes came home to me vividly when I was at Oxford many years ago. Nearing the end of my sabbatical stay, I knew something had gone awry. I was supposed to be researching a paper on the reception of George Sand in England, but spent most of my time caring for a willful five-year-old and keeping order in an antiquated thatched cottage outside the city. Sometimes on weekends, hoping to liven up my neutered state, I would go into town and attend a formal dinner party given by one of the Oxford faculty. The food was invariably bland and the conversation desexualized. Where were the playful innuendos I associated with European living?

"Enough," I silently screamed one day. "Enough of British dinners featuring stewed lamb and cauliflower. Enough of men who avoid my glance and make me feel like a talking block of wood. I'm going to France!"

As soon as school was out and I could place my son in an overnight boys' camp, I took off for Paris. The minute I dropped my suitcase in a small Left Bank hotel and strolled out into the street, I began to feel different. Outside my hotel, a street cleaner using one of those old-fashioned twig brooms looked me up and down admiringly and said, *"Bonjour, Madame"* in a suggestive tone I shall never forget. I was once again in France, a land where pleasing the ladies had not gone out of style.

I CANNOT RESIST ONE FURTHER ANECDOTE OF how French boys are, to this day, indoctrinated into the art of gallantry. My American friend Judy, who has lived in Paris since she married a Frenchman some twenty-five years ago, recalled this incident from the life of her son, Albert. He was three or four years old, playing on the floor, while she and her American brother discussed the differences between heterosexual relations in France and the United States. Her brother spoke of the ease with which Frenchmen attract women, while he lamented his own ineptness with the opposite sex. Judy agreed that Frenchmen certainly know how to turn on the charm. Witness her husband, who had wooed her away from less seductive Americans. These words were apparently not wasted on her son.

He looked up from his toys and carefully said: "Mommy, you have such pretty lips!"

I met Albert much later, when he was seventeen and in the last year of a prestigious French lycée. As he was considering various university possibilities, both in France and in the United States, I encouraged him to apply to my home university, Stanford. He was subsequently accepted, decided to go there, and ultimately made a name for himself, not only with his schoolwork but also with the ladies. Whatever elements of gallantry he had brought from France served him well on "the Farm."

CHAPTER THREE

Comic Love, Tragic Love

Molière and Racine

LOVE IS A GREAT TEACHER: WHAT ONE
NEVER WAS, IT TEACHES US TO BE.
Molière, *L'école des femmes*, 1662

THE CURSE OF VENUS IS FATAL.
Jean Racine, *Phèdre*, 1677

M OST FRENCH PEOPLE WERE STILL ILLITERATE DURING the seventeenth century. Only members of the nobility and the bourgeoisie could read and write. For those who could read with ease, a steady stream of novels, poems, fables, maxims, and memoirs familiarized them with the rules of gallantry. For the rest, as in Shakespearean England, you could keep abreast of the latest fashions by going to the theater, where there were comfortable boxes for the well-heeled and standing room in the pit for only fifteen sous. Paris, like London, was a mecca for playwrights, and even the

provinces had their share of theatrical productions. The illustrious names of Corneille, Molière, and Racine speak for an era when dramatic spectacle reached Olympian heights, never attained before or since in France, and most of these plays dealt directly or indirectly with love.

Molière and his younger contemporary Racine were first inheritors of and then contributors to the latest fashions in loving. Love showed its comic face in Molière's works, though sometimes those same comic faces betrayed inner anguish, whereas love was resolutely tragic in the world of Racine. Through the masks of comedy and tragedy, we can approach the meaning and practice of love during the 1660s and 1670s, the same period that gave rise to *La Princesse de Clèves*. At Versailles, in Paris, and in the major provincial cities, love onstage attracted spectators who could never get enough of beautiful young people magnetically drawn to one another despite the forces that conspired to pull them apart. As in real life, love knew no age barriers, with older men comically in love with younger women and older women tragically in love with younger men. In both instances, theater would take on a psychological dimension it didn't have before. Spectators who went to the theater to be entertained might come away with insights into their own amorous entanglements and erotic longings.

MOLIÈRE'S COMEDIES OF PASSION

During the years that Molière was traveling in the provinces with his theater troupe, from 1643 to 1658, *précieuses* controlled the salons that legislated correct French usage and refined modes of behavior. Yet even as preciosity dictated proper speech and conduct, its excesses would ultimately doom it to ridicule. *Les précieuses ridicules* (*The Pretentious Young Ladies*), the play that put Molière on the Parisian map in 1659, made a mockery of naïve young women bitten by the bug of romance. Better yet, listen to Magdelon, one of the two young protagonists, as she lays out her improbable vision of love to her incredulous father.

Father, my cousin will tell you, just as well as I, that marriage should never occur until after all the other adventures are over. A lover, in order to be acceptable, should be able to toy with noble fancies, and play the gamut of emotion, sweet and tender and impassioned. And he should woo according to the rules. . . . The day of the declaration arrives; this should usually take place on a garden path, while the rest of the party has gone out. . . . Then come the adventures: rivals who threaten an already established affection, persecutions by fathers, jealousies conceived on some false basis, reproaches, despairs, abductions and all the consequences. That's how matters are treated according to proper etiquette; those are rules of gallantry which can hardly be set aside.[1]

Magdelon's father has entirely different ideas. Marriage is where love should begin, and he has already chosen husbands for his daughter and his niece, Cathos, on the basis of their suitors' families and finances.

Magdelon reacts with outrage. "What? Begin with marriage?" And Cathos, in an oft-quoted line, adds: "As for me, all I can tell you is that I find marriage very shocking. How can one endure the idea of sleeping beside a man who is absolutely nude?"

The father warns the two young ladies: "Either you'll both be married very soon, or you'll go into a nunnery."

Magdelon dismisses her father's position as "utterly bourgeois," and Cathos condemns him as "coarse." But this is a play in which the common sense of the coarse bourgeois wins out over the affectations of the two damsels, who have come up from the provinces equipped with nothing more than precious language and far-fetched romantic notions acquired from books. While they hungrily look upon Paris as "the office of marvels, the center of good taste, wit, and gallantry," they are unable to distinguish between what is authentic and what is false and are taken in by two lackeys masquerading as gentlemen. Molière uses this old theatrical ploy to deflate the sentimental notions of two gullible young women and shame them into submission.

THE BOURGEOIS IDEAL OF MARRIAGE ESPOUSED BY Magdelon's father does not fare so well in Molière's subsequent plays. In fact, once settled in Paris after the success of *Les précieuses ridicules* and after Louis XIV had given him the Palais-Royal theater in 1660, he produced works that were more sympathetic to women's marital aspirations. *The School for Husbands* (1661), *The School for Wives* (1662), and *The Learned Ladies* (1672), written in the verse couplets that would become Molière's trademark, feature young women who succeed in marrying the men of their choice.

First, *The School for Husbands* pits old-fashioned patriarchal dominance against the new mode of love, which champions claims of the heart. These two positions are incarnated in two brothers, Sganarelle and Ariste, who have as their wards two sisters of marriageable age. Sganarelle, entrenched in the old order, insists that his ward, Isabelle, should live according to his reactionary ideas: she should stay at home and apply herself to domestic duties such as mending his underwear and knitting socks. She should shut her ears to romantic talk and never go out without a chaperon. Since he himself intends to marry Isabelle, despite their great difference in age, he is intent upon keeping her pure, or, in the language of Molière, "I don't want to wear horns on my head," the traditional symbol of cuckoldry.

His brother, Ariste, representing the new order, expresses the credo of gallant love: "I believe the heart is what must be won." He, too, wants to marry his ward, Léonor, and has brought her up according to an entirely different formula.

> *My care of Léonor has followed these maxims:*
> *I have not turned her slight liberties into crimes.*
> *I've always consented to her youthful desires.*
> *And, thank God, I haven't had to repent.*

I've allowed her attractive company;
Entertainment, balls, and comedies;
These are things, in my opinion, which are always
Very suitable for forming young people's wit;
And the school of the world, in that air which gives life,
Is better instruction than any book.

As for his marital plans, Ariste does not want to force Léonor's hand. He hopes that his great affection and kindness, plus a fortune of 4,000 crowns a year, will make up for the difference in age. But if not, she has the right to look elsewhere for a husband.

In the end, it is Ariste's version of female liberation that wins over Sganarelle's old-fashioned script. Léonor chooses Ariste rather than the blond-wigged fops who pursue her at balls, but Isabelle contrives to wed Valère, the young man who has secretly captured her heart, leaving Sganarelle to declaim misogynistically:

He who trusts a woman will always be deceived;
Even the best of them are fecund in evil;
It is a sex born to damn the whole world!

The real message is not so much the warfare between youthful love and parental authority, as one finds in many English and Italian plays of the same period, but the emergence of a radically new spirit announcing the partial emancipation of women. Early in the play Léonor's female attendant, Lisette, attacks Sganarelle's efforts to keep his ward a semiprisoner. She asks pointedly: "Are we among the Turks who lock up their women?" The Turkish harem was a symbol of female repression that seemed totally alien to seventeenth-century France, just as the Afghan burqa appears to Westerners today. Yet the liberties that many upper-class women enjoyed during the reign of Louis XIV were by no means universal, and they rarely included the choice of a marriage partner. Freedom, of a sort, was to begin only *after* marriage.

Not so long ago, Frenchwomen of the nobility and *haute bourgeoisie* were still brought up with this sequence in mind. When I was at Wellesley College in the 1950s, one of my housemates announced that she was returning to France to marry a man she hardly knew. Why, I asked, would anyone want to marry so young? Her answer was: to be free. Free? Weren't we free at college, despite curfews and overnight prohibitions? She was tired of such constraints and wanted to be "truly free." But how can one be truly free in marriage? Lillian had been brought up in an affluent family, without ever having been away from prying eyes. She went from a girls' boarding school to a women's college and was tired of her same-sex world. Marriage was the gateway into heterosexuality. She envisioned a life of relative independence, with opportunities to entertain and be entertained in the company of both men and women. So, back she went to France the summer after our freshman year, to marry, to live in Paris, and, God knows, enjoy the delights of gallant relationships. Though I once visited her in a luxurious Right Bank apartment, we lost touch over the years, and I wonder about the end of her story. Did her marital decision bring her the satisfaction she had anticipated?

The School for Husbands is a victory for female choice—Isabelle chooses Valère, Léonor chooses Ariste. But since one of the two women prefers to marry her older guardian, it does not argue against the marriage of an older man and a younger woman.

Indeed, in 1662, Molière, aged forty, would marry Armande Béjart, a woman twenty-one years his junior—a fact that undoubtedly contributed to his understanding of an older suitor's plight. Simultaneously, as he became caught up in the social whirl of Paris and the court, Molière limited his attacks against preciosity and gallantry to their most outrageous excesses. How could he not when Louis XIV honored him in 1663 as godfather to his first-born child (a son who died shortly after birth) and sponsored the production of Molière's plays at Versailles in the presence of the king himself and his first official mistress, Mademoiselle de La Vallière?

THE YEAR OF MOLIÈRE'S MARRIAGE IS BETTER known as the year of his controversial *School for Wives*, a fully developed five-act play that once again takes up the subject of an older man with a younger ward whom he intends to marry. Like Sganarelle in *The School for Husbands*, Arnolphe in *The School for Wives* is convinced that his ward Agnès's thorough education in the domestic arts and thorough ignorance of everything else will ensure that she will be the perfect wife. It should be enough for her "to know how to pray to God, to love me, and to sew."

His friend Chrysalde—the counterpart to Ariste in *The School for Husbands*—chides him for his narrow-minded views.

CHRYSALDE: A stupid woman is your delight?
ARNOLPHE: I would prefer a very stupid ugly woman
To a very beautiful one with lots of wit.

Arnolphe has tricked himself into thinking that a chaste adolescent brought up in a convent will be immune to the seductions of society. His major fear, one that haunts him from the beginning of the play, is that the "gallant humor" of the times will corrupt his future wife and force him to wear the horns of cuckoldry. Determined at all cost to prevent this scenario, he outlines to his ward, Agnès, his expectations for her after they are married.

> *Marriage is not a light-hearted affair.*
> *The rank of wife requires duties most severe.*
> *And you must not attain it, according to my view,*
> *To become a libertine and live at your ease.*
> *Your sex is there only for dependence:*
> *All power belongs on the side of the beard.*

Arnolphe's long speech to Agnès and "The Marriage Maxims or Duties of the Married Woman" that he makes her read out loud are a parody of patriarchy. To ask an upper-class woman to lower her eyes when talking to her husband and never look him straight in the face; to dress up only for him; to forgo all lotions that embellish the skin, as well as writing equipment—ink, paper, pens; and to make no attempt to please anyone but her husband would come across to Molière's audience as hopelessly and ridiculously outdated.

Of course, Arnolphe's plan to mold Agnès like a "piece of wax" is doomed to failure. Agnès, who leaves the convent wondering whether babies are born through the ears, quickly discovers romantic delights in the person of Horace, and, without tutelage, she surrenders to the force of love. Love helps her pierce the veils of ignorance and stupidity, which had enclosed her since birth, and teaches her to outwit her guardian with the skill of a practiced deceiver.

But Arnolphe, ridiculous as he is made to appear, is not a one-dimensional stock character. His profound love for Agnès, his anguished jealousy, his fear of becoming a cuckold all ring true and make him more sympathetic by the end of the play than one could have imagined at the beginning. Even knowing that Agnès is in love with Horace, he wants her more than ever and offers marriage on new terms.

> *Listen only to my amorous sighs,*
> *Look at my dying gaze, contemplate my person,*
> *Refuse this snot-nosed jerk and his proffered love.*
> *Surely he has thrown a spell over you.*
> *Surely you will be happier with me.*
> *As for your wish to be bold and sprightly,*
> *You will be all that, this I promise you.*
> *Ceaselessly, day and night, I shall caress you,*
> *Massage you, kiss you, eat you;*
> *You can conduct yourself just as you like.*

And he asks himself in a pathetic aside: "How far can passion go?" It is too late. The union of Arnolphe and Agnès was never meant to be. She and Horace, already joined by "mutual ardor," will marry with the good wishes of all but Arnolphe. It's a play that ends with thanks to heaven, "which arranges everything for the best."

IN THESE EARLY PLAYS, MOLIÈRE'S VISION OF love reflected his encounter with high society. After thirteen years in the provinces, he was not immune to the niceties of conversation and the suave exercise of gallantry found among the elite, as well as the freedom and wit of its sophisticated ladies. At the same time, he was not blind to stupidity and silliness wherever he found it: he mocked the affectations and euphemisms of overly purified women and he skewered fashionable men dripping with ribbons, along with their impromptu poems composed days in advance. When his *School for Wives* provoked heated controversy, he wrote his own *Critique of the School for Wives*, which ridiculed the prudes who had attacked him. And in his own defense, one of his male characters asserts: "All the ridiculous pictures that one exposes on the stage . . . are public mirrors." Despite their comic exaggerations, Molière's plays are indeed "public mirrors" of court and Parisian manners during the reign of Louis XIV.

In *The School for Wives*, the scene most criticized by Molière's detractors was Arnolphe's passionate declaration to Agnès. His heartfelt sighs and facial contortions and promises to massage and kiss her were judged out of keeping with the stolid bourgeois character presented earlier in the play. But Molière's defenders argued that "it is not incompatible for a person to be ridiculous in certain things and reasonable in others." The love of an older man—or woman— for a younger person can be the source of unspeakable desire and torment. Molière gave Arnolphe the heart of a hero for whom we feel compassion, even if the rest of him inspires ridicule. It is this paradox of love that Molière will explore more deeply in his greatest play, *The Misanthrope* (1666).

IF A TWENTY-FIRST-CENTURY SPECTATOR COULD SEE ONLY one play from the seventeenth century, I would recommend *The Misanthrope*. It is at once a comedy of gallant manners and a tragedy of true love unrequited. In the character of the young widow Cé-limène, we see a woman who has become fatally warped by the fraudulent world around her, and in the character of Alceste, we see a man so opposed to inauthenticity that he can find salvation only by being alone. Given their totally opposite natures, Alceste's love for Célimène is destined for defeat, but not before it has run the gamut of every emotion in the lover's book. He is captivated by Célimène's beauty and charm, jealous of her constant attention to other suitors, appalled by her propensity for bad-mouthing supposed friends, simultaneously willing to believe her private declarations of love and wary that she is as duplicitous with him as she is with everyone else. Smitten as he is, Alceste condemns society for Célimène's flighty behavior, and he lives with the illusion that she can be changed by his love. For he does indeed love her with an irrational force that borders on madness. (The lover, the poet, and the madman, as Shakespeare reminds us, have much in common.)

Alceste's friend Philinthe points out that the rectitude Alceste demands from "the whole human race" is conspicuously lacking in Célimène. Her coquetry and love of scandal, so close to the manners of the age, are faults that Alceste has managed to set aside. Yet he is not blind to her defects:

> *I see her faults, despite my ardent love,*
> *And all I see I fervently reprove.*
> *And yet I'm weak; for all her falsity,*
> *That woman knows the art of pleasing me.*
> *And though I never cease complaining of her,*
> *I swear I cannot manage not to love her.*[2]

Alceste's efforts to reform Célimène through his love are, of course, unsuccessful. While his love for her is earnest and exclusive, her feelings for him are playful and superficial. Their sparring duets reveal her inbred coquettishness, his churlish disposition, and their mutual incomprehension of one another. For example:

ALCESTE: Shall I speak plainly, Madame? I confess
Your conduct gives me infinite distress.
. . .
CÉLIMÈNE: You kindly saw me home, it would appear,
So as to pour invectives in my ear.
ALCESTE: I've no desire to quarrel. But I deplore
Your inability to shut the door.
. . .
CÉLIMÈNE: You're jealous of the whole world, Sir.
ALCESTE: That's true.
Since the whole world is well-received by you.
. . .
Well, if I mustn't be jealous, tell me, then,
Just how I'm better treated than other men.
CÉLIMÈNE: You know you have my love. Will that not do?
ALCESTE: What proof have I that what you say is true?
CÉLIMÈNE: I would expect, Sir, that my having said it
Might give the statement a sufficient credit.
. . .
ALCESTE: I make no secret of it: I've done my best
To exorcise this passion from my breast;
But thus far all in vain; it will not go;
It's for my sins that I must love you so.

. . .

CÉLIMÈNE: Yes, it's a brand-new fashion, I agree:
You show your love by castigating me,
And all your speeches are enraged and rude.
I've never been so furiously wooed.

Despite her worldly ways and skill in repartee, Célimène over-
plays her hand by sending declarations of love to two other suitors, exposing herself for what she is: *une femme galante*, a faithless
woman who confirms the stereotype of female inconstancy. Even
so, Alceste continues to love her. Like Arnolphe in *The School for
Wives*, he gives in to what he recognizes as an ignoble love and
offers to marry her, but only if she is willing to renounce her milieu
and flee with him to a deserted locale far from the perverting influences of society. Célimène refuses.

CÉLIMÈNE: What! I renounce the world at my young age,
And die of boredom in some hermitage?
ALCESTE: Ah, if you really loved me as you ought,
You wouldn't give the world a moment's thought;
Must you have me, and all the world beside?
CÉLIMÈNE: Alas, at twenty, one is terrified
Of solitude. I fear I lack the force
And depth of soul to take so stern a course.

So off Alceste goes to his desert, leaving behind the world of
gallantry for which he was so ill suited. Though we have laughed
throughout the play—at Alceste's monomaniacal fits, at Célimène's
satirical wit, at secondary characters who embody foolish human

weaknesses—we do not laugh at the end. Alceste, however impossible as a social being, has a strain of truth that Molière's contemporaries were loath to recognize. It would take succeeding generations, those bred on Rousseau in the eighteenth century, and the romantic poets in the nineteenth, to side with Alceste against society's compromises and betrayals. Gallantry was too firmly entrenched in the 1660s and 1670s for a spoilsport like Alceste to shake up the game of love. However, Molière's younger contemporary, Jean Racine, would have a different kind of success treating love with gravitas.

INCESTUOUS DESIRE IN RACINE'S *PHÈDRE*

In January 2010, I attended a production of Racine's *Phèdre* in San Francisco. A new translation of the play, commissioned by the American Conservatory Theater, had already been workshopped at Canada's Stratford Shakespeare Festival and was now making a rare appearance on an American stage.[3]

I went to the play in the company of my husband, hiding my fears from him. How could Racine's limpid poetry be gracefully translated into English, a language that does not lend itself easily to French verse? How could today's dual-career couples connect with the patriarchal mentality of seventeenth-century France? How would a sexually liberated audience react to the tortured passion and overwhelming guilt expressed by an author imbued with Jansenism, the most austere form of seventeenth-century Catholicism? Could the audience make the leap back to the requisite formality of court life under Louis XIV and a second leap back to ancient Greece, which furnished the original characters and plot for the play?

I feared incomprehension, even ridicule. And I was wrong. The audience sat transfixed through an hour and fifty minutes of elegant speech, without explosions or police chases, without even an intermission. My husband was among the first to initiate a standing ovation for a cast that had risen to the level of Racine and forcefully projected *Phèdre* into our hearts and minds. And I left the theater with the renewed conviction that Racine had given voice to the tyranny and turmoil of primordial passion as known through the ages, even if his voice was intrinsically seventeenth-century French.

The very first production of Racine's *Phèdre* took place in 1677, four years after the death of Molière and one year before the publication of *La Princesse de Clèves*. But unlike Molière and Madame de La Fayette, whose subject matter was French in every respect, Jean Racine looked to Greek and Roman literature for his subjects, following the example of Louis XIV, who used mythological figures to enhance his own grandeur. Racine took from Euripides' play *Hippolytus* the trio of Theseus, Phaedra, and Hippolytus. By the time of Euripides in the fifth century BCE, Theseus was already familiar to every Greek as the legendary king of Athens who had slain the Minotaur—a half-human, half-bull creature—in a maze on the island of Crete. Through this daring act, Theseus had freed his Athenian subjects from paying an annual tribute to Crete in the form of human sacrifices.

Phaedra was Theseus's second wife, daughter of Minos and Pasiphaë, the rulers of Crete. Hippolytus was the son of Theseus by his first wife, Hippolyta, queen of the Amazons. In Euripides' play, Hippolytus is the central character, a notoriously celibate young man devoted to Artemis, the virgin goddess of chastity. In Racine's play, the spotlight is moved to Phèdre, who finds herself in the familiar French triangle of husband, wife, and lover.

But what happens when the prospective lover rejects the advances of another man's wife, especially when that other man is his father? What happens when love that is already illicit by virtue of its adulterous nature becomes doubly illicit through connotations of incest? Then all hell breaks loose.

When Phèdre first appears onstage, she is wasting away from an unknown malady and has resigned herself to an untimely death. Her confidante, Oenone, forces her to reveal her shameful secret: that she, Phèdre, wife of the heroic king Theseus, is madly in love with her stepson, Hippolytus. Previously, Phèdre had been able to conceal her passion by treating Hippolytus rudely, by sending him away from the Athenian capital, and by concentrating on the well-being of her own younger son. Publicly, she has played the role of the good mother and the hateful stepmother. As far as her actions are concerned, she has nothing for which to reproach herself. But ever since her husband Theseus took off six months earlier on one of his long uncertain voyages, she has been obliged to reside in the coastal city of Troezen under the protection of Hippolytus, and carnal desire has returned with a vengeance. She describes herself, in one of the most famous lines of the play, as the victim of "Venus attached to her prey."

Venus, the Latin name for Aphrodite, is an implacable goddess. If she seizes you, you are doomed to love, no matter how tragic the consequences. In the world of Greek and Roman mythology invoked by Racine, to be caught in the claws of Venus has the same effect as a medieval love potion. Passion of this order is irreversible.

Phèdre has certainly struggled mightily against her incestuous desires, for she is not the remorseless pagan of ancient legend, nor the proud adulteress of medieval romance, but a Christianized version of woman subject to a guilty conscience. And how Phèdre's guilty conscience eats away at her! By the time she appears on-stage, she is already in a state of extreme frailty and mental disarray, which makes it easy for Oenone to pry out a confession. Once Phèdre has described her torments, there is no going back. Speaking out is in itself an irreversible act. In Racine's world, one talks one's way into a state of exultation and into the sequence of tragic events that follow.

The situation is further compounded by the fact that Hippolytus is secretly in love with Aricia, the only surviving offspring of an enemy dynasty with pretensions to the throne of Athens. Theseus has spared her under the condition that she remain in captivity and never marry. In both cases—Phèdre's and Hippolytus's—the love object is forbidden fruit, and in both cases, the smitten parties reveal the secret to a trusted confidant before confessing directly to the persons they love. Hippolytus unburdens himself to his friend Théramène, who encourages him to try his luck with Aricia. By the time Hippolytus declares himself to Aricia, and by the time Phèdre admits her longings to Hippolytus, the spectator is tense with anticipation.

We experience the emotions of the characters onstage as if they were our own. First, we witness Hippolytus's embarrassed tenderness toward Aricia and her dignified, yet subtly flirtatious response. At that moment, we are all young lovers susceptible to the charm of budding romance. For a moment we forget the dark clouds gathering in the background, the fate of kingdoms and empires and smaller nations doomed to destruction. We forget the catastrophic harm inflicted by evildoers and even the well-intentioned. We open our hearts to the possibility that love will conquer all when Hippolytus declares to Aricia:

> *My love speaks crudely, but do not reject it.*
> *Without you, I never could have known it.*[4]

After that bright interlude, the meeting between Phèdre and Hippolytus evokes an entirely different set of emotions. Believing her husband Theseus to be dead, Phèdre allows herself to be persuaded by Oenone that her love for Hippolytus is no longer unspeakable. We cringe with the knowledge, unknown to Phèdre, that Hippolytus loves Aricia. We are embarrassed as Phèdre works her way up to a declaration by invoking the physical similarities between Theseus and his son. Having unsealed her lips, she permits the words so long repressed to spill forth in an ardent tirade where love and guilt are inextricably interwoven.

> *I am in love.*
> *But do not suppose for a second*
> *I think myself guiltless*
> *For loving you as I love you.*
> *. . .*
> *You know too well how I have treated you.*
> *I not only shunned you.*
> *I acted like a tyrant, I had you banished.*
> *I wanted you to hate me. . . .*
> *Yes, you hated me more. And more and more—*
> *But my love never lessened.*

Phèdre's interior struggle between her passion for Hippolytus and her sense of guilt are now acted out onstage. Condemning herself as "utterly corrupt," she begs Hippolytus to punish her, to kill her, or lend her his sword so that she can kill herself. Instead, he flees to join his friend, Théramène, and depart for Athens, where turmoil has broken out at the news of his father's death.

At the beginning of act 3, Phèdre is at the nadir of despair. She has uncovered her love to an incredulous, horrified Hippolytus and realized, too late, that she should have kept her feelings to herself. Oenone advises her to try to find peace in the obligations now imposed on her by the power vacuum in Athens, to which Phèdre responds:

> *Me, rule? Me take control*
> *Of a state flying to pieces*
> *When I cannot control myself?*

Such protestations soon become moot because—to everyone's surprise—Theseus turns out to be alive and about to return. Now Phèdre is tormented by a new fear: what if Hippolytus reveals to Theseus her lovesickness? Once again Phèdre expresses her preference for death to disgrace, and once again Oenone comes up with a solution: "Accuse him first—of the same crime."

When Theseus arrives home, Oenone follows through on her own suggestion and accuses Hippolytus of attempting to seduce Phèdre. In response, Theseus curses Hippolytus and calls down the wrath of the gods. By the last scene of the play, both Phèdre and Oenone have joined Hippolytus in death, but not before Phèdre confesses all to Theseus. And in this last scene she regains some of her lost dignity and honor. With poison in her veins and only a few moments to live, she admits her unrequited love for Hippolytus and affirms his innocence.

> *Listen to me carefully, Theseus.*
> *Every moment now is precious to me.*
> *Hippolytus was chaste. And loyal to you.*
> *I was the monster in this riddle.*
> *I was insane with an incestuous passion.*

As Phèdre expires at his feet, Theseus goes off to honor the remains of his son and to take Aricia as his surrogate daughter.

How did Racine, a seventeenth-century Frenchman, refashion the subject of love for his time and place? If we compare his *Phèdre* to the Greek model on which it was based, the first obvious change is that he transferred the leading role from a male to a female. Ten years earlier, Racine's first major theatrical success, *Andromaque* (1667), had born the title of its female protagonist, played by the seductive actress Thérèse du Parc, whom Racine secretly married. After her death, he took up with the greatest actress of his day, La Champmeslé, who would play the lead in *Phèdre*. Even Racine's last plays, *Esther* and *Athalie*, written in 1689 and 1691 when he had become a sage married man and prolific father, would feature a woman as the central character. With Racine's *Phèdre* in 1677, and Madame de La Fayette's *La Princesse de Clèves* in 1678, the French were getting used to seeing women with top billing.

A second significant change in *Phèdre* was the addition of the character Aricia, who did not exist in the Euripides play. She brings another feminine dimension into the drama and one that incarnates normative ideas about love. She is young, beautiful, noble, and a captive. Little wonder that Hippolytus finds her irresistible! Under her sway, the hero, supposedly immune to love's flame, becomes humanized—one might even say feminized.

This French feminization of love, with its roots reaching back to troubadour poetry and medieval romance, contrasts markedly with the ancient Greek masculinist ideal. It is true that Euripides and the other great Greek tragedians—Aeschylus and Sophocles—have given us several imposing female characters, such as Antigone and Medea. And it is true that Racine learned from Euripides how to make even monsters like Medea—a woman who murdered her own children!—sympathetic to an audience. Yet Racine goes one step further. He makes Phèdre's torment understandable and her person not to be despised. A woman who falls in love with her stepson, who resists revealing this love until she is practically dying, who feels guilty for a crime she has not committed, who allows herself to be manipulated by her most loyal confidant, who is rejected and humiliated by the young man she lusts after, and who ultimately atones for her sins through confession and suicide—this woman is not a monster. She is human, all too human, and could exist in any age.

If we set aside the royal setting with its crowns and swords, it is not impossible to imagine a similar scenario in certain American families today. Stepmothers and stepfathers living in close proximity to the offspring born from their partners' earlier unions sometimes find themselves sexually attracted to these children. We know that fathers and stepfathers sometimes lust after their daughters and stepdaughters and may even force them into sexual relations, usually with devastating effects on the child. Mother-son incest is considerably less common.

Incestuous desire always defies societal proscriptions. It would certainly have horrified those brought up in the morally strict Jansenist branch of Catholicism, like Racine. And it is this stern version of Christianity, however disguised under the names of Greek gods, that Racine implants in Phèdre's conscience and which contributes to her overwhelming sense of guilt. Even if her sin remains hidden in her heart, even if it is not acted upon, it is seen by the eye of God and causes her unbearable anguish. Phèdre's struggle between the claims of passion and the relentless attacks of her conscience resonate with the moral dilemmas of many historical eras, including our own.

This is the paradox of Racinian love, and of French love. On the one hand, no people in the Western world understand the claims of passion better than the French. No one extols love more—with the possible exception of the English in their poetry and the Italians in opera. No one better conveys the obsessive nature of romantic love and its tendency to take precedence over all other human relations.

And yet the French cannot avoid their Catholic heritage, which has had a notably troubled relationship with carnal desire. While the French have difficulty conceptualizing love without a sexual component and are generally much less moralistic about sex than Americans, they are nonetheless imbued with Judeo-Christian beliefs that impose numerous restraints on sexual behavior. The tension between these collective beliefs and an individual's erotic longings is palpable in many French novels, plays, and films centered on love.

Which brings us to a second facet of Racine's *Phèdre* that is peculiar to the French. The French love to talk about love. For all of

Phèdre's initial silence, once she begins to speak, she is inexhaust-ible. She evokes every aspect of her seething desire, burning body, and tortured mind, without, of course, ever using a vulgar word. Hippolytus, too, for all his previous career as an enemy of love, suddenly knows how to turn a phrase when he declares himself to Aricia. Like all classical French writers, Racine followed the dic-tates of linguistic good taste that had become operative in salon and court culture. And he elevated this constrained style to the level of tragedy through his sublime poetry.

With or without the craft of poetry, a French man or woman who doesn't know how to talk the language of love is considered a boor. In the French mind, conversation is almost as essential to love as physical attraction. Of course, Molière made fun of those gentlemen who felt obliged to carry ready-made love poems with them at all times, and he ridiculed those ladies who used so many euphemisms in conversation that you couldn't understand what they were saying. Still, the tradition of gallant love talk has never disappeared from France. Think of Edmond Rostand's Cyrano de Bergerac, who lent his flowery speech to the word-challenged Christian, so that Christian could become an acceptable lover for Roxane, the woman both men adored. Think of the characters in Eric Rohmer's films, who spend most of their time talking lucidly about the love obsessions that devour them.

The emphasis on language is ubiquitous in France, from poli-tics and medicine to lovemaking. The late French psychoana-lyst Jacques Lacan categorized human beings as *des êtres parlant*: "speaking beings." In France, you are expected to be able to articu-late desire. Declarations of love help to define one's feelings and encourage the loved one to reciprocate in kind.

When Phèdre begins to talk in the hope of finding release through confession, the opposite occurs: speaking out inflames her ardor. She works herself up to a pitch of erotic excitement in her conversations with Oenone and then with Hippolytus, despite the moralistic self-censure that weaves through her words. Only in her confrontation with Theseus does she learn to curb her tongue, and eventually shut up.

Theseus is both husband and father figure to Phèdre, as well as king of Athens and father to Hippolytus. He represents ultimate authority in both public and private life. The kings of the *ancien régime*, the leaders of the French Revolution, Napoleon I and Napoleon III, the Restoration monarchs, and the French Republic presidents of the nineteenth and twentieth centuries—they all represented the rule of the father.

The father is always there lurking in the background of French literature, as he is in traditional life. He may have been a great womanizer, as was Theseus in his early manhood; he may be a foolish dupe or ridiculous *arriviste*, as are Molière's fathers, but whatever his foibles, his authority is pervasive. Phèdre cannot loosen Theseus's hold on her, even when he is away, even when he is presumed dead. Hippolytus, too, must brave Theseus's sanction if he is to love Aricia.

Perhaps one source of Phèdre's uncontrollable lust for Hippolytus springs from repressed rage against Theseus. Preferring a younger edition of the man she had married is one way of throwing off the shackles she has worn as a wife. But let us not get carried away with psychoanalytic investigations into Phèdre's unconscious, nor apply a patently feminist interpretation to the institution of marriage. Phèdre is an older woman who falls in love with a younger man. This could happen to any woman. The irresistible attraction of youth fuels her desire, and when she hears of Hippolytus's love for Aricia, jealousy, too, increases her turmoil. In the end, totally distraught, she turns to Theseus to set things right. In the end, the rule of the father prevails.

Despite the social advances made by Frenchwomen in the seventeenth century, Racine, Molière, and most of their contemporaries had no intention of disavowing male authority. With Louis XIV firmly on the throne, autocratic power was at its zenith. Moreover, Frenchmen would have seen the male principle embodied not only in government and family but also in the mental capacity of reason. Women, they averred, were more given to sentiments, like love, which reputedly clouded their judgment. Witness Phèdre. Nevertheless, it was one of Racine's fellow writers, a French scientist and faith-affirming Christian philosopher named Blaise Pascal, who came up with the best-known credo for those addicted to love: "The heart has its reasons, which Reason does not know."

IN THE THREE WORKS I HAVE CHOSEN from a wealth of seventeenth-century material—*La Princesse de Clèves*, *Le Misanthrope*, and *Phèdre*—love is always involuntary. It thrusts itself upon us. We do not choose to love or not to love. Call it the consequence of a love potion, or Cupid's arrow, or "chemistry," love defies rational explanations. The husband who should be loved in *La Princesse de Clèves* is never able to inspire within his wife one ounce of the craving she feels for a man she should not love. Alceste is a temperamentally unsuitable suitor for Célimène, and even though he knows it, he cannot free himself from the love trap she has set for him. Phèdre is doubly inappropriate as a partner for Hippolytus, for she is married to his father, which makes her desire both adulterous and incestuous. Such loves cannot have happy endings.

Still, some lovers do enjoy brief moments of bliss. If they are young, physically well-endowed, and drawn to one another by a robust magnetic pull, all external efforts to pry them apart will fail. Such is the case for the *jeunes premiers*, the youthful lovers in many of Molière's comedies. Despite the increasingly problematic picture of human relations that he presents in his later plays (for example, *Tartuffe* and *Don Juan*), despite the somber portrayal of illicit or unrequited love found in most of Racine's tragedies, despite Madame de La Fayette's sober renunciation of sexual love in her fiction, the ideal of true love remained entrenched within the French mentality. While gallantry often acquired a world-weary tinge and could degenerate into cold-blooded seduction, claims of the heart were never silenced. Both of these currents would find their voice in the following century.

CHAPTER FOUR

Seduction and Sentiment

Prévost, Crébillon fils, Rousseau, and Laclos

YES, MY FRIEND, WE SHALL BE UNITED IN SPITE OF OUR
SEPARATION; WE SHALL BE HAPPY DESPITE FATE. IT IS THE
UNION OF HEARTS WHICH CONSTITUTES THEIR TRUE FELICITY.

Jean-Jacques Rousseau, *Julie, or The New Eloise*, Part II, Letter XV, 1761

SHE IS CONQUERED, THAT PROUD WOMAN WHO DARED TO THINK
SHE COULD RESIST ME! YES, MY FRIENDS, SHE IS MINE, ENTIRELY
MINE; AFTER YESTERDAY, SHE HAS NOTHING LEFT TO GRANT ME.

Choderlos de Laclos, *Dangerous Liaisons*, Part IV, Letter CXXV, 1782

EIGHTEENTH-CENTURY FRENCH ART AND FICTION ARE PRACTI-
CALLY synonymous with lovemaking. If we were to judge
only by paintings, we would conclude that members of the upper
classes had nothing to do other than disport themselves as lovers.
The *fêtes galantes* series of Jean-Antoine Watteau portrayed delicate and wistful figures embarking to the Isle of Cythera—the

legendary birthplace of Venus. This pastoral paradise inhabited by dreamy ladies and lazily attentive men acted as prelude to the openly erotic works of Watteau's celebrated successors, François Boucher and Jean-Honoré Fragonard.

Boucher's female figures were overtly sexual, sometimes exposing their breasts and derrières to anyone wanting to gape at them. He also painted seductive women, their luxurious clothing enhancing their curves, as in his portraits of Madame de Pompadour, the third of King Louis XV's official mistresses. Boucher's sumptuous colors and sensual overtones fulfilled to perfection the libidinous taste of the century.

Fragonard's less fleshy creatures kiss tenderly in bucolic settings, send each other love letters, soar in garden swings, and vow to love each other forever. The museums and châteaux of France are filled with the rococo paintings of Boucher and Fragonard, but Americans don't have to go that far to see their work. Superb examples hang on the walls of many American museums, including New York's Frick, which contains Fragonard's magnificent series known as *The Progress of Love*. Though these paintings were originally commissioned by Madame du Barry, the last of Louis XV's official mistresses, and intended for her garden pavilion, she never had them installed. Ultimately they wound up at the Frick, where they can be found in a room with delicately carved wall paneling and elegant pieces of furniture from the same period.

Gallantry was the order of the day, "the taste of our century" according to the Abbé Girard in his 1737 dictionary of French synonyms; these are practically the same words that the fabulist Jean de La Fontaine had used in his 1669 preface to *Psyché*. Had nothing changed in the dominion of gallantry during the seven decades that separated these two works?

What had changed was the meaning of the word "gallantry." More and more, it implied a short-term sexual affair, with little if any emotional depth. The Abbé Girard distinguished clearly between gallantry and love in the following manner:

> *Love* is more ardent than *gallantry*. Its object is the person . . . whom one loves as much as one loves oneself. . . . *Gallantry* is a more voluptuous passion than love; it has sex for its object. . . .
>
> *Love* attaches us uniquely to one person . . . so that we feel only indifference for all others, whatever beauty and merit they have. *Gallantry* draws us to all persons who have beauty and charm . . . *gallanteries* are sometimes endless in number, and follow one another until old age dries up its source.
>
> In *love*, it is mainly the heart which experiences pleasure . . . the satisfaction of the senses contributes less to the sweetness of pleasure than a certain contentment in the interior of the soul. . . . In *gallantry*, . . . the senses are more eager to be satisfied.[1]

This shift in the meaning of gallantry, with its primary emphasis on sexual satisfaction, was due, in part, to the rulers of France who succeeded Louis XIV. After his death in 1715, the underside of gallantry came out in the open. What had been tolerated in secret during his reign no longer bothered to stay hidden. During the scandalous Regency period (1715–1723) when Louis XV was a boy, gallantry gave up the pretense of true love, and openly promoted serial seduction. Under the regent, Philippe d'Orléans, known to sleep with anyone he could lure into his bed, there was little place for heartfelt emotions or moral concerns. What counted was the sheer pleasure of voluptuous lovemaking, not love in any permanent sense.

Certainly Louis XV did little to stop that trend when he took control of the kingdom. Like his predecessors, he enjoyed a long succession of mistresses, among them the Marquise de Pompadour and the Comtesse du Barry mentioned above. But unlike his great-grandfather, Louis XIV, who turned religious at the end of his life under the influence of Madame de Maintenon, Louis XV became notorious in his old age for the harem of very young women he bedded on the royal budget. Poor Marie Leszczynska, his Polish wife, was kept busy bearing him children, eleven in all, while in her husband's quarters, the line between gallantry and debauchery was simply effaced.

What happened to true love in this cynically gallant world? At best, gallantry accommodated the love of two individuals, as long as they played according to the rules. In polite society, lovers—like everyone else—had to make a show of meticulous manners and clever conversation. Public displays of affection were frowned upon, even between married couples. In fact, among the nobility, it was considered *déclassé* for married people to demonstrate their love in social settings. Rémond de Saint-Mard wrote in his *Lettres galantes et philosophiques*: "The Marquis de ★★★ . . . is insufferable: he's always caressing his wife in public; he always has something to say to her. In short, you would say he acts like a lover."[2] And that, Saint-Mard added, makes the Marquis de ★★★ appear infinitely ridiculous in the eyes of society. Of course in private, far from censorious eyes, lovers of every stripe voiced their feelings and acted out desire. We get a peek into those secret spaces from a series of eighteenth-century novelists, most notably Abbé Prévost, Crébillon fils, Jean-Jacques Rousseau, and Choderlos de Laclos, whose works opened up new territory on the map of tenderness.

THE NOVEL WAS THE CONSECRATED HOME OF love. Love peopled its pages and set off vibrations in the skins of readers eager to experience romance in all its forms, from gallantry to true love. While love was and is essentially a personal affair between two people, gallantry was and is a social phenomenon with similar rules for everyone. It can easily spend itself in artificial gestures and become a caricature of authentic emotion, as we have already seen in *La Princesse de Clèves* and *Le Misanthrope*. During the Regency and the reign of Louis XV, the excesses of gallantry baldly degenerated into libertinage.

A libertine would seduce a woman by any means, take advantage of her youth or modest parentage, and then abandon her after "he had had his way with her." Often she was left pregnant, which could reduce her to outcast status. This was not merely the stuff of literature; it was an old story in France, as in other European countries, but it seems to have garnered more print attention in the eighteenth century than at any other time. Seduction novels proliferated in France and England, to be imitated by pulp fiction for years to come, well into our own benighted era.

Women were not always the victims of libertinage. They, too, knew how to play the game of seduction, both as gallant ladies and as coquettes. The eighteenth-century *Encyclopédie* distinguished between the two, reserving the greater opprobrium for the coquette who kept several lovers dangling at once. In contrast, the gallant lady, motivated by the desire to please and to be thought lovable, limited herself to one lover at a time. Regardless of the fine distinctions presented in encyclopedias and dictionaries, novels portrayed a messier reality. The important thing was not to be the one who got dumped—that could ruin anyone's reputation, gallant lady, gallant man, base seducer, or frank coquette.

The Goncourt brothers, in their classic study, *The Woman of the Eighteenth Century*, took the position that "woman equaled man, and may even have surpassed him, in that libertinage of gallant wickedness."[3] Given the Goncourts' notorious misogyny, it is not surprising that they judged women to be equally as responsible as men, if not more so, for the century's moral decadence. It is true that many aristocratic women took lovers after they were married and some even got away with giving birth to illegitimate children without unpleasant consequences for themselves. The same cannot be said for their children, often abandoned at church doors and raised under harsh conditions. The stories of unfortunate "love children" popularized in fiction had their roots in verifiable history, as we shall see in the following chapter on the life of Julie de Lespinasse.

If we are to believe the novelists—and I suggest we do, to the extent that their characters mirror eighteenth-century social realities—love was in a state of constant warfare between claims of the heart and claims of the flesh. On the one side, the heart, the soul, the mind, sentiment, tenderness, and sensibility lined up to defend the rights of true love. On the other, sensuality, pleasure (*plaisir*), taste (*goût*), and above all voluptuousness (*volupté*) infiltrated upper-class life and often triumphed over authentic emotion. Only the hyphenated term *amour-passion* gave expression to both cravings. To this day, the French speak of *amour-passion* as a special category, the kind of love you would hope to experience at least once in a lifetime.

Abbé Prévost's novel, known popularly as *Manon Lescaut* (its full title can be found in the bibliography), brought an obsessive form of love-passion to the French in 1731 and to the rest of the world in Puccini's late-nineteenth-century operatic version. Passion was still, in Prévost's novel, an affair of love at first sight, as it had been in medieval romance, as it was for the Prince de Clèves, and as it would be for innumerable romantic heroes and heroines. Here is how Prévost's hero, the seventeen-year-old Chevalier des Grieux, experienced the first sight of the woman who would constitute his love-passion: "I found myself enflamed all of a sudden to the point of rapture."[4] Though her background was modest, she had the beauty and manners of a woman well above her station. Discovering that she was being sent by her family to a convent to become a nun, Des Grieux was immediately transformed from a naïve adolescent to an active lover. He managed to dine alone with her that evening and experienced the full force of first-time love.

I soon realized that I was less of a child than I had thought. My heart opened up to a thousand pleasurable emotions, of which I had not had the least idea. A gentle warmth spread through my veins. I was in a kind of transport, which for a time deprived me of the power of speech and found expression only through my eyes. Mademoiselle Manon Lescaut— for so she told me she was called—seemed well pleased with the effect of her charms.

Before we know it, Des Grieux and Manon have fled from Amiens to Paris. Since they were both minors and would have needed their parents' consent to marry, they skipped the projected nuptials and found themselves living as man and wife "without giving the matter a moment's thought." Des Grieux asserts that he would have been happy with Manon for his entire life if she had remained faithful to him. And here we arrive at the kernel of the story: a virtuous young man of noble extraction falls for a lower-class woman given to all the excesses of the century. Over and over again, her need for pleasure, amusement, and luxury will do them in. Manon brings into French literature *la femme fatale*, the direct ancestor of Carmen and a string of ill-famed women who ensnare ostensibly good, but weak, men and cause their ruin.

Gone are the standards of virtue that aristocrats at least pretended to uphold in the past. Whenever money runs out, Manon runs into the arms of lovers more affluent than Des Grieux, returning to him afterward with expressions of love and remorse, which he—permanently enamored—always accepts. Like many men of Prévost's generation, Des Grieux sees little harm in cheating at cards when it comes to providing Manon with the affluent lifestyle she craves. Worse yet, he too gets entangled in schemes that will defraud wealthy aristocrats of vast sums in exchange for Manon's charms, twice landing them both in jail. The second time, Manon is deported to New Orleans with a band of other women convicts deemed fit only to populate that distant primitive colony. Des Grieux, still love-struck, follows after her.

Does Manon, or Des Grieux for that matter, have any redeeming qualities? The author tries to make us believe that they do. *Amour-passion*, he tells us, was their undoing. Over and over and over again, Des Grieux attributes any wrongdoing to his fatal love for Manon: "I love her with so violent a passion that it has made me the most unhappy of men." Love of this sort is its own justification. And while Manon is notoriously liberal with her favors, she too professes an undying love for Des Grieux. She explains at one point that the only faithfulness she values is that of the heart. At heart, Manon may not be evil, but she is clearly thoughtless, flighty, and amoral.

There is little in the novel to convince us that Manon merits Des Grieux's undying flame. He tries to endow her with the tragic dimension of a Racinian heroine like Phèdre, but she comes across more like the duplicitous character of Célimène in *Le Misanthrope*, without her wit and class. How can we understand Manon's solid hold on Des Grieux?

She undoubtedly knows how to manipulate him. After her third infidelity, he calls her a false-hearted girl, a cruel and fickle lover, a perfidious mistress, a deceiving slut. Yet, a few moments later, instead of walking out the door as planned, he responds to her tears by taking her in his arms, kissing her tenderly, and begging for forgiveness. He tries to convince himself: "She sins, but without malice . . . she is frivolous and imprudent, but she is straightforward and sincere." Straightforward and sincere? Only if we see her through his biased eyes. He will confess to his father: "It is love, as you know, love alone—fatal passion!—that has caused my errors. . . . Love has made me too tender, too passionate, too faithful, and too ready, perhaps to indulge the desires of a mistress who is all enchantment. These are my crimes."

However criminal his actions, we are expected to believe that Des Grieux has an inner goodness. His enduring feelings for

Manon, in spite of her failings, are presented as the mark of an exceptional person. You must have a martyr's strength to submit to love-passion, often to the point of humiliation or even self-destruction. This emotion-driven love would find its ultimate voice later in the century in *La nouvelle Héloïse* (*Julie, or The New Eloise*) by Jean-Jacques Rousseau. But before we come to him, we must consider another ingenious novel, also published in the 1730s, that traces the amorous adventures and misadventures of a young man in search of love.

LES ÄGAREMENTS DU COEUR ET DE L'ESPRIT (literally "the wanderings of the heart and mind" but translated as *The Wayward Head and Heart*), written by Crébillon fils, starts out by imitating initial aspects of *Manon Lascaut*. Like Des Grieux, the hero of Crébillon's novel is a seventeen-year-old, completely unversed in the ways of the world. But this is all the two men have in common, for the Chevalier de Meilcour sets about seducing a fortyish woman, before, and even after, he falls in love with Hortense de Théville, a beauty his own age. This youthful lover quickly learns that the pursuit of women is a full-time affair, filled with lies and pitfalls he could never have anticipated. Where was the true love he had heard about from the past, "so respectful, so sincere, so delicate"? Instead, he saw before him sexual liaisons undertaken in the interest of passing pleasure rather than enduring attachment. The ease with which the two sexes became physically involved was described in these much-quoted lines:

> You told a woman that she was pretty three times; . . . The first time she would certainly believe you; she would thank you the second; and not uncommonly reward you the third.[5]

The young chevalier has everything to learn and little to offer other than his prepossessing appearance and noble name. But others—the fortyish Madame de Lursay, the *femme galante* Madame de Senanges, and the libertine Comte de Versac—are eager to instruct him. They take him on a romp through salons, dining rooms, boudoirs, carriages, parks, and the opera, as Meilcour attempts to discover the meaning of such words as pleasure, passion, heart, and, of course, love itself. (The Flammarion 1985 French edition of this work provides an "Index to the Vocabulary of Love" with one hundred entries and over a thousand references!) Suffice it to say that *The Wayward Head and Heart* offers an ironic portrayal of love *à la française*.

Meilcour's ignorance of the rules of seduction and his maladroit behavior occasion many moments of comic ridicule. He does not understand that he, as a man, must make the first declaration of love, even when Madame de Lursay gives him ample opportunity to do so. Half-reclining on her sofa, ready to be seduced, she is confronted with a tongue-tied suitor experiencing the most horrible fright of his life. The only words he can utter concern the type of decorative sewing she has taken up. "'Are you tying bows, Madame?' I asked in a trembling voice. At this witty and interesting question Madame de Lursay stared at me in astonishment." Meilcour has several other comic experiences before he learns how to take advantage of the situation. During his apprenticeship, he is always surprised by his volatile emotions in response to a society that keeps moving faster than his apprehension of it, like a constantly changing kaleidoscope.

That society, modeled on the pleasure-driven Regency period, hastened the shift toward libertinage that became one of the two main erotic currents of the century. Versac, the spokesman for libertinage, advises Meilcour to seek gratification of the senses without concern for sentiment. Indeed, at one point Versac makes an important distinction between the "heart" and "taste." He dismisses the former as "novelists' jargon" and defines the latter as an intense friendship that resembles love in its pleasures without its "silly" refinements. Though Versac's arguments will have lasting influence on Meilcour's impressionable character, there is an unresolved contradiction in the novel, as there was in eighteenth-century society. Sentiment, feeling, emotion never disappear. They inflame the hearts of the young and continue to erupt throughout life as long as one is not thoroughly jaded. And despite Versac's low regard for the heart, the society in which he plots his seductions never dismisses its importance.

Sentimental love remains the major justification for giving in to desire. Madame de Lursay explains to Meilcour that she might mistake desire for love if she were younger, but at her age, she could only yield to a lover's entreaties, without self-reproach, if she believed herself loved. "I will not surrender myself except to true feeling." When Meilcour finally succeeds in bedding Madame de Lursay, he convinces himself that what he feels for her is more than desire. He says to himself: "The work of my senses appeared to me [to be] the work of my heart." The verb "appeared" is the operative word here. It reflects the discrepancy between Meilcour's experience of sensual pleasure and his quest for true love.

Although the book ends at this point, we are led to believe that Meilcour will continue his erotic career beyond his affair with Madame de Lursay. How do we know? We know from the interjections of an older version of Meilcour, who comments from time to time on the adventures of his younger self. Like *Manon Lescaut*, *The Wayward Head and Heart* is a memoir-novel told from the point of view of an older, chastened, narrator. Yet however cynical he has become in later life, this middle-aged Meilcour has not forgotten the feeling of what it was like to be young, naïve, and hungry for love.

The Wayward Head and Heart has been credited with (or accused of) inaugurating the novel of libertinage in France. It also bears numerous hallmarks of the sentimental novel popular at this time in both France and England. The most famous English novels of this genre, Samuel Richardson's *Pamela* (1740–1741) and *Clarissa Harlowe* (1747–1748), would be widely imitated in France, not only for their amorous content but also for their epistolary form—that is, a novel written entirely in letters. Prévost, who had lived in England, translated *Clarissa* into French in 1751, and Jean-Jacques Rousseau appropriated the letter-novel style in his one long work of fiction, *La nouvelle Héloïse* (1761).

Even allowing for English influence, Rousseau must be granted the lion's share of credit for launching the cult of sensibility in France, a cult that championed nature above culture, emotion above reason, and spontaneous love above all the contrivances of gallantry. His novel, *La nouvelle Héloïse*, offered an idealized romance between Julie, a young woman of noble birth, and Saint-Preux, her love-struck tutor, who was unacceptable to her family because he lacked both title and fortune. Their story became an unprecedented best-seller in its day, and made Rousseau the darling of countless readers, the young and the old, aristocrats and bourgeois, and even literate members of the working class. In the course of forty years, from 1761 to

1800, *La nouvelle Héloïse* was published in seventy-two separate editions, and those who could not afford to buy the book could rent parts of it from bookstores for twelve sous per half hour! So jealous were Rousseau's fellow authors that some, like Voltaire, parodied the book and tried to make its author a laughingstock. All to no avail: Rousseau's admirers won the day. His one novel eclipsed all those that had previously depicted sentimental love, and in time it would be seen as the forerunner to the early nineteenth-century movement known as romanticism.

Today Rousseau's literary reputation rests more on his posthumously published memoirs than on *La nouvelle Héloïse*. We recognize in his *Confessions* the ancestor of all the self-revealing autobiographies that have proliferated for the past 250 years. As for *Émile*, his treatise on education, today's critics have faulted him primarily for his treatment of women, who were, according to Rousseau, created solely to serve the needs of men and children. You can imagine how that sticks in the craw of feminists, like me.

But *La nouvelle Héloïse* is ambiguous enough to provoke differing interpretations of how men and women should interact. We shall have to judge for ourselves as we examine it. Then, by comparing Rousseau's novel with Laclos' *Liaisons dangereuses*, we shall see two very different faces of eighteenth-century love, one sentimentally sacred, the other perversely profane.

AMONG THE LETTERS THAT WERE SAVED FROM my time at Wellesley College, there is one from my sophomore year dated October 29, 1951, written to my future husband, Irvin Yalom, then a premed student in Washington, D.C. In those days, a train ride from Boston to Washington took eight hours or more, so Irv and I, sweethearts since high school, saw each other only on holidays and during the summer. That Sunday night in the autumn of 1951, as I was reading *La nouvelle Héloïse* for a course on French romanticism, I was inspired to translate for Irv a passage from one of Saint-Preux's letters to Julie, which seemed applicable to our situation.

> When I have pleasure, I don't know how to enjoy it alone, and I call you to share it with me. Ah, if you knew how terrible my torment is when we are separated, you should certainly prefer your position to mine. Think, think, Julie, that we are already seeing years lost to pleasure. Think that they will never come back. And that the years of the future, when age will have calmed our first fires, shall never be the same as those of today.

Hmm. I won't check over my translation with the original to see how I would have done it differently today. What matters is that Rousseau's words expressed my very feelings. Two centuries after Rousseau had captivated an astonishing number of readers, I became one of those women who embraced Julie and Saint-Preux as kindred spirits. Like them, I felt a thwarted desire to share my pleasures with my soul mate, and I suffered from the sense that our best years were passing us by. Such is the intensity of youthful love.

What made *La nouvelle Héloïse* such an unparalleled success? Why did women in particular become its devotees? Rousseau told his contemporaries that true love was pure and ennobling. He managed to infuse a jaded society with his own fierce belief in the virtue of feeling. His vision of love was irresistible, especially to women, because it validated the rights of the heart. He authorized men and women to express themselves in heated declarations that imitated his own ecstatic style, and to cry tears of joy at every opportunity.

First, a word about the title. You've already met Héloïse in the prologue to this book. The reference to her love affair with Abélard would have been recognized by any eighteenth-century French man or woman with a smattering of education. Even today, a novel titled *Bélard et Louise* (2010) about a university professor and one of his students recalls the medieval couple for a French audience. Saint-Preux acknowledged the parallel of his situation and Abélard's in one of his early letters to Julie, while at the same time dissociating himself from the man he called a "vile seducer."

> I have always pitied Eloise. She had a heart made for love, but Abelard has ever seemed to me only a miserable creature who deserved his fate and who was a stranger as much to love as to virtue.[6]

At this stage in his relationship with Julie, Saint-Preux can pride himself on the dissimilarities between his passion and Abélard's, for he and Julie have not yet crossed the line between "virtue" and "vice"—they have not yet consummated their love. But they cross that line very quickly. Within a few letters, Julie writes to Claire, her friend, cousin, and confidante, that she is "ruined," that she now lives in "disgrace" brought about by "that cruel creature" Saint-Preux, and that "vice" has corrupted her soul. Then she accuses herself as well.

> Without knowing what I was doing, I chose my own destruction. I forgot everything but love. Thus, one unguarded mo-

ment has ruined me forever. I have fallen into the abyss of shame from which a girl never returns, and if I live, it is only to be more wretched. [Part I, Letter XXIX]

It may be difficult for a contemporary reader to swallow such passages. Today, most of us do not think of an unmarried woman as ruined if she goes to bed with a man. Indeed, in both France and the United States, we have come to accept nonmarital sex as a norm. This was not the case in eighteenth-century France (not to mention colonial America), nor would it be until the late twentieth century. The theme of the "fallen woman" would continue to be a constant in literature until the post–World War II period, when sexual fulfillment began to be accepted as a good in itself. How can we empathize with literary figures who define virtue and vice so narrowly? Did Rousseau, following the dictates of continental and British culture, believe that it was enough for a woman to remain chaste for her to be virtuous? No, he did not. Though he used the vocabulary of virtue so dear to his contemporaries, it took on a new meaning with his pen.

Virtue, for both men and women, was a question of character. The "virtuous" person was imbued with a heightened sensibility that made him or her more compassionate than the ordinary lot of humankind. Virtue became synonymous with sensibility: you had to have the capacity to feel, and hence to suffer, in order to empathize with the misfortunes of others. Only the person who had experienced suffering could put himself or herself in the place of others in distress. Sensibility was a prerequisite for suffering, and suffering was a prerequisite for acts of charity. Here and elsewhere in Rousseau's oeuvre, the heart was to be trusted over the head in creating a moral life.

Virtue was also linked to a sense of awe before the wonders of nature and a rejection of socially constructed artifice. Like Rousseau himself, notorious for his plain attire and rustic manners, Saint-Preux rejected the witticisms and formalities of high culture in favor of simplicity and sincerity. All the characters in *La nouvelle Héloïse*, with the exception of Julie's father, are supreme examples of virtuous individuals. They create an ideal community of generous souls ensconced in a bucolic setting, far from the corrupting influences of big cities like Paris and London.

When reduced to the plot, *La nouvelle Héloïse* does not shine among works of fiction. For modern readers, it probably lacks the suspenseful turn of events and subplots featured in today's bestsellers. It is long, too long, and sometimes frankly boring. What saves *La nouvelle Héloïse*, even in a condensed version, is its dithyrambic style. It is hard not to be carried away by its poetic language. Every page has a passage worth reading aloud. Try this one from Saint-Preux after he receives a letter from Julie.

I lose my reason, my head strays in continual delirium, a devouring flame consumes me, my blood takes fire and boils over, a frenzy causes me to tremble. I imagine I see you, touch you, press you to my breast . . . adored object, enchanting girl, source of delight and voluptuousness, seeing you, how can one not see the angelic companions created for the blessed? [Part II, Letter XVI]

And here is Saint-Preux after Julie has sent him her portrait.

Oh my Julie! . . . Once more you enchant my eyes. [. . .] With what anguish the portrait reminded me of the times which are no more! Seeing it, I imagined I was seeing you again; I imagined I found those delightful moments again, the memory of which now creates my life's unhappiness. [. . .] Gods! What torrents of passion my avid eyes absorb from this unexpected object! [Part II, XXII]

What torrents of words Saint-Preux unleashes in describing his feelings for the incomparable Julie—his pupil, friend, mistress, and lifelong love! How can she resist such an emotional onslaught? She cannot.

It is too much, it is too much. Friend, you have conquered. I am not proof against so much love; my resistance is exhausted. . . .

Yes, tender and generous lover, your Julie will be yours forever; she will love you always. I must, I will, I ought. I resign to you the empire which love has given you; it will be taken from you no more. [Part III, Letter XV]

Saint-Preux's spirits are revived, at least temporarily.

We are reborn, my Julie. All the true sentiments of our hearts resume their courses. Nature has preserved our existence, and love restores us to life. Could you doubt it? Did you dare think you could take your heart away from me? No, I know it better than you do, that Heart which Heaven created for mine. I feel them joined in a common existence which they can lose only in death. [Part III, Letter XVI]

Can you stand such hyperbolic language? It is likely that you are used to more reticent lovers. Living in an age of casual sex, serial commitments, and frequent divorce, we are all in danger of becoming as jaded as *ancien régime* aristocrats. Does the notion of undying love still have any meaning for us today? It does when brides and grooms vow to love each other forever, even if subsequent reality cuts short their vows. Who does not treasure the belief in a soul mate? Who does not wish to find someone to love, with the hope of being loved in return? If we still hold on to those hopes, it is partially due to *La nouvelle Héloïse*, which showed us what it felt to be alive at a time when the "divine union of virtue, love, and nature" captured the French imagination.

The romance of Julie and Saint-Preux, however intense, is only one half of the story. The other half concerns Julie's reluctant marriage to Monsieur de Wolmar and the family she creates with him. Julie and Saint-Preux do not end up marching down the aisle together. Yet her marriage to a man more than twice her age does not turn out to be unhappy. Quite the contrary! Julie discovers that life with a wise husband and two sons can be fulfilling, even without *amour-passion*. A different kind of love based on *amitié* (friendship) proves to be enduring. Wolmar is the antithesis of the stereotypical jealous husband; he has so much confidence in Julie that he even allows her to receive Saint-Preux as a part-time lodger in their country home after his return from a four-year voyage! Julie's cousin, Claire, completes the idyllic foursome as they all pursue virtue in harmony with the bounties of nature.

What are we to make of this unexpected turn of events? How does the second half of the book complement the first? Has Rousseau rejected his belief in fervent emotion as the source of virtue and felicity? To answer these questions about a novel with a thousand pages would require another book at least half that long, and, indeed, many such critical works have already been written. My advice is to read large chunks of *La nouvelle Héloïse*, if you can't bear to read all of it. Only then can you decide whether it is merely a literary curiosity or whether its romantic transports and pragmatic solutions still have meaning for inhabitants of the twenty-first century.

ON THE PLANE TO PARIS IN SEPTEMBER 2010, I read in a newspaper that *Les liaisons dangereuses* by Choderlos de Laclos was still on the required list of readings for what the French call *terminale*—the last year of lycée studies. If ever there were a single example of the difference between French and American attitudes to education and sexuality, this is one! I can't imagine any American high school allowing, much less requiring, the reading of a book like *Les liaisons dangereuses* in twelfth grade. We would have such an outcry from decency organizations as to make all previous protests seem like a whisper. No one in France thinks to critique this choice, but when I read it as a graduate student in my twenties, it struck me as the most subversive book I had ever read. It taught me the meaning of sexual perversity, albeit perversity with charm. As much as I condemned the leading characters, the Vicomte de Valmont and Madame de Merteuil, I was fascinated by them. And, I must admit, their machinations aroused me and filtered into my dreams. By then, I was a married woman with children and able to handle such erotic provocation.

Les liaisons dangereuses is perhaps the most wickedly erotic book ever written. I defy anyone to read it without feeling the fires of lust. With Madame de Merteuil and Valmont engaged in a contest of seduction that ends catastrophically for everyone, this book has enjoyed a *succès de scandale* since it first appeared in print in 1782, and more recently in French and American films.

In *Les liaisons dangereuses*, two young people, Cécile de Volanges and her music tutor, the Chevalier Danceny, experience the intense delights of first-time love. Modeled on Julie and Saint-Preux, they communicate their timid declarations and high ideals in carefully hidden letters. Their budding love is a world apart from the proprieties that would separate them on the grounds that Danceny lacks sufficient fortune. Though he is of noble birth like Cécile, her family rejects him, just as Julie's family had rejected Saint-Preux. If this were a sentimental novel in the mode of Richardson's *Pamela*, true love would win out in the end. But this is no ordinary novel. Instead, Laclos undermines the novel of sentiment; he reverses every feeling held sacred by the author of *La nouvelle Héloïse* and demonstrates how easily lovers can betray their own ideals when led astray by determined seducers.

And what seducers! The Marquise de Merteuil and her former paramour, the Vicomte de Valmont, are utterly enticing, diabolically clever, and pragmatically evil. As representatives of *ancien régime* decadence, they live only for sensual pleasure, moving from one lover to the next with little concern for the person who has been left behind. As long as they are the ones who do the abandoning, their self-esteem will remain intact. Valmont can also boast publicly about his conquests, whereas Madame de Merteuil must keep hers hidden. Even as a widow, she must feign chastity if she is to be received in the best circles. Not so for Valmont. The more women he is known to have seduced, the higher his stock. This difference between the sexes features prominently as the plot unwinds.

At the beginning of the book, the Marquise de Merteuil and the Vicomte de Valmont, once lovers, remain friends who share a common agenda: to indulge their erotic appetites through successive affairs but never to fall in love. Both think of these affairs as conquests and, following the military vocabulary that informs their speech, they must always be the ones who decide when to invade, when to withdraw, and when to seek revenge. Madame de Merteuil's desire for revenge sets the plot in motion. She enlists Valmont to seduce the young Cécile, who has been promised by her family to the Comte de Gercourt, one of the Marquise's former lovers. Because Gercourt had left Madame de Merteuil for another mistress, she will not be satisfied until he finds himself with a thoroughly debauched bride.

But Valmont has his own program. When he receives his orders from the Marquise to seduce Cécile, he is already in pursuit of Madame de Tourvel, the notoriously chaste wife of a provincial dignitary. Valmont has built his much-envied reputation on the basis of multiple conquests, and he has no intention of flubbing this one. Handsome, endowed with title and fortune, he represents the consummate libertine seducer. The three female characters incarnate various aspects of womanhood. Cécile is a sensuous ingénue, ready to be plucked. Madame de Tourvel is a repressed sentimentalist, also ready to be plucked. Madame de Merteuil is a perverse feminist, in her words to Valmont, "born to avenge my sex and to dominate yours."[7]

Compared to the sublimely virtuous characters in *La nouvelle Héloïse*, the main figures in *Les liaisons dangereuses* are either perpetrators of vice or their victims. The perpetrators—Valmont and Merteuil—are ingeniously cruel, she even more than he. The victims—Cécile, Danceny, and Tourvel—are trusting and gullible. Two of them end up dead, one retires to a convent, another becomes a knight of Malta, and one lives on with disfiguring smallpox and the loss of an eye. You will have to read the book to find out who gets what. Believe me, once you start to read it, you'll be transfixed till the end.

Yes, I cannot deny it—*Les liaisons dangereuses* is a more compelling work than *La nouvelle Héloïse*. As in Dante's *Divine Comedy*, which offers better material for the Inferno than for the Paradiso, Laclos' depiction of evil has an irresistible demonic appeal. In addition, the epistolary style he borrowed from Richardson and Rousseau turns out to be the perfect medium for conveying the relentless progress of Merteuil and Valmont's infernal strategies. Not a single word is wasted. Everything proceeds with machine-like efficiency. Whatever goodness existed in the fledgling love between Cécile and Danceny, and in Madame de Tourvel's tender feelings for Valmont, and even in Valmont's attentions to Madame de Tourvel, will be swept away by gallantry run amok. Laclos' contemporary, the writer Nicolas Chamfort, succinctly expressed this dissolute and solely materialistic aspect of gallantry in one of his most famous epigrams: "Love, as it exists in society, is only the contact of two epidermises."

And yet, hidden within *Les liaisons dangereuses*, one finds whispers of Valmont's love for Madame de Tourvel and even that of the Marquise de Merteuil for Valmont. Ironically, it is this tender love—this love engaging the heart as well as the body—that dares not say its name. Madame de Merteuil spots true love in Valmont's letters about Madame de Tourvel, and, motivated by jealousy, she forces him to live up to his reputation as a coldhearted seducer. So true love, though still capable of sprouting within a hostile environment, is ultimately crushed by sadistic libertinage.

Having consciously avoided the word "sadistic" up till now, I have intentionally used it here to imply that at least one of the perpetrators—Madame de Merteuil—gets pleasure out of inflicting pain on others. The word "sadism," meaning a sexual perversion characterized by the enjoyment of cruelty to others, derives specifically from the work of the Marquis de Sade. His novel *Justine*, published in 1791 at the height of the French Revolution, and others that appeared despite his many years in prison and the madhouse, carry the libertinage of Crébillon fils and Laclos to new depths of horror. Sade's heroines are submitted to verbal abuse, physical torture, rape, and other repugnant forms of violence. His fictional libertines lack guilt and remorse and do not get their just desserts. What, you may be asking, does any of this have to do with love? It's a good question, one that I pondered when asked by a French friend if I intended to address Sade in this book. My friend insisted that I must do so since Sade understood the link between love and evil better than any other thinker. To admit that I can't bear to read Sade, that he makes me sick, and that I don't intend to inflict him on my readers may speak to intellectual cowardice. So be it.

I've heard enough personal stories in my life to know that some people, mostly men, get their sexual highs by manipulating, abusing, or beating up on women. Here is one told to me not long ago by a Frenchwoman.

Dominique is a lively lady nearing sixty, well bred, nice looking, divorced, and the mother of two ravishing daughters. Since her divorce, she has worked part-time in a fine jewelry store, where her taste and warmth are much appreciated. I've never met a person who seemed happier.

Yet, as I learned recently, Dominique lived a secret horror for almost thirty years. Her husband was a sadistic pervert. He could make love only by humiliating her, insulting her, making her cry, then taking her violently.

On top of that, she discovered fairly early in the marriage that he was bedding anyone else he could lay his hands on, mostly young women working in the company he directed, women wanting to get ahead professionally in return for sexual favors.

Why did Dominique stay in the marriage so long? Her answer: because of the children. She got some satisfaction by taking a lover, who helped restore confidence in herself as a sexual being. Then, with the aid of a *psy* (that's the French term for a shrink), she ultimately asked for a divorce, at which point her husband ran off with someone the age of their daughters. Dominique still has nightmares about her husband's sadistic practices, but in the daytime she leads a very active life. No, she is no longer with her former lover, who was offered a job in another country. She would like to find someone else, just a decent man who has normal sexual needs. Still, she considers herself lucky to be rid of a husband who was, in her words, "right out of a novel by the Marquis de Sade."

To schematize the period stretching from the death of Louis XIV in 1715 to the end of the century, I have tried to show how the French repackaged love in two competing brands: libertinage and sentimentalism. The first brand exaggerated the immoral aspects of gallantry, spreading sexual license from the nobility to the middle and lower classes, and to women as well as to men. The fictions of Prévost, Crébillon fils, and Laclos bore witness to the corrosive presence of libertinage in *ancien régime* France. The second brand of love accentuated feeling. Sentiment, emotion, tenderness, passion—these were the hallmarks of a true lover. With Rousseau leading the charge, sentimentalism spread its empire among the entire reading public, starting with the bourgeoisie and extending upward to the nobility and downward to the lower classes. Lawyers and administrators, the wives of merchants and doctors, unmarried governesses and shop girls—all professed devotion to sentimental love.

These four novels reflected the practice of love in prerevolutionary France. And they did more than that: they created new ways of feeling, behaving, and expressing oneself. How many men read and reread the pages in which Versac told them how to conduct themselves so as to seduce as many women as possible and still maintain the reputation of a gentleman? How many parents advised their offspring to read *Manon Lescaut* and *Les liaisons dangereuses* as cautionary tales? How many men and women, reborn as sons and daughters of Saint-Preux and Julie, turned their own lives into epistolary novels? One of the latter group, Julie de Lespinasse, provides an extraordinary example of this interplay between fiction and life, so much so that I'll devote the next chapter to her alone.

CHAPTER FIVE

Love Letters

Julie de Lespinasse

I REGULARLY RECEIVED TWO LETTERS A DAY FROM
FONTAINEBLEAU. . . . HE HAD ONLY ONE OCCUPATION,
HE HAD ONLY ONE PLEASURE: HE WANTED TO LIVE
IN MY THOUGHTS, HE WANTED TO FILL MY LIFE.

Julie de Lespinasse, Letter CXLI, 1775

J ULIE DE LESPINASSE THOUGHT OF HERSELF AS the heroine of a
novel. She considered the facts of her life more fantastic than
the fictions of either Samuel Richardson or Abbé Prévost.[1] While
she never wrote her memoirs for public consumption, the hundreds of letters she left behind read like one half of an impassioned
epistolary novel.

During her lifetime, letters were the staples of human com-
munication within cities, throughout Europe, and across the seas.
What the telephone was to the twentieth century, and email, text-
ing, and tweeting are today, letters were to our ancestors. People
stayed in touch with each other on a regular basis, sometimes

weekly, biweekly, or daily, and these letters were not just short tele-graphic messages. They were well-written and lengthy, containing descriptions of one's experiences and observations, as well as feelings that might have been awkward to express face-to-face. Within Julie's Parisian circle, which contained many of the best-known figures of her day, letters were often written so as to be read aloud to others or copied for circulation or saved for posterity.

Love letters constituted a prized category. Would he have the nerve to declare himself in writing? Would she respond with the appropriate dose of encouragement? Would they manage to keep their correspondence free from snooping eyes? How could they endure silences due to illness or distant travel or letters that simply went astray? What should she surmise if he sent letters less frequently than before? If she was approached by another suitor, could she write to the second man as well as the first? Love letters were meant to be treasured, to be read over and over again while passion burned, and again in old age when the fires of youth had cooled. If the affair didn't turn into a lifetime attachment, the right thing to do was return the letters to their author. People died with love letters stashed away in boxes and desks, leaving instructions in their wills that all their papers should be destroyed. Though most of the love letters written to Julie were indeed burned right after her death, a few others managed to survive; and, above all, the 180 letters she wrote to the Comte de Guibert bear witness to her incredible life story.[2]

When Julie de Lespinasse died at the age of forty-four in 1776, she was famous as the muse of the *Encyclopédistes*—d'Alembert, Condorcet, Diderot, and so many other luminaries who had been regulars at her lively salon. For twelve years, the cream of French literary, scientific, and artistic society streamed into her apartment almost every day from five to nine in the evening for the sole pleasure of conversation. Her demise was mourned by Enlightenment leaders from Paris to Prussia. Frederick II sent his condolences to Jean le Rond d'Alembert, and d'Alembert wrote her two intensely moving love letters several weeks after she had died.

Who was d'Alembert and why would he have written to Julie after her death? D'Alembert was a renowned mathematician and philosopher and Diderot's first collaborator on the *Encyclopédie*—a mammoth dictionary of eighteenth-century knowledge. Between the ages of twenty-five and thirty-five d'Alembert wrote the numerous treatises that would place him in the ranks of the greatest Enlightenment intellectuals: Fontenelle, Montesquieu, Buffon, Diderot, Voltaire, and Rousseau. Nearing forty, he fell in love with Julie, who was fifteen years his junior. For twelve years, from 1764 to 1776, their shared life was a matter of public record. For the sake of form, they lived in separate quarters of the same building, although everyone assumed they were lovers. They probably were for a time, and then they were not. But whatever the exact nature of their relationship during all the years they were together, d'Alembert never stopped loving her and treating her as the exclusive mistress of his heart.

But Julie, after her first years with d'Alembert, was not satisfied with the love of one devoted man, however distinguished. There would be two other lovers during this same period. Somehow she managed to keep the depths of her great passion for the Marquis de Mora hidden from d'Alembert. Similarly, he didn't know the true nature of her relations with her last lover, the Comte de Guibert.

Julie's letters to Guibert, which were published by his widow in the early nineteenth century after all the principal parties had died, revealed a woman who was proud to be driven by passion. She wrote of herself that she had "the good fortune of loving and of being loved" and that if she had to live her life all over again, she would devote herself a second time to "loving and suffering, heaven and hell." She had no desire to live in the temperate climate inhabited by "all the fools and all the automatons by whom we are surrounded" (Letter XCIX). This credo certainly reflected the mentality of a generation who had fallen under the spell of another Julie, Saint-Preux's beloved in *La nouvelle Héloïse*.

And what about d'Alembert? How did he interact with this excitable creature and how did he survive her demise? In the first of the two letters that d'Alembert wrote to Julie after her death, he poured out his heart to the one who could no longer hear him. It is one of the strangest love letters in history, for he articulates not only the devastating loss felt by a surviving partner, but also his sense of betrayal in discovering that the woman he adored had been madly in love with another. This came about because Julie had asked d'Alembert to burn her papers, which contained many of the love letters she had received from the Marquis de Mora as well as a memoir of their affair.

D'Alembert's first words to Julie convey a state of utter despair. He feels abandoned, horribly alone, and inconsolable.

Oh you who can no longer hear me, you whom I loved so tenderly and so constantly, you who I thought loved me for a few moments, you whom I preferred to everything, you who would have taken the place of everyone for me, if you had wanted to; alas! If you can still feel some emotion in that dwelling place of death for which you have so deeply sighed, and which will soon be mine, look at my misfortune and my tears, the solitude of my soul, the horrible emptiness you have placed there, and the cruel abandonment in which you leave me!

This tone of general grief fills several pages before d'Alembert turns to the subject of his second affliction: the discovery of her lover.

Cruel and unhappy friend! It seems that by making me responsible for the execution of your last wishes, you wanted to add more to my pain. Why did the duties which this execution imposed upon me teach me what I should never have known, and what I would have liked to ignore. Why didn't you order me to burn that disastrous manuscript without opening it—that manuscript which I thought I could read without finding in it more subject for grief, and which taught me that, for at least eight years, I was no longer the first object of your heart, in spite of all the assurances you so often gave me? Who can say, after this distressing reading, that during the eight or ten additional years when I thought I was so loved by you, you had not already betrayed my tender love? Alas, didn't I have reason to believe such a thing when I saw, in that immense multitude of letters which you ordered me to burn, that you had not saved a single one of mine?

There is something so touching about d'Alembert's reaction. That Julie saved a multitude of letters from Mora, and not one of his, wounded him to the marrow. His pain rings true. Here was a man totally shattered by the loss and duplicity of a woman. Here real life seems to have imitated art, and surpassed it.

In a second letter to Julie written six weeks after the first, he visits her tomb in a somewhat more forgiving mood. He remembers:

> You who no longer loved me, it is true, when you were delivered from the burden of life! But you who did love me once . . . you loved me at least for a few instants, and no one loves me now and will ever love me again. Alas! Why must you now be nothing more than ashes and dust? Let me at least believe that these ashes, as cold as they are, are less insensitive to my tears than all the icy hearts that surround me.

Julie had been d'Alembert's greatest love, and he had no hope of ever loving again. It is impossible to read these two letters without feeling the agonizing pain of this aging philosopher, who never got over his attachment to his irreplaceable mistress, though he lived on for seven more years in the shadow of her death.

Now I shall turn to the beginning of her life and you will see why Julie had reason to believe that it was stranger than fiction. Julie's baptismal certificate, dated November 10, 1732, and issued in Lyon, stated that her parents were Claude Lespinasse and Julie Navarre. Neither of these two adults had ever existed. Julie's real mother was the Comtesse Julie-Claude d'Albon, a member of an illustrious family whose nobility went back to the Middle Ages. Her father? Ah, there's the problem. Like the heroes and heroines of many English novels, Julie's father was unknown, but instead of turning up at the right moment to claim his daughter and elevate her to her proper place in society, Julie's father remained forever hidden from her. One thing was certain: he was not her mother's legal husband, Claude d'Albon, the cousin whom Julie-Claude had married when she was sixteen and the man with whom she had had two surviving children, a girl and a boy. Soon after the boy's birth in 1724, the parents legally separated.

The Comtesse d'Albon remained at the country manor with her two children and in time took a lover. In 1731, she gave birth to a son named Hilaire, whose baptismal certificate also bore the names of false parents, like her daughter—our Julie—born twenty months later. Hilaire was sent off under an assumed name to be raised in a monastery, whereas Julie was raised at home in the company of her mother's legitimate children. No one publicly acknowledged the mother-daughter connection; no one publicly revealed the identity of Julie's father. She grew up within a bubble of mystery, the "bastard child" protected by a mother who could not acknowledge her own daughter.

In her adult correspondence with Guibert, Julie wrote: "Heroines in novels have little to say about their education: mine will merit being written because of its peculiarity" (Letter XLVI). It was a strange childhood, indeed, and one from which Julie could never entirely shake herself free. Guibert, her confidant and last lover, would write after her death: "Several times she had related to me the first years of her life. Everything one hears at the theater, everything one says in novels, is cold and devoid of interest in comparison with that tale." Both Julie and Guibert looked to novels and plays as the only appropriate references for the storybook quality of her life.

And then that story became even more improbable. In 1739,

when Julie was seven, a dashing officer and distant relation turned up at the manor house. At forty, Gaspard de Vichy was still an attractive man and succeeded in winning the heart of Julie's half-sister, Diane, aged twenty-four. Nothing unusual about that, except . . . it appears that Gaspard was Julie-Claude d'Albon's former lover and the father of her two illegitimate children, Hilaire and Julie! It must have been a tormenting experience for the countess to see Gaspard turning his affection to her daughter instead of to her. Yet everyone kept up appearances (the French are very good at this), the wedding took place, and Diane went off to live with her husband at his château, leaving behind her mother and Julie, who was now not only Diane's unacknowledged half-sister but also her unacknowledged stepdaughter. Did Diane know this at the time of her marriage? In the atmosphere of half-truths that surrounded the d'Albon family, she probably had her suspicions, which would be revealed to her in time.

The story worsens. The Comtesse Julie-Claude d'Albon died nine years later from tuberculosis, leaving her sixteen-year-old daughter Julie to the mercy of Gaspard and Diane, now the parents of two children. (Try to figure out their relationship to Julie.) Before her death, Julie's mother left her a sum of money in a small desk, which ended up in the pocket of the legitimate son, and an annual pension of 300 pounds to cover her food, upkeep, and education—a pittance, considering the family fortune. At sixteen, Julie was hardly of an age to live alone, so off she went to live with Gaspard, Diane, and their two children, as the poor relative, half-governess, half-maid.

Still, with the education she had received in her mother's home, where she had been bred on classical French writers like Racine and La Fontaine and learned to read English and Italian, she was able to continue her studies and, however unknowingly, prepare herself for the day when she would entertain France's greatest intellectuals.

The transition from poor relative to Parisian star took place through an unlikely intermediary—Gaspard's younger sister, the Marquise du Deffand. In 1752, when the widowed marquise arrived at her brother's home for a visit, she had a history she no longer talked about. While her husband had been alive, they had lived largely apart. Among the provincial nobility with means, it was not uncommon for a wife to leave her husband to his hunting and estate management in the country while she enjoyed the bounties of Paris. Sometimes the situation was reversed, but in her case, it was the wife, rather than the husband, who established herself as a welcome presence in Parisian society.

She was received at the court of the regent, Philippe d'Orléans during the years when sexual liberties were notably flamboyant. What we have seen in Crébillon fils's novel *The Wayward Head and Heart* is a pale reflection of the orgies characteristic of Philippe's reign. Suffice it to say that he slept with the young marquise and with every other female in reach, including, according to rumors, his own daughter. But it was also at the court of Philippe d'Orléans that Madame du Deffand met Voltaire and began her social ascendance among the philosophers. Thanks to the magnificent correspondence she carried on with him and other notables, we have precious information about the cultural life of her century.

Madame du Deffand was already past fifty when she met Julie de Lespinasse. Since 1745, the marquise had run a noteworthy salon at the apartment she rented from the sisters of Saint Joseph in the parish of Saint-Sulpice, in today's fashionable sixth district. Voltaire and d'Alembert were her intimate friends. She had at her disposal a considerable fortune, left to her by her long-neglected husband, and was still one of the most sought-after women of Paris. But she was going blind, and she was bored. The meeting with Julie at twenty, a charming young woman with an uncertain future, revived her spirits. Here was someone through whom she could live again. She invited her to come to Paris and live under her protection. It took two years of complicated negotiations with Julie's "family" before she found herself at the Marquise's side.

No one ever said that Julie de Lespinasse was beautiful, or even pretty. But everyone agreed that she had something special— charm, intelligence, wit, sensitivity, vivacity, spontaneity, and, above all, passion. In short, she captivated through her mind and speech, rather than through the usual attributes of female pulchri- tude. If she was physically ugly, as some have said, she was what the French call *une jolie laide*—an ugly woman who knows how to make herself attractive. With Madame du Deffand as her mentor, Julie metamorphosed into a warm and gracious woman, at home in the marquise's salon, at home answering letters from French *phi- losophes*, at home at the theater and the opera, at home in her skin. Finally, it seemed, the female bastard had found her rightful place.

Would-be lovers and prospective husbands pressed their suits. The Chevalier d'Aydie, seventy-two years old, asked for her hand in mar- riage. She rejected him. D'Alembert, the marquise's faithful friend, also fell for Julie, but was not in a position to offer her marriage, since he lived frugally on limited means with the woman who had nursed him as a baby. Like Julie, he was the illegitimate child of an aristocratic woman, but unlike Julie, he had been abandoned by his biological mother and had transferred his filial feelings to the low-born wet nurse who had raised him as her own. Although his true mother, Madame de Tencin, one of the most influential salon leaders of her day, refused to see d'Alembert and gave him nothing, his father, Louis-Camus Destouches, provided for the modest education from which d'Alembert would rise to astronomical heights.

Julie entertained the men frequenting Madame du Deffand's salon, without taking any of them seriously. And then, inevitably, she fell in love. She was twenty-eight when an Irish viscount named John Taaffe began to visit. Soon he was coming regularly and paying more attention to her than to the marquise. For the first time in her life, Julie felt those delicious pulsations that she had only read about in novels. With the sexy Irishman filling her head and her heart with love talk, she turned to her protector for advice. The marquise was outraged. What! She, a young woman without name or fortune, should imagine that an Irish lord would marry her! It was unthinkable.

Julie threw herself into despair. Her emotional crisis was so severe that she started taking calming medications, most notably opium, the drug of choice for various nervous disorders grouped under the term "vapors." It was the beginning of a habit she would depend on increasingly as she aged. In the meantime, Madame du Deffand wrote to Mr. Taaffe to probe his intentions, and, as she had expected, he did not have marriage with Julie in mind, once he had been enlightened as to her lack of legitimacy and fortune. Though Julie would live four more years under Madame du Deffand's protection, their relationship had suffered what would prove to be a mortal blow.

Julie's room was on the mezzanine level above the marquise's apartment, at a distance that allowed her a certain amount of privacy before she descended to the role of companion every day around three in the afternoon. She and the marquise would spend time together answering the mail and discussing their social activities. Julie would return to her room to prepare herself for the arrival of guests around seven o'clock. Madame du Deffand's lavish dinners for twelve or fourteen were as notable as the witty conversations that filled her salon. Sometimes the two women went together to the theater or the opera, and when they returned in the wee hours of the morning, Julie sat by the marquise's bed, reading her to sleep.

The disastrous episode with John Taaffe eventually receded from Julie's psyche, especially when d'Alembert, after years of silence, finally managed to convey his sentiments to her. D'Alembert was Madame du Deffand's most intimate friend, a man with an international scientific reputation but little in his physical appearance or finances to recommend him as a lover or husband.

Surely Julie admired him. He had shown such loyalty to her benefactress, such devotion to his work, such disinterest in societal advancement, such modesty and independence. How could one not admire a man who was solicited by Catherine the Great of Russia and King Frederick II of Prussia? In 1763, Julie encouraged him to spend three months at the king's court. While there, he wrote her every day. These were letters that Julie did not share with Madame du Deffand.

Upon his return, d'Alembert got in the habit of visiting Julie in her separate quarters before presenting himself to the marquise. There they could spend an hour or two in guarded intimacy. Yet, unlike lovers in novels, they also began to share that time with some of the other salon regulars, a few of d'Alembert's closest friends who enjoyed a light conversational prelude to Madame du Deffand's more formal program. When the marquise got wind of the goings-on in Julie's rooms, she became enraged. How dare Julie usurp the position of salon leader that belonged exclusively to herself!

The break between them was immediate and permanent. It was not so much a matter of the liberties Julie had taken in the social world but of her ascendance over d'Alembert. The marquise forced the issue by asking him to choose between her and Julie. He chose Julie. Many of her other friends also chose to follow Julie, rather than stay behind in Madame du Deffand's now reduced circle. Julie managed to rent two floors in a small house not far away, using the income of 300 pounds left by her mother and several other small pensions obtained by friends. This was the beginning of a new life following her own star.

Although this new life would be Julie de Lespinasse's time of glory, it began very badly. She came down with a severe case of smallpox. Remember, this was before inoculations were common, and many people either died from the disease or survived with disfiguring facial marks. Julie hovered for days between life and death. D'Alembert stayed at her side, feeding her, encouraging her, taking upon himself the duties of nurse, husband, and faithful friend. With his support, Julie slowly recovered, though she would bear on her face the pockmarks that wounded her vanity as much as her appearance. They did not daunt d'Alembert, who wrote to the philosopher David Hume: "She was rather marked by smallpox. But, without being disfigured in the least."[3]

No sooner did Julie get her strength back than d'Alembert fell sick as well. Now it was her turn to nurse him. He, too, lingered near death, and she exerted every effort to bring him back to life. When he began to recover, she insisted on one thing: that he move out of the small quarters he still shared with his old nurse. She could take care of him better in more comfortable rooms, first at the home of a friend and then in her building where he rented rooms on the floor above hers. Let the world talk, and they did! David Hume referred to Julie as d'Alembert's mistress, while others—the philosopher Marmontel, for example—maintained that their relationship was innocent. While rumors circulated, d'Alembert continued to insist that he and Julie were linked only by mutual esteem and friendship, not by love. As for marriage, he asked Voltaire rhetorically: "My God! What would I become with a wife and children?"[4]

There are two different motivations at work here. On the one hand, d'Alembert was trying to protect Julie's reputation. A woman known to have a lover was censured by a hypocritical society that looked the other way for married women but came down hard on single women. Our morality today goes in the opposite direction: an unmarried woman has the right to take as many lovers as she pleases, while married women are expected to remain monogamous.

D'Alembert had another reason for denying his love for Julie. He saw himself in a tradition, going back to Socrates in ancient Greece and Abélard in the Middle Ages, that considered marriage incompatible with philosophy. He did not want to be ridiculed as a "married philosopher," even if certain other well-known *philosophes*, like Helvétius and the Baron d'Holbach, had taken that perilous step.[5]

While d'Alembert and Julie did not wed, there is no doubt that he loved her deeply and exclusively. The bonds established between them in the intimate circle presided over by Madame du Deffand had only been strengthened by their break with her. Then the care they had taken of each other during their illnesses added a new layer of meaning to their intimacy. They became family to one another. Henceforth, d'Alembert's first loyalty was to Julie de Lespinasse, whom he would serve with the legendary dedication of a medieval knight.

Julie also loved d'Alembert, if not passionately, then certainly with respect and gratitude. Their shared interests in literature, philosophy, and science brought them closer together every day. She read Racine to him; he countered with Montesquieu. They enjoyed the same music, the same plays, and the society of their peers who received them as a de facto couple. The wealthy and highly influential Madame Geoffrin, whose salon rivaled Madame du Deffand's, took them under her wing. With d'Alembert at her side, Julie shared the spotlight with France's most illustrious *salonnières*. D'Alembert had reason to believe that Julie loved him: in his letter of July 22, 1776, written after her death, he remembered that ten years earlier she had said she was actually afraid of being so happy.

The honeymoon period of their relationship lasted about three years. Then the arrival of the Marquis de Mora, son of the Spanish ambassador, would open Julie's heart in a new way. Gonçalve de Mora was young, handsome, well built, personable, and, like Julie, passionate. He captivated everyone not only with his winning appearance but also with his open mind. Here at last was a Spaniard who would bring the spirit of the Enlightenment back to his conservative country. In a letter of introduction, d'Alembert wrote to Voltaire: "I have seen few foreigners of his age who have a more sound mind, more exact, more cultured, and more enlightened. You can be sure that, as young, and as *grand seigneur*, and as Spanish as he is, I am by no means exaggerating." Irony of ironies, it was d'Alembert who helped pave the way for Mora's brilliant success among Paris intellectuals, including Julie de Lespinasse.

She was thirty-six, while Mora was about ten years younger. Let me pause to reflect on this difference of age. If he had been ten years older than she, no one would have said a word. But a woman ten years older than the man set the gossips' tongues in motion: the philosopher Friedrich Melchior, Baron von Grimm, probably echoed public sentiment when he wrote that "she had passed the season for love affairs." When a woman is older than a man, or when a man is much older than a woman—say twenty or thirty years—there is usually a power differential in favor of the younger person. The older man may be taken for his wife's father and mocked behind his back or, worse yet, made a cuckold. The older woman, comparing herself to her young lover's female contemporaries, often finds herself wanting. And even if she isn't prone to jealousy, she fears he will lose interest in her as her physical charms fade. In most love relations, there is often one person who loves more, and when there is a significant age discrepancy, it is often the older party.

And yet, in the case of Lespinasse and Mora, it seems as if the passion was mutual. Even in public, their attraction to each other was visible to all. The historian Marmontel wrote in his memoirs that she inspired a passionate feeling in Mora, who made no effort to hide his adoration for her. Only d'Alembert was blind to what everyone else saw so clearly.

Like many of their contemporaries in the 1760s, Julie and Mora were marked by Rousseau's *Nouvelle Héloïse*. They saw themselves as reincarnations of Julie and Saint-Preux, destined to love madly and suffer excruciatingly. Mora was in every way the noble figure worthy of her passion, especially with the tragic demeanor he took on after the death of his only son. By his midtwenties, Mora had lost the sickly wife he had married at the age of fifteen, a daughter, and a son, and he was about to lose his mother. He was also beginning to experience the symptoms of tuberculosis, which would end his life in 1774. Mora threw himself into his relationship with Julie and never looked back. Despite his father's attempts to separate them—a grandee of Spain simply didn't marry a bastard woman with no fortune who was already living publicly with another man—Mora refused to abandon the one woman whose cultural sophistication and passion equaled his own.

Much of the time they were separated, either by Mora's career and family obligations or by his worsening health. While he was away, they wrote each other almost daily. Here is how Lespinasse described a separation of ten days when Mora was at the French court in Fontainebleau.

I regularly received two letters a day from Fontainebleau. He was away ten days: I had twenty-two letters; but even while he was in the middle of the dissipation of the court, having become a fashionable object and the craze of the most beautiful women, he had only one occupation, he had only one pleasure: he wanted to live in my thoughts, he wanted to fill my life. And, indeed, I remember that during those ten days I did not go out a single time: I waited for a letter and then I wrote one. [Letter CXLI]

These twenty-two letters must have been among the multitude that broke d'Alembert's heart.

Since most of Julie's letters were burned, how is it that we know so much about her intimate relationship with Mora? The answer, adding another layer of duplicity to Julie's love life, lies in the letters she wrote to Guibert, whom she met in May 1773. Yes, even while Mora was still alive—he would expire a year later, in May 1774—Julie was fatally drawn to another man. It is not for us to judge Julie but to try to understand how she balanced three major relationships: (1) daily life with her honorary husband, d'Alembert; (2) her great passion for Mora, which began around 1767; and (3) the intense attachment to Guibert that consumed the last three years of her life.

Jacques Antoine Hippolyte de Guibert was a military man and a writer. His 1772 treatise, *A General Essay on Tactics (Essai général de tactique)*, was the talk of Paris among intellectuals and courtiers and would in time inspire the young Napoleon. What's more, he wrote tragedies that he read aloud with a captivating voice, and one of them would even be performed under the patronage of Marie-Antoinette. With Gonçalve de Mora's deteriorating health causing Julie endless torment, she turned to Guibert for consolation.

From the start, Julie found in Guibert an empathic confidant. She poured out her heart to him about her liaison with Mora—that perfect creature who loved her without reserve, just as she loved him. Guibert reciprocated with the story of his attachment to Madame de Montsauge, a worldly mistress lacking the passion and perception he discovered in Julie. Shared confidences can bring people together in unexpected ways, especially when the confidences concern romantic love. Talking about love can easily become love talk.

Mora left Paris in the summer of 1773 with the hope that the weather in Spain would be better for his health. Julie waited impatiently for the biweekly courier that would bring news of her beloved. And in the meantime, she fell under the spell of Guibert, an increasingly fashionable figure in the circles they both frequented. Julie added her assent to the voices lauding him as a military genius and the next Corneille. Guibert basked in his newfound glory among the *Encyclopédistes* and their acknowledged muse, the oh-so-engaging if not so pretty Julie de Lespinasse. He was also a great hit in aristocratic homes and at court, especially among the ladies.

Yes, Guibert was a ladies' man, already known for his amorous conquests by the time he met Julie, and with many more to come. Yet we should not think of him as a seducer in the coldhearted manner of a Valmont; he seems to have been considerate of Julie's feelings, responding as best he could to her increasing passion. But as she herself realized: "I love you madly . . . and something tells me that you should not be loved in this way" (Letter XXXIV).

Let's back up and see how this came about. After their first meeting in the spring of 1773, Julie and Guibert were constantly in contact with one another. He would arrive a little before her open salon in the afternoon when, according to custom, the doors were not shut to her numerous friends. Guibert usually balanced two or three other social engagements—lunches, dinners, the theater, country outings. Occasionally they met at the home of a mutual friend or at the opera, where Julie rented a box for the year. Oddly enough, it was at her box in the opera that they could enjoy the greatest privacy, and, strange as it seems, it was here that they became lovers.

Try to imagine a large loge with an adjoining salon, to which one retired for refreshments. On the evening of February 10, 1774, exalted by music and deferred pleasure, Julie surrendered to Guibert's persuasive advances and became his mistress. A year later, on the anniversary of this date, she would write to Guibert: "It was on the tenth of February last year that I became intoxicated by that poison, the effect of which still endures. . . . By what fatality is the most intense and sweetest feeling of pleasure linked to the most overwhelming misfortune" (Letter XCII). Why does she speak of this event as both a poison and a pleasure? Because the pleasure she experienced with Guibert was linked in her mind to the tragedy of Mora's death in May 1774, as he was returning to France from Spain in a final effort to see her once more. By then, Julie was already madly in love with Guibert, and she considered herself guilty of betraying Mora. It was as if she had transferred her passion *in toto* from Mora to Guibert, even though she felt from the start that he would never love her as Mora had.

Like Mora, Guibert was ten years younger than Julie, and in his case, the rule of the older lover loving more held firm. When we read her letters, it seems that Julie loved enough for both of them. She was constantly writing to Guibert "I love you" or "I adore you" and suffering agony for that love. "My friend, I love you as one must love, with excess, with madness, violent emotion, and despair" (Letter XX). Since she burned his first batch of letters on June 2, 1774, when she received the news of Mora's death and tried to kill herself with an overdose of opium, and since few other letters from Guibert have survived, we cannot fully judge his feelings, but from her letters to him, it is clear that she was much more invested in their affair than he was. Indeed, he would still see his former mistress from time to time, and, during the last year of Julie's life, he would marry another.

And where was d'Alembert in all this? Just as he had blindly suffered Julie's passion for Mora, he closed his eyes to her affair with Guibert. Worried mainly about her health, for she too would die of tuberculosis before long, he looked in on her regularly, was at her bedside during her illnesses, ran her errands, and continued to believe that he was as essential to her as she was to him. They were still a couple in the eyes of the world, so much so that he himself wrote letters to Mora's family inquiring after the young man's health, and when Mora died, the renowned philosopher composed a moving funeral oration at Mora's father's request. Both d'Alembert and Julie were in tears when he read it aloud to her.

Julie closed the doors of her salon to all but her most intimate friends. And while she genuinely mourned the sublime Marquis de Mora, she was tormented by her ineradicable love for Guibert. She now lived exclusively for his visits and his letters as she had previously lived for those of her former lover. Her letters to Guibert are one long cry of the heart, begging him to assuage the feelings that were tearing her apart:

Oh, my friend, commiserate with me! Have pity on me! You alone in nature can penetrate my mortally wounded soul with feelings of sweetness and consolation. [Letter LIV]

Oh my friend, my soul is aching. I have no more words, I have only cries. I have read, I have reread, I shall read your letter a hundred times. Oh my friend, how many boons and how many ills are joined together. [Letter LVI]

I hate myself, I condemn myself, and I love you. [Letter LVII]

I am waiting for the hour of tomorrow's post with an impatience that you alone can perhaps understand . . . of course, it would be sweeter to be in a dialogue, but a monologue is endurable. [Letter LXV]

Months later she is still crying out: "My God! How I love you!" (Letter XC) even as she implores him: "My friend, deliver me from the misfortune of loving you" (Letter CII). Julie conceptualizes herself as a creature whose entire being is given over to "loving and being loved" (Letter CIX). And however sick she becomes, with a wracking cough and high fever, it is always some sign from Guibert that brings her back to life. "My friend, I live, I shall live, I shall see you again; and whatever fate awaits me, I shall once more have an instant of pleasure before dying" (Letter CXIX). "I am condemned to love you as long as I shall breathe" (Letter CXX).

As I made my way through her letters, I asked myself: Could this be the same woman known for her charm, intelligence, and culture? Love had turned her into the slave of overripe passion, like Racine's Phèdre, whom she often cited in her letters to Guibert. At times hysterical, at times calmed by opium, often reproachful, but steadfast in her declarations of love, Julie must have become a burden to Guibert long before she died. How many times does a man want to hear that he is madly loved, without being able to reciprocate in kind? How many times does he want to be reproached for his neglect or coldness or interest in other women?

And yet, even amidst what she called her *sottes écritures* (her stupid writing), we espy the sophisticated woman who merited the esteem of her contemporaries. She critiques Guibert's paper in praise of Catinat, which he will submit to the Academy of Sciences for a prize and lose out to La Harpe. She goes almost daily to the opera to hear *Orphée* by Gluck, her favorite composer. She cites the great classical authors—Racine, La Fontaine, Molière, Boileau—often finding lines that are applicable to her present reality. She mingles with the best-known Enlightenment figures of her day—Condorcet, Holbach, Voltaire, Marmontel, Grimm, La Harpe—and dines with the upper crust of Parisian society. It is breathtaking to see her shift from the self-abasing stance she takes in voicing her unhappy love for Guibert to accounts of her social calendar, without even opening a new paragraph.

There are moments when she regains her dignity, asking Guibert to refrain from visiting. In September 1775, when he marries a young aristocrat with a sizable fortune, she insists they break off their liaison. "Oh my God! The moment has come when I can say, or I must say: *I shall live without loving you.*" She compares the passion she has had for him to "a great sickness" and asks that he return her letters. In October she senses that she is dying and pronounces dramatically, "I must submit to my horrible destiny, to suffer, to love you, and soon to die" (Letter CXXXVI). Still, she languishes for seven more months, during which time she writes Guibert forty-four more letters. Her last written words to him carry her love credo to the grave: "Goodbye, my friend. If ever I return to life, I would like to spend it once more in loving you; but there is no longer any time" (Letter CLXXX).

Julie de Lespinasse died on May 23, 1776. Several hours before her death, she asked d'Alembert to pardon her. In his words: "You asked me for that harrowing pardon, a last testimony to your love, of which the sweet and cruel memory will always remain in the depths of my heart."

Julie was buried the next day at the Church of Saint-Sulpice. D'Alembert and Condorcet led a crowd of mourners, which included a tearful Guibert. Grieved to the depths, d'Alembert had no way of knowing that worse was yet to come. When he waded through the thousands of letters Julie had left behind, including those from Mora, and the memoir she had written of their affair, he was torn to pieces, lacerated, destroyed. What words can convey the agony he felt?

Thank God he was spared the knowledge of Julie's second passion, since those letters were locked in a little writing desk, and d'Alembert followed Julie's instructions by sending it, unopened, to Guibert. The extent to which he was willfully blind and ignorant of their liaison shows up in the letter he sent Guibert along with the desk. Taking Guibert for a confidant in his discovery of Julie's love for Mora, he wrote: "Commiserate with me. . . . I was never the first object of her heart; I have lost sixteen years of my life and I am now sixty. Would that I could die while writing these sad words and would that they were engraved on my tomb. . . . Everything is lost for me, and I have only to die."[6]

IF EVER THERE WAS *UNE GRANDE AMOUREUSE*—A woman whose existence was synonymous with loving—it was Julie de Lespinasse. Intemperate by nature, excessive by choice, she forces questions about the nature of love itself. What does it mean to love not just one man but three, more or less at the same time? The French have accepted Julie as one of their own, a variant on the theme of *l'amour fou* (crazy love) that reappears in different incarnations from century to century: think of Racine's *Phèdre*, or the writer George

Sand, or the singer Edith Piaf. In France, for all her eccentricity, the woman who loves too much assumes a heroic dimension.

To love excessively, wildly, madly, to sacrifice and even humiliate oneself for love, is a radical but not unrepresentative expression of French culture. It was, after all, the French who invented romantic love with such all-or-nothing characters as Tristan and Iseult, and Lancelot and Guinevere. Julie shares with her fictive predecessors a seemingly inexhaustible fund of passion, but she does not invest it all in a single love object. She loves different men differently—d'Alembert with tender affection, Mora with mutual enthusiasm, Guibert with obsessive passion. She belies the idea that love must always be exclusive.

Julie's story also exemplifies the pervasive interchange between an individual life and the culture of her time and place. The sentimental novel, popularized in England and France by Richardson and Rousseau, was not merely a literary artifact: it had consequences in the lives of real people. Julie de Lespinasse, Mora, Guibert, and even d'Alembert fashioned their behavior on the models they had discovered in books. In an age that celebrated feelings, they could not appear to be lacking in sensibility. Obviously there were differences in the depth of their emotions and differences in their manner of expression, ranging from Guibert's studied gallantry to Julie's overwrought declarations, which resembled professions of faith, but for all of them, the ability to love was considered a reliable measure of worth.

By the 1740s when Julie was a girl and Richardson's epistolary novels were gaining international celebrity, letters had become a conventional accompaniment to love affairs. The eighteenth century is famous for its correspondences between intellectuals and between lovers. In the latter category, those of Julie rank at the top of the list. They make a stunning contrast with the letters of her transatlantic contemporaries, Abigail and John Adams, who bequeathed to posterity the richest marital correspondence in American history. The Adamses' enduring love was bound up in the proprieties of marriage, religion, and politics, all of which were firmly grounded in the virtue of subordinating pleasure to duty. We see this principle at work during the many trying years when the couple was separated by John's public service in Philadelphia, Paris, and the Netherlands, while Abigail raised their children and managed their Massachusetts farm. When she finally joined John in Paris, she was—not surprisingly—uncomfortable with the sexually charged mores enjoyed by the French. She was taken aback by men and women who were physically expressive in public and openly discussed private matters that were not considered fit for polite conversation in her homeland. She was shocked when Madame Helvétius, widow of the famous philosopher, threw her arms around Benjamin Franklin's neck and bussed him on both cheeks. She was embarrassed and offended when ballerinas showed their ankles at the opera. As representatives of a provincial and still-puritanical American culture undernourished by passion, the Adams family set a tone of domestic harmony that neither Franklin nor Jefferson, unencumbered by wives during their overlapping ministries in Paris, had reason to convey. John and Abigail's carefully preserved letters document a loving commitment that lasted more than half a century. In contrast, Julie's love letters to Guibert have the operatic extravagance we have come to associate with a notable current in French literature and life.

A love letter had the task of conveying one's feelings to its recipient in the hope that such feelings were and would be reciprocated. Letters could create an ongoing dialogue while the lovers were apart, but, as Julie wrote to Guibert, even a monologue was better than nothing. Writing to her lover allowed her to vent explosive emotions, like a bloodletting that ostensibly purged the body of excess humors. Julie's emotions were larger than life, and the men she found to share them with, albeit their distinction, were rarely as passionate as she. Yet, it is perhaps d'Alembert's story that I find the most moving. His love for Julie was the one great love of his life. He loved her blindly, sincerely, deeply, loyally. He deserved a better fate than to discover her duplicity after her death.

She, however, had the death she longed for. She died with her reputation intact, beloved and admired by the best of French society. Among the many words of posthumous praise, Guibert's eulogy would have made her very proud. He wrote of her gift for friendship and her generosity. The friends who gathered around her were united by "the desire to please her, and the need to love her." He wrote of the harmony that reigned between her thoughts and her manner of expression. "Her letters had the movement and warmth of conversation." He admitted: "I made a tour of Europe, and her letters followed me, consoled me, supported me." And in a final personal note that would have touched Julie deeply, he said: "If ever I do anything good or honest, and if I attain something great, it will be because your memory will perfect and still enflame my soul."

CHAPTER SIX

Republican Love

Elisabeth Le Bas and Madame Roland

NATURE HAS GIVEN ME THE GIFT OF A PURE HEART
AND GOOD AND TENDER PARENTS, WHO HAVE
BROUGHT US UP WISELY AND GIVEN US AN EDUCATION
CAPABLE OF MAKING US VIRTUOUS WIVES.

Elisabeth Le Bas, "Manuscrit de Mme Le Bas," 1842

WHEN I ARRIVED IN PARIS IN THE spring of 1988, my friends were anticipating the bicentennial of the French Revolution the following year. They were still debating whether the Revolution had done more harm than good, as if it had occurred just yesterday. I couldn't help adding my two cents gleaned from the work I was doing on women memoirists from that period. Before I knew it, a publisher offered me a contract to turn my research into a book, provided that I write it quickly and in French. That book appeared in 1989, just in time for it to be cited as one of twelve focusing on women among the 750 publications concerned with male-dominated revolutionary events. Four years later, I published a more comprehensive version in English on the same subject.[1]

What I discovered from researching those two books was that women remembered the Revolution in a more personal way than men. (Not surprising!) The memoirs of the leading male figures who survived the Revolution highlighted public events, with little mention of their private lives, but because women were primarily ensconced within the domestic sphere, their accounts were likely to include portraits of themselves as girls, sisters, wives, and mothers. It is from their stories that I was able to discover how love manifested itself in a time of revolution—how it did, and did not, conform to the politically correct discourse of its time.

This chapter is based on the little-known forty-nine-page autobiography written by Elisabeth Le Bas at the end of her long life, and on the now-famous memoirs written in prison by Madame Roland. Separated by a generation and by differences in education, the two women had little in common beyond their husbands' republican politics, which they shared. Each saw herself, justifiably, as a victim of the Revolution, since it had already destroyed Le Bas' husband and would be responsible for the deaths of Madame Roland's husband and Madame Roland herself.

Elisabeth Le Bas, née Duplay, was a young woman from a comfortable bourgeois family, who offered lodgings to the Revolutionary leader Maximilien Robespierre. Her future husband, Philippe Le Bas, was one of Robespierre's closest associates. She was scarcely twenty years old when she first encountered Le Bas in 1792. They were married on August 13, 1793, and she was a mother and widow less than one year later, imprisoned with her baby and ostracized after her liberation. How did all these tumultuous events come about in so short a time?

Elisabeth began her memoirs in medias res:

It was on the day that Marat was carried in triumph to the Assembly that I saw my darling, Philippe Le Bas, for the first time.

I found myself, on that day with Charlotte Robespierre. Le Bas came to greet her. He stayed with us a long time and asked who I was. Charlotte told him I was one of the daughters of her elder brother's host.[2]

The narrator knew how to make the most of the historical moment. The beginning of her romance was linked to the day when the radical journalist and Convention delegate, Jean-Paul Marat, overcame his adversaries and was carried on the shoulders of a jubilant crowd back to the assembly. Such intoxicating circumstances were decidedly favorable to the flowering of love.

Charlotte Robespierre, Maximilien's sister, played the role of friend, confidante, and mediator for the young woman and her future spouse. She chaperoned Elisabeth at the Convention sessions, introduced her to the deputy Le Bas, witnessed their first exchange of words and trinkets, and counseled the younger woman on the early flutterings of love. At one session, the two women brought sweets and fruit to offer to Philippe Le Bas and to Charlotte's less famous brother, Augustin Robespierre, also a deputy.

At the next Convention session, the stakes rose from oranges to jewelry. Le Bas took Elisabeth's ring and lent the women a lorgnette. Elisabeth remembers:

I wanted to give him back his lorgnette. . . . He begged me to keep it. I asked Charlotte to ask him again for my ring; she promised she would, but we did not see Le Bas again.

. . . I had my regrets not to have my ring and not to have been able to give him back his lorgnette. I was afraid of displeasing my mother and of being scolded.

Budding love, as Elisabeth depicts it, is a comedy of errors, the mishaps contributing to its intensity and leading in a roundabout way to love's ultimate victory. The would-be lovers are presented as chaste and above reproach, the purity of their actions guaranteed by the watchful eye of a respectable chaperone and the ever-present fear of a stern mother. Their love, consecrated within hallowed halls, must write itself according to a republican script in which women and men eschew the libertine ways of *ancien régime* aristocrats in favor of virtue, sincerity, and affection.

After the suggestive exchange of objects initiated by Le Bas—a ploy that produced anxiety in the heart of a naïve young woman—a serious obstacle presented itself. Le Bas fell sick and could not return to the Convention. Elisabeth responded to his illness with signs of sorrow that perplexed her friends. "Everyone noted my sadness, even Robespierre, who asked me if I had some secret sorrow. . . . He spoke to me with kindness: 'Little Elisabeth, think of me as your best friend, as a kind brother; I shall give you all the advice you need at your age.'"

Robespierre played a major role as marriage broker. In Elisabeth's memoir, he comes across as kindly and warm, in contrast to his austere reputation. But another legendary revolutionary figure, Danton, is cast as a villain. Meeting him at a mutual friend's country house, Elisabeth was repelled by his ugliness and even more so by his forthright sexual advances.

He said I appeared to be unwell, that I needed a good [boy] friend—that would bring back my health! . . . He approached, wanted to put his arm about my waist and kiss me. I pushed him away with force. . . .

I immediately begged Madame Panis never to bring me back to that house. I told her that man had made vile propositions to me, such as I had never heard before. He had no respect whatsoever for women, and even less for younger ones.

The picture of a wanton Danton is not out of keeping with his reputation; one didn't have to be an aristocrat to model oneself on the likes of Crébillon's Versac or Laclos' Valmont. In his presence, Elisabeth's first duty was to protect her virginity and her good name.

After two months of illness, Philippe Le Bas returned to public life. Elisabeth ran into him by chance at the Jacobin meeting hall where she had gone to reserve seats for the evening session featuring a speech by Robespierre. As she tells the story, it is clear that this encounter with Le Bas was a turning point in their relationship.

Imagine my surprise and my joy when I saw my beloved! His absence had caused me to spill many tears. I found him very changed. He asked for news of myself and all my family . . . he asked me many questions and tried to test me.

He asked if I was not going to be married soon, if I loved someone, if clothes and frivolous pleasures were to my taste, and, when married and a mother, whether I would like to breastfeed my children.

All these questions constituted a kind of premarital test to determine whether Elisabeth had the appropriate character to become a republican wife. She clearly passed the test, for Le Bas ended up saying: "I have cherished you since the day I saw you."

The lovers continued to reveal their true feelings. Le Bas had thought ten times a day of writing her but refrained for fear she would be compromised by his letters. (Any reader of novels knew what mischief such letters can lead to.) A visit from Maximilien had assured him that the Duplays were pure people, "devoted to liberty." Augustin also agreed that the Duplay household "breathed virtue and pure patriotism." With this background check, Philippe was ready to ask for Elisabeth's hand.

Because Le Bas was ten years older than Elisabeth, well educated and well placed, he was able to speak to her mother as an equal, while Elisabeth remained mutely on the sidelines. Her mother's major objection was that she wanted to see her two older daughters married before Elisabeth, who was still very young and flighty. Le Bas insisted: "I love her like that. . . . I shall be her friend and mentor." The next day, when he addressed both parents together, Elisabeth was not even allowed to be present. But eventually, her parents consented to the marriage and Elisabeth was called in to share the good news. "Imagine my happiness! I could not believe it. . . . We flew into my father's and mother's arms. They were moved to tears." It is a scene out of a painting by Jean-Baptiste Greuze, who captured the spirit of sentimental love better than any other artist of that period. Like figures in one of Greuze's paintings, Philippe, Elisabeth, her family and friends (Robespierre was there too) shed tears of joy as they toasted their engagement with hot chocolate.

Yet, as in a novel, there were still obstacles to overcome. One appeared in the form of a villain who slandered Elisabeth so as to make Philippe believe she had had past lovers. It turned out that the scoundrel wanted Philippe to marry his own daughter. Elisabeth held her own, defending herself as an innocent person raised by her parents to remain chaste before marriage and to become a virtuous wife.

Ultimately, of course, Philippe saw the truth and a wedding date was set, but then another major obstacle occurred. Philippe was sent on a special mission by the Committee of Public Safety. While the lovers were separated, Elisabeth bombarded Robespierre with entreaties to bring Philippe home. She readily admitted: "I was having so much pain that I did not want to be a patriot any longer. I was inconsolable. . . . My health suffered considerably." Lovesickness held on to its literal meaning.

Finally Philippe was brought home long enough for the wedding to take place and long enough for Elisabeth to become pregnant. They would have barely a year of conjugal intimacy before Le Bas lost his life in the catastrophe of the ninth of Thermidor. Based on the revolutionary calendar, this date referred to the coup of July 27, 1794, when Robespierre and his close associates were brought down by their own excesses and their political enemies.

In Elisabeth's account, we witness revolutionary trauma invading the household. As soon as her husband was arrested, government officials came to close their apartment and take away all their personal papers. Le Bas went to face his destiny at the Hôtel de Ville. Elisabeth recorded his last, patriotically inspired words, intended for their son. "Nourish him with your own milk . . . inspire in him the love of his country; tell him that his father has died

for her; adieu, my Elisabeth, adieu! . . . Live for our dear son; inspire him with noble sentiments, you are worthy of them. Adieu,
Adieu!"

She writes that she never saw Le Bas again. She does not say
that he shot himself several hours later in the same room in which
Maximilien was already gravely wounded and from which Augustin Robespierre threw himself out the window. Instead, she paints
her own despair in the Duplay house.

> I went home distraught, almost crazy. Imagine what I felt when
> our dear infant stretched out his little arms to me. . . . From the
> ninth to the eleventh [of Thermidor] I remained on the floor. I
> no longer had strength nor consciousness.

As Elisabeth lay unconscious on the floor, the mob carried
Robespierre and the rest of his political clan past her house on their
way to the guillotine. Shortly thereafter, members of the Committee of Public Safety came for Elisabeth and her baby. Judged guilty
by association with her husband, she was incarcerated with her son
in the Talarue Prison. Her life situation could not have been worse:
"I had been a mother for five weeks; I was nursing my son; I was
less than twenty-one years old; I had been deprived of almost everything."

The prison ordeal bred in Elisabeth a wild rage. When propositioned by government agents to marry one of the deputies and
thus "abandon the infamous name" of her husband, she cried out,
"Tell those monsters that the Widow Le Bas will never abandon
that sacred name except on the scaffold." Such defiance in the face
of prolonged incarceration derived from an imperishable love for

her dead husband and an intractable belief in the righteousness of his cause. Clinging to her married name, she emerged from prison after nine months as a force to be reckoned with. Until her death in 1859, she proclaimed republican principles and continued to cherish Le Bas' memory.

The Revolution had nourished and then destroyed her one great love; she clung to that memory in old age as to a life raft. For the rest of her days—a full sixty-five years—she would look back nostalgically to the period from the fall of 1792 to the summer of 1794 as the paradise from which she had been violently ejected.

WHILE ELISABETH LE BAS' SHORT MEMOIR IS virtually unknown, that of Madame Roland is the best-known eyewitness chronicle of the Revolution.[3] She, too, was a political prisoner by virtue of her husband's involvement in revolutionary politics. During her five-month incarceration, before she was sent to the guillotine, she wrote both a history of revolutionary events and her private memoirs. The latter interest us here because they touch upon love both inside and outside a long-standing marriage.

Before her marriage, Marie-Jeanne Manon Phlipon was something of a bluestocking, dissatisfied with her lot as a woman. She wrote to a friend in 1776: "I am truly vexed to be a woman: I should have been born with a different soul or a different sex . . . then I could have chosen the republic of letters as my country." Later, converted to the cult of domesticity by her passion for Rousseau, she followed the path of Julie in the second half of *La nouvelle Héloïse* by marrying a man twenty years her senior and giving herself unstintingly to wifehood and motherhood. Hers was a marriage of mutual esteem, nourished by shared values and goals. There was none of the passion we find in eighteenth-century novels or in the life of Julie de Lespinasse. Manon's husband, Jean-Marie Roland de la Platière, was a distinguished lawyer who became minister of the interior from 1791 to 1793. In that role, he relied heavily on his highly literary wife, his secret aid in drafting many of his letters and circulars. In the eyes of the world, they formed an exemplary couple.

But Manon had a secret. She had fallen in love with another man, François Buzot, a member of the extreme-left deputies. They wrote letters when one or the other was away from Paris, and Manon admitted in her memoirs that her liaison with him had become "intimate, inalterable" and "binding." Elsewhere, without mentioning Buzot's name, she wrote: "I cherish my husband as a sensitive daughter adores a virtuous father to whom she would sacrifice even her lover; but I found the man who could be that lover . . ." What happened then? Manon tells us only that she confessed this love to her husband. One wonders: was she inspired by the confession in *La Princesse de Clèves*? Or by Wolmar's acceptance of Julie's prior passion for Saint-Preux in *La nouvelle Héloïse*? Those husbands were fictional paragons of understanding; hers was not. He "could not support the idea of the slightest change in his dominion; his imagination blackened, his jealousy irritated me, happiness fled far from us."

Although Madame Roland never named Buzot as the man responsible for the change in her marital relations, elsewhere she described him in terms more befitting a lover than a statesman. He was "sensitive, ardent, melancholic and lazy. . . . A passionate contemplator of nature . . . he seems to be made to taste and procure domestic happiness; he would forget the universe in the sweetness of private virtues with a heart worthy of his own." That heart worthy of Buzot's could only be hers. Madame Roland does not seem to have been troubled by the existence of Buzot's wife, dismissed parenthetically as not being on the level of her spouse.

The secret story of Madame Roland's unconsummated love had created a breach between husband and wife that was still unreconciled at the time of his flight from Paris and Manon's imprisonment. A memoir to perpetuate her husband's glory would be one way of expunging the blemish on her marital record. As a disciple of Rousseau, Madame Roland would not deny the claims of the heart; she believed that she and Buzot, like Julie and Saint-Preux, would be united beyond the grave. In a final farewell she cried out to Buzot: "And you whom I dare not name! . . . who respected the barriers of virtue . . . will grieve to see me go before you to a place where we shall be free to love each other without crime."

BOTH ELISABETH LE BAS AND MADAME ROLAND were born into the bourgeois milieu that prescribed chastity for unmarried women and monogamy for spouses. Parents were the final arbiters of marital choices, and husbands had dominion over their wives. As opposed to the aristocratic culture of the *ancien régime*, infidelity was not tolerated, especially for women. At the same time, the subversive voices of philosophers, political thinkers, dramatists, and novelists were beginning to shake up the system. Questions about authority, be it in government or family, were raised openly as never before.

Rousseau, of course, led the critics of existing society by laying bare its vices, and by proposing a morality that issued from the heart. His elder contemporary and sometime adversary Voltaire attacked him for his trust in emotion, just as he attacked the German philosopher Leibniz in his satiric masterpiece, *Candide* (1759), for his optimistic belief in divine providence. Attacks against religion and traditional hierarchies were the order of the day, even if they had to be published in Amsterdam or London to avoid the French censor.

One attack that succeeded on home ground was Beaumarchais' phenomenally successful play *The Marriage of Figaro* (1784). Beaumarchais dared to question the right of aristocrats to command wealth, rank, and public office, while others had to use all their wits just to survive. The family servant, Figaro, vilifies his master, Count Almaviva, behind his back: "What have you done to have so much? You've hardly given yourself the trouble to be born." Figaro's fury had been aroused by the count's attempts to sleep with the countess's lady-in-waiting, Suzanne, whom Figaro wants to marry. Aided by Figaro and Suzanne, the countess turns the tables on her philandering husband: she disguises herself as Suzanne, seduces her own husband, and then, in a hilarious scene, exposes him publicly and forces him to retreat from his predatory plan.

Some women in real life went further: they expected equality with men and even dominance over them. Think of the social and political power that Madame du Barry and Madame de Pompadour exercised as official mistresses of the king. Think of Madame du Deffand, Madame Geoffrin, and Julie de Lespinasse, who showcased philosophers, scientists, authors, and artists in their prestigious salons and pulled strings throughout society to advance their favorites. Think of Olympe de Gouges, who issued her own proclamations in favor of women's rights during the Revolution and ended up on the guillotine. Several notable women, like Sophie de

Condorcet, the wife of the mathematician and statesman Antoine-Nicolas de Condorcet, and Marie-Anne Lavoisier, the wife of the famous chemist Antoine-Laurent Lavoisier, enjoyed happy companionate marriages, before their husbands were destroyed by the Revolution.

Madame Roland came close to this ideal of companionate felicity. For most of her marriage, she seems to have been a good wife and mother and a helpmeet to her husband in every way. Following the code of conduct advocated by Rousseau, she practiced the virtues of simplicity, economy, and breast-feeding. A return to breast-feeding, as opposed to the common practice of sending babies out to wet nurses, was one of the fundamental changes considered necessary for the regeneration of society.[4] Philippe Le Bas maintained that position when he asked Elisabeth during their courtship if she intended to breast-feed her babies and, right before his death, when he reminded her to nurse their son with her own milk.

Republican love was supposed to take into account the greater society and become part of the general good. It was expected to go hand in hand with virtue, which meant refraining from sex until marriage and remaining monogamous within marriage. It also meant producing children for the nation and nursing them with the mother's milk. Gone were the excesses of gallantry, with its seductive retinue of affairs, mistresses, and lovers. Republican lovers and spouses were equated with good citizens, taught to sacrifice their personal desires for the well-being of their families and their country. But as we saw in the case of Madame Roland, the heart's reasons were not always politically correct.

DE

L'Amour;

PAR L'AUTEUR
DE L'HISTOIRE DE LA PEINTURE EN ITALIE, ET DES
VIES DE HAYDN, MOZART ET MÉTASTASE.

That you should be made a fool of by a young
woman, why, it is many an honest man's case.
THE PIRATE, tome III, page 77.

TOME PREMIER.

PARIS,

LIBRAIRIE UNIVERSELLE,
DE P. MONGIE L'AINÉ.
BOULEVART POISSONNIÈRE, No. 18.
ET RUE NEUVE DE MONTMORENCY, No. 2.

1822.

CHAPTER SEVEN

Yearning for the Mother

Constant, Stendhal, and Balzac

THE COUNTESS ENVELOPED ME IN NOURISHING PROTECTION,
IN THE WHITE DRAPERIES OF AN ENTIRELY MATERNAL LOVE.
Balzac, *The Lily of the Valley*, 1835

THE SEXUAL INITIATION OF A YOUNG MAN by an older woman is what the French call a "sentimental education." The roots of this tradition reach back to the Middle Ages, when courtly love privileged the attachment of a young knight to a high-born lady, and to the Renaissance, when no less a personage than King Henri II took as his official mistress Diane de Poitiers, a woman twenty years his senior. And, as we have seen in *The Wayward Head and Heart*, the adolescent protagonist made his sexual debut with his mother's friend when he was seventeen and she was around forty.

But it was not until Rousseau's *Confessions*, published posthumously in 1782 and 1790, that the maternal component of such liaisons was laid bare. Jean-Jacques Rousseau had lost his mother in childbirth and was raised in Geneva by his unstable watchmaker father. Then, when Rousseau was ten, his father simply decamped and Rousseau found himself both motherless and fatherless. He received minimal schooling and underwent two apprenticeships before taking off from Switzerland on his own at the age of sixteen. Wandering about France, he found a benevolent protectress in Louise de Warens, a woman twelve years his senior, who had left her husband and settled in the Savoy region of France. She sheltered Rousseau on and off for twelve years. When she suggested that it was time for his sexual initiation, he was a reluctant lover. Yet, once *Maman* (Mommy) had made up her mind, he could not refuse. Afterward, he was grateful for this further proof of her love: "I became her work, totally; her child, totally, and even more than if she had been my true mother."

Similar liaisons became the theme of countless eighteenth- and nineteenth-century novels. For ambitious young men, sleeping with an older married woman was a rite of passage that launched them, not only into sexuality but also into society and professional opportunities. The following examples, taken from life and literature, explore this particular socio-erotic variation on love.

LIKE JEAN-JACQUES ROUSSEAU, BENJAMIN CONSTANT LOST HIS mother in childbirth and thereafter yearned for a mother substitute. He found one in a number of women, including the amazing Isabelle de Charrière, twenty-seven years his senior, and the even more amazing Germaine de Staël, only one year older than he was but already a wife, a mother, and a formidable cultural force when he first met her in 1794. The story of their stormy relation over a period of fifteen years has inspired numerous biographies and fictionalized accounts, and none better than Constant's own compact novel, *Adolphe*.

Madame de Staël (1766–1817) was, without a doubt, the most impressive woman of her generation. As the only child of Jacques Necker, Louis XVI's Swiss-born finance minister, and his influential wife, Suzanne, Germaine Necker was brought up to take her place both at the French court and among France's most brilliant thinkers. With her dowry of 650,000 pounds, she made a prestigious marriage to the Swedish ambassador, Baron de Staël-Holstein, though she never learned to love him. Never mind: marriage was the gateway to freedom and to her many lovers, starting with the Abbé de Talleyrand, who would become the most cynically immoral and politically successful ecclesiastic of his age. By the time she encountered Constant, she had already been madly in love several times, and her passionate affair with the Vicomte de Narbonne had produced a son, whom she passed off as her husband's. She had also been actively involved in revolutionary politics as the salon leader of a moderate group that argued for a constitutional monarchy and tried, unsuccessfully, to save the king and queen from the guillotine.

Constant shared Madame de Staël's liberal views and would become not only her lover but also her political protégé after the Revolution. Under her tutelage, he was appointed to the twenty-member Tribunate, a position he held for three years until Napoleon dismissed him. Napoleon lost no opportunity to inflict pain upon Madame de Staël. It was not in his nature to tolerate a brilliant, articulate woman who supported liberal causes. By 1803 Napoleon ordered her exile to Switzerland, and it was there at her

Château de Coppet that she and Constant played out their tempestuous drama. Constant depended on her for almost everything. Without a career, without a family of his own, he lived under her wing. Moreover, Constant was the father of Germaine's last child, Albertine, born on 1797, again passed off as her husband's. But life at Coppet was a torment for both of them. Constant noted in a diarylike text called *Amélie et Germaine* on January 6, 1803: "For a long time now, I have felt no love for Germaine. . . . A great intellectual rapport draws us together. But can this last? My heart, my imagination, and above all my senses crave love."

From his diary entries, we know that Constant had frequent recourse to prostitutes. We also know that he and Germaine quarreled incessantly, sometimes until three or four in the morning. Words like "torture," "fury," and "anguish" explode on every page of his private writing. He could no longer tolerate her dominating nature but vacillated in his desire to break away. She knew he no longer loved her, yet she could not let him go. At times he wanted to marry her, but she refused on the grounds that such a marriage would be beneath her station and compromise her children's future. It was a nightmare for both of them.

This is the "maternal" nightmare that Constant activates in his novel. Adolphe, Constant's fictional alter ego, becomes entangled with Ellénore, a woman of Polish origin who is ten years his senior. She leaves her aristocratic protector, with whom she has had two children, for a man in his twenties with no position. What began in sensual delight soon metamorphosed into a prolonged battle between Adolphe's fluctuating commitment and Ellénore's impassioned tenacity. The echoes of Constant's tumultuous relationship with Madame de Staël reverberate throughout the novel.

The scene became stormy. We broke out in mutual recriminations. . . . There are things which for a long time are left unsaid,
but once they are said, one never stops repeating them. . . . Had
I loved her as she loved me, she would have been calmer. . . .
A senseless rage took hold of us; all circumspection was abandoned, all delicacy forgotten. It was as if the Furies were urging
us on against each other.[1]

Despite their mutual recriminations and Adolphe's waning love
for Ellénore, he follows her to Poland, where she, unexpectedly,
has regained her inheritance. His father tries to dissuade him: "So
what do you expect to do? She is ten years older than you; you are
twenty-six; you will look after her for ten more years; she will be
old; you will have reached the middle of your life, without having
started anything, without having completed anything that satisfies
you." His father's warnings are to no avail.

Isolated in his mistress's Polish retreat, the narrator becomes
increasingly dejected and bitter. Whatever love he had felt at the
beginning of their liaison dissolves into mere pity and a sense of
duty. She, however, never loses her passion for him. The emotional
disparity between them results in endless rows.

Whereas in real life Constant eventually broke away from
Madame de Staël and went on to a distinguished career as a politician and writer, Adolphe finds his freedom only when Ellénore
dies. It's the oldest ploy in fiction: kill off the woman. But as he
realizes retrospectively, his freedom does not bring him happiness. "How heavily it weighed on me, that freedom for which I had
longed so much! . . . I was indeed free; I was no longer loved; I was
a stranger to everyone."

Adolphe will always be a stranger adrift in the world because his own core is hollow. His attachment to a mother figure from whom he cannot escape, even after her death, begs a psychological interpretation. There are some men who, for want of satisfactory mothering, never grow up, or grow up very late in life. A surrogate mother, like Madame de Warens for Rousseau, like Madame de Staël for Constant, may help repair early maternal loss, but not without painful struggle. The filial nature of the erotic relationship with a substitute mother is fraught with classic ambivalence: the young man comes to resent the older woman's authority and protectiveness while simultaneously craving it. Can one truly love the mother in another woman? This is the question animating the greatest novel of sublimated maternal love: *The Red and the Black* by Stendhal.

IN 1976, I PUBLISHED AN ARTICLE ON Stendhalian love.[2] It was a strictly Freudian interpretation of how Stendhal's unconscious Oedipal struggle filtered into his novels, *The Red and the Black* and *The Charterhouse of Parma*. At that time in my life, I was heavily influenced by psychoanalytic theory, due largely to the life I shared with my husband, psychiatrist Irvin Yalom. The following discussion is based mainly on that article, amended by latter-day feminist insights.

In Stendhal's autobiography, *The Life of Henry Brulard*, the fifty-two-year-old writer recalled his passionate childhood love for his mother and concurrent intense hatred for his father.

I wanted to cover my mother with kisses, and without any clothes on. She loved me passionately and often kissed me; I returned her kisses with such fervor that she was often forced to go away. I abhorred my father when he came to interrupt our kisses. I always wanted to kiss her bosom. Please be kind enough to remember that I lost her in childhood when I was barely seven.[3]

With an intuitive comprehension of the psychology of love that antedated Freud's clinical observations, Stendhal understood that this original love for his mother served as the prototype for later love experiences: "When I loved her at about the age of six in 1789, I showed exactly the same characteristics as in 1828 when I was in love with Alberthe de Rubempré. My way of pursuing happiness was basically unchanged." He was, however, not fully aware of the essentially triangular nature of his feelings, which always included a father figure.

Triangular love permeates both *The Red and the Black* and *The Charterhouse of Parma*, with a triad consisting of the hero (the author's alter ego), the woman he loves, and another man, either the husband or the father of the beloved woman. The adult Stendhal had often found himself in the position of the *terzo incomodo* (the third wheel). What sweet revenge to transfer that unflattering role to a fictive husband or father figure!

In *The Red and the Black*, Julien Sorel's original family configuration resembles that of Stendhal after the age of seven: mother deceased, father despised, mutual incomprehension between father and son. Barely nineteen and with the pretty-boy face of youth, Julien seeks both father and mother substitutes at the home of the mayor of Verrières. The mayor, Monsieur de Rênal, is hardly a likable character, but he does have the advantage of a charming wife.

Freud might say that Rênal becomes the "injured third party," an opponent who satisfies the hero's psychological need to take a woman away from a patriarchal male, as in the primal family scene.

Let me backtrack and lay out the bare outline of the novel. Julien Sorel, the son of a carpenter with brutal peasant ways, is taken under the wing of a retired surgeon who had served under Napoleon. Napoleon's fall and the restoration of the Bourbon monarchy make it necessary for Julien to hide his Napoleonic sympathies, especially after he becomes the protégé of the village priest, Chélan. With Chélan's instruction, Julien learns to read, write, and speak Latin, and becomes a local prodigy capable of reciting from memory any part of the New Testament in Latin.

Such impressive, if limited, erudition earns him a place as tutor in the home of Monsieur de Rênal. Before long, Julien seduces Madame de Rênal, a mother in her thirties. No doubt Stendhal was influenced by *La nouvelle Héloïse*, as he himself acknowledged in many ways throughout the novel; yet *The Red and the Black* strikes an entirely new note in literature. Julien is an original type, lucidly aware of his own failings and cynically conscious of the hypocritical society in which he must make his way. He also demonstrates genuine passion and generosity: what began as willful seduction on his part turns into a great reciprocal love.

It is true that after his first night with Madame de Rênal, Julien pronounces those words that have troubled many readers: "My God! To be happy, to be loved, that's all it is?"[4] His main concern is whether he has lived up to expectations. "Did I play my role well?" Apparently he had played it well enough, for from that night forth Madame de Rênal loves him with the strength of a lioness defending her cub. She will prove herself daring and resourceful, playful and passionate, youthful and mature in responding to the needs of her ardent lover.

Her only worry lies in their age disparity. "Alas, I'm too old for him; I'm ten years older than he." Julien never consciously thinks about their age difference. He cannot get over the fact that he—a poor, unhappy, lowborn creature—could be loved by such a noble and beautiful woman. During the idyllic months when Madame de Rênal receives Julien in her bedroom late at night, his love for her and his confidence in himself grow exponentially. But like all paradises, this one, too, will be lost.

An anonymous letter sent to Monsieur de Rênal by a jealous party forces Julien to leave the mayor's home and enter a seminary in Besançon, where he is to train for the priesthood. Once again he finds a father figure, in the person of the austere seminary director, Abbé Pirard. However miserable he is among the seminarians, Julien manages to distinguish himself through his learning and apparent probity. Then, through Pirard's good offices, he lands an unexpectedly fortunate position in Paris as private secretary to the Marquis de La Mole, a nobleman of great lineage and influence. Once again Julien has to prove himself the equal of those born to rank and fortune, and he does. After all, this is a novel. Where else do all our wishes come true?

In Paris, Julien embarks upon another love affair, this time with the proud and beautiful Mathilde de La Mole, the nineteen-year-old daughter of Julien's protector. While she is socially superior and initially treats him with disdain, she proves no match for Julien's cunning and daring. Ultimately she finds herself pregnant and wants to marry him. Only a genius like Stendhal could have imagined the convoluted plot that ultimately satisfies Mathilde de La Mole. Here I won't say more for fear of spoiling the pleasure of the first-time reader.

Suffice it to say that Julien ultimately returns to Madame de Rênal with the realization that she is the only one he has truly loved. Why does he reject Mathilde de La Mole, a woman his own age, and fall back upon a married mother a decade older than himself? One can scarcely avoid the incestuous dimension of this love, so satisfying to the hero (and author). It is she, the mother-mistress, who corresponds most completely to his deepest needs, for she loves him naturally, spontaneously, totally, sexually, and maternally. Julien's ultimate return to Madame de Rênal demonstrates the hero's inability to transfer his love from the mother figure to a more suitable love object. The primary bond remains unsevered and proves stronger than any subsequent relationship.

But Julien does not get off lightly. Union with the mother is tabooed. It implies an injured third party in the husband-father, and an accompanying sense of guilt, however unconscious. The father may be done in, as in *Oedipus the King*, but he is never done away with. He exists in the very idea of the judicial system that arrests and tries Julien for attempted murder. As the pace quickens, the reader is swept along breathlessly to the sensational end.

ROUSSEAU AND CONSTANT NEVER KNEW THEIR MOTHERS. Stendhal lost his at the age of seven. Balzac's mother sent him to a wet nurse in the country and barely visited during the four years he remained there. Then, when he returned to the family home in Tours, neither she nor her husband paid him much attention. If we are to believe his later memories, he was brought up in a cold, intimidating atmosphere that stunted his psychological growth for years to come. The fictive re-creation of a loveless childhood in his novel *The Lily of the Valley* is bathed in pathos. I would call it Dickensian if it weren't for the fact that Balzac influenced Dickens, rather than vice versa. Both were masters in depicting monstrously egotistic adults and pitiful children.

Félix de Vandenesse, the young hero of *Lily of the Valley*, cries out in pain: "What physical or moral disgrace in me caused my mother's coldness? . . . Sent to a wet nurse in the country, forgotten by my family for three years, when I returned to the paternal home, I counted for so little that people looked upon me with compassion."[5]

Unsure of himself and mistrustful of everyone, he spent eight years in a Catholic boarding school living the life of a pariah. It didn't help that his father gave him only three francs a month for spending money, whereas the other boys could permit themselves toys and sweets and other marks of parental largesse. Even when he won the two most important school prizes, neither his mother nor his father came to the awards ceremony. At fifteen he was sent to live with a conservative family in Paris, while he attended the Lycée Charlemagne. There too he suffered from his parents' indifference and frugality and was as miserable as before. Like most adolescents, he began to feel the stirrings of sexuality, but finding no outlet, he passed his twentieth year tormented by "repressed desires . . . I was still small, skinny, and pale . . . a child in my body and old in my thoughts."

It is necessary to keep Félix's background in mind as we read the scene of his decisive encounter with a woman. When Félix returns to Tours, his mother still treats him as an "unnatural son," but because political events have unseated Napoleon and brought about the restoration of the Bourbon monarchy, Félix is called upon to represent his royalist family at a ball given for Louis XVIII. Suddenly he has decent clothing. Suddenly he finds himself in the midst of elegant women with dazzling attire and sparkling diamonds. "Carried like a straw into this whirlpool," he becomes unwell and takes refuge on a bench, where he slumps down like "a child ready to fall asleep while waiting for his mother." At this moment, a woman sits down on the bench with her back to Félix. He is so overcome by her perfume and by the whiteness of her neck and shoulders that he does the unthinkable. Suddenly he takes to kissing her back "like a child who throws himself upon his mother's breast." The woman is, to say the least, astonished. She draws herself up with the "movement of a queen" and leaves the besotted young man to contemplate how ridiculously he has behaved.

Henceforth Félix goes in search of the woman with the beautiful shoulders. Since this is a Balzac novel, he finds her immediately and almost by chance. Madame de Mortsauf lives with her older husband and two young children in the poetic Touraine countryside. She is as divinely beautiful from the front as she was from the back and corresponds exactly to Félix's dream of an ethereal angel. And that is exactly what she will remain throughout the book, despite his need for a flesh-and-blood woman. Madame de Mortsauf, whom he privately addresses as Henriette, is given to maternity and to religion as others are given to sex, sports, or business affairs. She calls Félix her child and refers to herself as his mother. They talk together of love, but only on an airy plane where spirits commune with each other like angels. For the most part, Félix accepts the angelic contract she offers him, content to kiss her hand even when his body calls out for fuller pleasures. He tells himself: "I had no other ambition than that of loving Henriette."

It takes little effort for the reader to understand why Félix regresses to the state of a baby and experiences in his early twenties the love he was deprived of as a child. At the same time, he is not a baby, and adult demands refuse to be silenced: "I loved her with a double love that unleashed, one by one, the thousand arrows of desire."

Ultimately, after six years of platonic love, Félix succumbs to the seductive wiles of an energetic Englishwoman, Lady Dudley, who trails behind her a husband and two sons. By now Félix has attained a position in the world as private secretary to the king, Louis XVIII. He should be content with his lot as the acknowledged lover of a passionate woman while still retaining his filial ties to his chaste beloved. But of course he is not. As he explains to Henriette, "you soar victoriously above her, she is a woman of the earth, the daughter of fallen races, and you are the daughter of heaven, the adored angel." He tells her that Lady Dudley knows "you have all of my heart and she has only my flesh. . . . For you the soul, for you my thoughts, for you, pure love, for you youth and old age; for her desires and pleasures of a fugitive passion."

Balzac has conveniently divided womanhood into the prototypes of the madonna and the whore, each satisfying a different part of his nature. That one of these figures is French and the other English allows him to praise the Frenchwoman excessively at the expense of her English counterpart. Rarely will you find pages so outrageously chauvinistic as those written to compare the love of a Frenchwoman with that of an Englishwoman. Balzac is not known for his moderation.

In the end, Balzac kills off Henriette, as so many French authors have done to heroines before and after him, but not before delivering a whopping surprise in her final death agony. I leave that for you to discover. And in the very last pages of the book, in a letter written to Félix by a certain Nathalie, we see that Balzac is capable of critiquing his own creation. However heartfelt his identification with the young Félix, however idealistic his portrayal of the angelic mother, Balzac turns the tables on his hero and takes him to task for his refusal to grow up. Nathalie, to whom Félix has turned for affection, writes him that he can "taste happiness only with dead women." She is not about to step into the perilous space left empty by Henriette and Lady Dudley. For the moment, Félix de Vandenesse is left stranded in a loveless no-man's-land, still craving the woman who will bring together his yearning for the mother and his physical need for a mistress-wife. I say "for the moment" because Félix will reappear in nine other novels, all part of the capacious oeuvre Balzac called *The Human Comedy*.

Is it possible for any living woman today to identify with these mother figures created to fill the psychological needs of men with incestuous longings? As a woman and a mother, I feel no sisterhood with either the mindlessly passionate Ellénore or the saintly Henriette. Only Madame de Rênal comes across as the reflection of a real person, someone whose hesitations and anxieties, transports and fleeting happiness, concerns for her greater age and fear of losing her lover, and simultaneous worries about her children and husband all ring true. More than any other male author, Stendhal endowed women with a credible female psyche. Perhaps he could do this because he carried within him vestigial memories of a loving mother and was not merely prey to unrealistic fantasies of a mother he had never known.

Any lovers who have a double-digit age disparity between them would do well to read *The Red and the Black*. I recommended it several years ago to a young man in his twenties who had come from Brussels to study in Paris soon after his mother's death. He was lodging with his French aunt—his mother's younger sister—and her husband in the Latin Quarter while attending the Sorbonne. At the request of his aunt, I met with him to discuss the possibilities of literary studies in the United States. During the course of our conversation over a glass of wine in a café near the Panthéon, his mood changed from cautious to confiding. He let me know that he and his aunt were on intimate terms. Since she was over fifty, I wondered how that made him feel. "It's a problem for her, but not for me." And how did he feel about the uncle? "Now that's a problem." He felt guilty receiving bed and board at his uncle's expense and wondered how long he could possibly stay with them. At the end of our conversation, he promised me he would read *The Red and the Black*.

His aunt had put him in her grown son's room. She took him with her to various social events, called him "my adoptive son," and spared no effort to help him in his career. He eventually became a journalist and returned to his home country. Within a year of his departure, his aunt developed cancer and rapidly met a premature death. When I visited her mournful husband, he told me that he had not been blind to the affair. "David came along just when she needed him." Their own son had recently moved away and she had keenly felt his absence. "At least she had a little pleasure before she disappeared." It was strange for me to sit in that familiar apartment, where I had come to offer my condolences and where every piece of furniture and *bibelot* spoke to the dead woman's presence. It was stranger still to hear her husband speak dispassionately, almost nostalgically, about his wife's affair with a man half her age. I can't imagine this scene taking place in my American homeland, or anywhere else but in France.

The motif of the young man in love with an older woman, and vice versa, is quintessentially French. It does not appear significantly in German, English, Italian, Spanish, Scandinavian, or American literature, though surely—if Freud is correct—boys from these countries are also subject to the same Oedipal evolution. So what is there in French culture that gets added on to a person's psychological development to create this socio-erotic pattern? Here are a few of my musings on that question.

1. The French eroticize everything, including the relation of mother and son. Most French mothers have no trouble caressing their children, boys and girls, and words like *mon chéri* and *ma chérie* fall from their lips even when the children are adults. I have seen French boys of twelve and fourteen cuddling up to their mothers in ways that would be unthinkable to most American boys of that age. Some of us remember the film *Le Souffle au Coeur* (*Murmur of the Heart*), in which a mother sleeps with her adolescent son and nothing terrible happens to either of them. Once again, a film that could have been made only in France!

2. The French value erotic love to such an extent that women of all ages make an effort to retain their sex ap-

peal. This means staying thin, having one's hair done, and dressing fashionably even when one is eighty. Not for the Frenchwoman to bury herself in comforting fat or dowdy black weeds! True, class and region enter into all of this: a Parisian of the upper bourgeoisie may resemble a peasant in the Auvergne only to the extent that a thoroughbred horse looks like a plow horse.

3. Court society, which encouraged the love of a young man for a mature woman during the Middle Ages, privileged older aristocratic women throughout the *ancien régime*. For example, the Marquise du Deffand reigned over her prestigious salon long after Julie de Lespinasse's departure, and when she was sixty-eight and blind, fell so in love with the fifty-year-old Englishman Horace Walpole that he was obliged to assume the role of a younger suitor. It was about this same period that wealthy bourgeois women, like Madame Geoffrin, also began to establish salons that served as gateways for young men into "the world." Whether they were writers, philosophers, scientists, or just plain social climbers, these men counted on older women to provide a showcase for their talents and lobby on their behalf for prizes, entrance into academies, and social acceptance among their peers.

4. The medieval romances and sentimental novels that French girls and boys read in childhood and adolescence offer models of behavior for the adult years. Each

generation that acts out these models adds a new chapter and inspires further stories in this vein.

Today, a woman of thirty, as in Balzac's novel with that title, has become a woman of fifty, or more. Both in the United States and in France, it has become increasingly common for some women—single, married, widowed, or divorced—to take a younger partner.[6] With increased longevity, careful diet, good medical care, cosmetic surgery, and often her own earnings, it is possible for a woman to keep her sex appeal well into her later years. That is, if she wants to, and many Frenchwomen seem to want just that.

Of course, it is still more common for an older man to take a younger mistress or wife, especially if he is rich and famous. How many well-known actors, politicians, and industrialists are pictured in the newspaper alongside first, second, or third wives who look like their daughters? Yet French novels and plays contain comparatively few accounts of an older man's passion for a much younger woman.

On the other hand, the theme of the young man in love with an older woman had become almost commonplace by 1869 when Flaubert published his eponymous novel, *L'Education sentimentale* (*Sentimental Education*). By then, even a few women writers had taken up the subject, most notably George Sand, whose life and work were inscribed from a female perspective. But as we shall see in the next chapter, the theme of older woman–younger man was only one aspect of Sand's peerless romantic career.

CHAPTER EIGHT

Love Among the Romantics

George Sand and Alfred de Musset

ANGEL OF DEATH, FATAL LOVE, OH MY DESTINY,
UNDER THE FACE OF A BLOND AND DELICATE
CHILD. HOW I STILL LOVE YOU, ASSASSIN!
George Sand, *Intimate Journal,* 1834

QUITE EARLY IN LIFE, I CAME TO love the English romantics. Lines from Wordsworth, Shelley, and Keats circled in my head as I walked to school or meandered in Washington D.C.'s Rock Creek Park. The mental picture of Wordsworth hiking the Lake District accompanied me as I asked my own questions about "nature's holy plan" and lamented "what man has made of man." The romantics were poets, prophets, philosophers, and they all came from England.

When I encountered the French romantics in college, it took me a while to understand how the two groups could share the same name. Yes, they were poets given to bucolic reverie. Yes, they were misunderstood individuals at odds with society. But what did a

group of Parisian bohemians have in common with the demigods who retreated to the English countryside or made pilgrimages to Italy and Greece?

The French poet Lamartine, to be sure, contemplated nature with a romantic sensibility. His verses conjured up the majestic mountains and soothing streams craved by troubled souls, as in these words, from "Le Vallon" (The Valley).

> . . . *la nature est là qui t'invite et qui t'aime;*
> *Plonge-toi dans son sein qu'elle t'ouvre toujours.*

> . . . *there is nature, which invites and loves you;*
> *Plunge into her breast, which she offers you always.*[1]

However, the unprecedented success of Lamartine's *Méditations poétiques* in 1820 sprang mainly from something even dearer to the French than the love of nature: his poems were inspired by a tragic love story, by love itself (*l'amour tout court*). Behind the solitary sojourner hoping to find consolation in nature's bosom is the lover who had lost his mistress. Lamartine's beloved Julie Charles went to an early death in December 1817. Under the name of Elvire in his poetry, she would be granted eternal life. Is there any French person who doesn't know the line "Un seul être vous manque, et tout est dépeuplé" ("A single person is missing, and the whole world is depeopled"). Lamartine's poignant loss, his melancholy tone and mystical longings—all resonated within the hearts of Rousseau's spiritual descendants.

One now-famous poem, "Le Lac," born from Lamartine's personal experience, offered an art of love intended for everyone. Returning to the lakeside where the lovers had once shared ecstatic moments, Lamartine recalled Elvire's moving words: "O temps, suspends ton vol!" ("O time, suspend your flight!") In response, the poet threw himself into love's incessant flux as a counterforce to despair.

> *Aimons donc, aimons donc! De l'heure fugitive,*
> *Hâtons-nous, jouissons!*
> *L'homme n'a point de port, le temps n'a point de rive;*
>
> Let us love, let us love, in this passing hour,
> Hurry up, let's enjoy!
> Man hasn't any port, time hasn't any shore.

What is left of our frenzied existence? Only the memory. As a site of remembrance, the lake has the power to evoke the only words that matter: "Ils ont aimé!" ("They have loved!") This will be the creed for a whole generation of writers born around 1800—Alfred de Vigny, Honoré de Balzac, Alexandre Dumas, Victor Hugo, Charles Augustin Sainte-Beuve, Prosper Mérimée, George Sand, Gérard de Nerval, Alfred de Musset, Théophile Gautier.

By 1830, almost all these French romantics had gathered in Paris. Writers from abroad, like the German poet Heinrich Heine and the Polish poet Adam Mickiewicz, would join them, as well as famous musicians like Chopin, Liszt, and Meyerbeer, and painters of every stripe. Once again Paris was the European capital of literary and artistic creation, as it had been during the reign of Louis XIV and the Enlightenment.

The year 1830 was marked by two major cultural events: Dela-

croix's painting *Liberty Leading the People,* in honor of the July revolution that forced the abdication of Charles X and ushered in the
liberal reign of the citizen-king Louis-Philippe; and Victor Hugo's
revolutionary play *Hernani.* First performed at the Comédie Française on February 25, 1830, *Hernani* officially launched French romanticism. It is true that the play is less memorable today as a work
of art than for the demonstrations it provoked, pitting young en-
thusiasts against entrenched conservatives. The bandit Hernani's
love of Doña Sol, contested by two high-born men who are also
in love with her, brought Spanish passion to the stage as seen by
French eyes—that is, cloaked in violent melodrama. This vein of
Spanish exoticism had already been mined by Musset in his *Contes
d'Espagne et d'Italie (Stories from Spain and Italy,* 1829) and would be
reworked by Prosper Mérimée in his story *Carmen* (1848), which
provided the plot for Bizet's world-famous opera. In all of these
works, Spain was represented as the country of fatal love.

French romantics projected upon Spanish princes, bandits, and
gypsies their own roiled emotions. Love combined with suffering,
jealousy, infidelity, honor, and death inspirited their lives and made
for marketable literature. If previous generations had given love its
due as prescribed by the codes of *fin'amor,* gallantry, or sensibility,
the romantics raised the stakes: love or death, love and death, love
in death, love, love, love as the supreme value in life. Love was
worth living for and dying for. In novels and plays, women and
men died of broken hearts, even as their authors recovered and
went on to new romances.

No one incarnates the French romantic spirit better than George
Sand. From the start, even before her birth, Sand's story was what
the French would call *romanesque,* meaning "like a novel." Sand

was born on July 1, 1804, only one month after her parents, Maurice Dupin, a dashing Napoleonic officer, and Sophie-Victoire Delaborde, a woman with a shady past, legalized their union. She was baptized the next day as Amantine-Aurore-Lucie Dupin. Her parents' liaison of four years had been hidden from Maurice Dupin's aristocratic mother, since she would never have accepted his marriage to the disreputable daughter of a bird vendor. But when Dupin met an untimely death, his mother, Madame Dupin de Francueil, was obliged to look out for her daughter-in-law and her four-year-old granddaughter, Aurore. Growing up in her grandmother's country manor at Nohant (today a pilgrimage site for Sand aficionados), Aurore Dupin experienced a divided sense of loyalty between the mother she fiercely loved and the grandmother she profoundly respected. Although she attributed her artistic genes to her parents, it was probably the education she received under her grandmother's tutelage that deserves equal credit for her ability to compete in the male literary arena.

As a child, Aurore caroused with peasant children of both sexes. She spoke their patois and joined in their rustic activities—milking cows and goats, making cheese, dancing country dances, eating wild apples and pears. Up to the age of thirteen, she could roam according to her fancy and read whatever she liked. In the twelve months between her twelfth and thirteenth years, Aurore grew three inches, attaining a maximum height of five feet two. It was then that she began to show the signs of adolescence that became the despair of her grandmother—irritability, temper tantrums, outbursts toward her tutor. At this point, her grandmother decided to send her off to a convent school in Paris so as to transform her from an unmannered country girl into a marriageable young lady.

Sand's autobiography *Histoire de ma vie* (*Story of My Life*) presents the picture of an active, energetic, curious thirteen-year-old who had trouble adapting to convent ways.[2] But gradually she settled in and formed close friendships. Sand, at the age of fifty, remembered in detail a large number of girls she had loved with great tenderness. She also wrote of the nuns who served as mother figures, including "the pearl of the convent," Madame Alicia, for whom she developed a great worshipful love, and the lowly lay sister, Sister Hélène. These intense attachments, all the more intense because they were formed in the absence of boys, can be seen as the prototype for the highly charged friendships the future author would form throughout adulthood.

We mustn't leave Aurore's school years without speaking about her conversion experience. During her second year at the convent, she had an epiphany in the chapel: "I felt faith grab hold of me." That episode inaugurated "a state of calm devotion" that she maintained throughout her third and final school year. For the rest of her life, despite her unconventional existence as a novelist, an adulteress, a cigarette-smoking woman in male clothes, and a political radical, she held onto her faith in God.

At sixteen, Aurore Dupin returned to her grandmother's estate and renewed the freer existence she had known before. Reading books, playing the harpsichord, going out horseback riding, befriending the locals, and taking classes with her old tutor filled her days, until her grandmother had a stroke and died in December 1821. Then, with mixed emotions, Aurore went to live with her mother in Paris. Her relations with her mother were always extra sensitive: as a child she had idolized her; as a young woman she recognized her mother's character flaws. Temperamental, uneducated, unpredictable, and disorderly, the younger Madame Dupin was in every way the opposite of Aurore's dignified grandmother.

Before her marriage to Maurice Dupin, when she was thirty-one and he was twenty-six, Sophie Delaborde belonged to that class of women known as demi-mondaines—women of doubtful reputation supported by their lovers. One of her previous lovers had fathered Aurore's half-sister, Caroline. On the paternal side, Aurore also had to deal with an illegitimate half-brother, Hippolyte Chatiron. And for all her grandmother's haughty sense of class, she, too, had been the illegitimate daughter of the field marshal Maurice de Saxe and his mistress, Aurore de Königsmark. Aurore Dupin, one month short of being illegitimate herself, was surrounded by the fruit of irregular unions. Ironically, or perhaps fittingly, the man she was to marry was the illegitimate son of a baron, who legally recognized him and passed on the baronial title.

Nine months after her grandmother's death, Aurore Dupin married Casimir Dudevant, a thin, elegant-looking military man with the friendly air of a companion. She was eighteen and he was twenty-seven. The first year of their marriage passed congenially enough for Aurore, elevated to the rank of a baroness and blessed with a son named Maurice. Though her affection for Casimir seems to have been relatively short-lived, her great love for her son would last a lifetime.

Sand's maternal capacity would be manifest not only to her son and later to her daughter, but also to her younger lovers. In these relations, she was wont to refer to her lover as *enfant* (child) and to herself as *mère* (mother) and take the lead in helping him advance both professionally and personally. Her standards were high, too high for some of the men, whom she abandoned or who broke away on their own. But most agreed, at least in retrospect, that she had played the combined role of lover and mother at a time when they needed both.

Much has been written about Sand's successive love affairs, a good deal by Sand herself in her correspondence, intimate journal, autobiography, travel literature, and semiautobiographical fiction. Numerous biographies have attempted to capture the intensity of a woman given to love, who was also a tireless writer, a wage earner, a concerned mother, a devoted friend, a sometime political activist, and an estate manager. I shall try to extract from her life story those elements that are quintessentially romantic.

George Sand—she took that pen name in 1832 for her novel *Indiana*—was a force of nature, endowed with physical energy and mental vigor that lasted into her seventies. Whether she was horseback riding at night to meet her lover Michel de Bourges, traveling abroad with Musset to Venice or with Chopin to Majorca, launching a political magazine or promoting a friend, Sand gave herself heart and soul to the enterprise. And all the while, she was writing from late evening till five in the morning in order to provide for herself, her children, some of her lovers, and numerous hangers-on. Like Hugo and Balzac, Sand was an indefatigable writing machine.

Sand had a great romantic imagination, by which I mean that she imagined love as a sublime experience and would settle for nothing less, both in her personal life and in the lives of her fictive heroines. She believed in the power of love to elevate, rather than degrade, and clung to this idealistic vision in spite of the suffering caused by her love affairs. Placing herself in the camp of Rousseau, she espoused emotion above reason as a spiritual guide to life.

Her husband, Casimir, did not share her idealism. He was not a bad sort but simply an ordinary mortal with down-to-earth tastes, like hunting, drinking, and bedding the household help. Sand knew fairly early in the marriage that he was not a match for her. But then, who was?

Her great platonic love for the magistrate Aurélien de Sèze lasted about three years, from 1825 to 1827. Their chaste affair survived mainly on the lofty sentiments they expressed in their correspondence and in rare face-to-face meetings in his native Bordeaux. Her short-lived liaison with Stéphane Ajasson de Grandsagne, a neighbor in the town of La Châtre near her grandmother's estate, was decidedly more corporeal and may have produced Sand's daughter, Solange, born in 1828. Whatever her paternity, Solange was much loved by Sand when she was a child, though she never took the central place in her mother's heart occupied by her son, Maurice.

During these years, the future writer was finding her voice, first in her letters to Aurélien de Sèze and their mutual female friend; then in four semiautobiographical texts that would remain unpublished until after Sand's death. By 1830 the writing machine was running nonstop and was ready to relocate to Paris. It was not an easy thing to persuade Casimir Dudevant that his wife could make a go of it in the literary capital, but with the revolution of 1830 inciting freedom even in the provinces, the fledgling writer was not to be denied. Casimir granted her a leave of three months twice a year and a modest pension of 3,000 francs to cover expenses. So off she went to Paris in January 1831, for what was to be an amazingly successful literary career, second only to that of Victor Hugo among the romantics.

Sand's first novel, *Rose and Blanche*, was a collaborative effort with a young man named Jules Sandeau, whose name appeared alone on the book jacket since it was not considered proper for a woman of her class to use her own name. Jules Sandeau became not only Sand's collaborator but also her lover—her third or fourth, depending on whether we include Aurélien, but who's counting? At nineteen, Sandeau tapped into the maternal tenderness that Sand was to show over and over again with her younger lovers. Trying to convince herself that Sandeau was worthy of her love, she wrote to a friend: "Doesn't he merit my loving him with passion? Doesn't he love me with all his soul and am I not right to sacrifice everything to him, fortune, reputation, children?"[3] Such was the importance romantics like Sand attributed to love that she was ready to abandon everything for what proved to be a relatively short affair. Sandeau turned out to be a lightweight, no match for Sand in energy and talent. She wrote her second novel, *Indiana*, without him and published it under the name of G. Sand, which would become George Sand in her later works. By the summer of 1832, Sand was a waxing star on the Parisian literary horizon.

Her novel *Indiana* is the story of one women's struggle to free herself from an oppressive marriage and, of course, to find true love. The heroine, Indiana, is married to Colonel Delmare, a middle-aged man still loyal to his Napoleonic past. Two other men vie for her attention: Raymon de Ramière, an archetypical aristocratic seducer, who casts a spell over Indiana despite her resistance, and her cousin Sir Ralph, a silent soul mate, who reveals his true nature only at the end of the novel. It was characteristic of Sand at this period of her life to conceptualize women primarily in terms of their relationships with men. Indeed, Sand always believed that what distinguished women from men was the feminine capacity for boundless love.

Sand's much admired contemporary, the English poet Byron,

understood the imaginative hold of romantic love over nineteenth-century women when he wrote: "Man's love is of man's life a thing apart; 'Tis women's whole existence." Today, women have other outlets, but in nineteenth-century France, it was possible for women of the upper classes to focus exclusively on love, if not romantic, then conjugal and maternal. And if we are to believe the novels, some Frenchmen also turned to love for the fabric of their "whole existence."

Certainly Raymon de Ramière in *Indiana* seems to have nothing to do beyond courting Indiana and her servant, Noun. And here we see the psychological genius of George Sand at work, for Indiana and Noun are doubles representing a basic duality in European culture—that of the idolized spiritual woman and her fleshly counterpart. Consider the following passage:

> Noun was Mme Delmare's foster sister, and the two young women, who had been brought up together, loved each other dearly. Noun was tall and strong, vividly alive, full of the ardor and passion of her Creole blood, and strikingly beautiful in a way that far outshone the delicate, fragile charms of the pale Mme Delmare; but their tender hearts and mutual affection eliminated all possibility of feminine rivalry.[4]

The words "foster sister" do not fully convey the original French expression *soeur de lait* (literally, "milk sister"), which indicates that Noun and Indiana had shared the same wet nurse, probably Noun's mother. Having nursed at the same breast, they are symbolic sisters, despite the difference in their social positions. Each is endowed with the physical attributes deemed appropriate to her station: Noun is tall, strong, healthy, and passionate, whereas Indiana is pale, frail, and implicitly less hot-blooded than her Creole counterpart. Individually they are stereotypes of their respective classes; together they constitute a whole person who has been fragmented by social proscriptions. Indiana's sense of sisterhood with Noun far exceeds the conventional bonds between mistress and maid. It suggests the union of a "respectable" woman and what the psychiatrist Carl Jung would have called her "shadow" self.

It is Noun who carries on the behind-the-scenes affair with Raymon. She is the free, uninhibited female who delights in love-making. She is the body experiencing pleasure. Raymon loves her "with his senses," but he loves Indiana "with all his heart and soul." During the day he declares his chaste and undying love to Indiana: "You are the woman I have dreamed of, the purity I have worshiped." But at night he returns to Noun to exchange "voluptuous caresses" that banish all vestiges of reason.

Alone with Noun in Indiana's bedroom while Indiana is out of the house, Raymon confuses the two women.

Little by little a vague memory of Indiana began to float in and out of Raymon's drunken consciousness. The two mirrored panels that reflected Noun's image into infinity seemed to be peopled by a thousand phantoms, and as he stared into the depths of that double image he thought he could see, in the final and hazy and indistinct reflection of Noun, the slender, willowy form of Mme. Delamare.

The confusion in Raymon's mind between the two women is not accidental. They are complementary characters, each half of a full person. Despite their spiritual sisterhood, Indiana and Noun are, on the underground level of the novel, engaged in psychological warfare. That neither knows of the other's involvement with Raymon adds to the tension and suggests the hidden reality of two hostile forces operating simultaneously within the writer's psyche. In *Indiana*, as in Sand's fourth novel *Lélia*, the double characters act out the author's split self. In life, Sand was also struggling to reconcile her lofty ideals and her erotic appetite.

In June 1833, approaching her twenty-ninth birthday, George Sand met Alfred de Musset, not yet twenty-three, at a literary dinner. Each had earned a coveted place at the table alongside other romantics. Musset the dandy, with his golden hair and supple body, was already famous for his poems and stories. He was also the darling of society ladies, courtesans, and prostitutes, and no enemy to alcohol, opium, and debauchery. In comparison, George Sand was a dark-headed, hardworking, tranquil saint. On July 26, Musset wrote to Sand: "I am in love with you." On July 27, she responded: "I love you like a child." On the night of July 28, the saint and the child slept together.

The following month the lovers took off for Fontainebleau, where they could isolate themselves from curious onlookers. Sand's novel, *Lélia*, was creating quite a stir in Paris, garnering both positive and negative press.[5] Who was this G. Sand who dared to speak the unspeakable about a heroine's sexual frigidity? The elderly writer René de Chateaubriand was already predicting that Sand would become France's Lord Byron, high praise from one whose own novels had sounded the note of romanticism even before it had a name.

Like Indiana, Lélia is another beautiful, superior woman, but she has lost some of the innocence of Sand's earlier heroine. Having idolized a man she took for a demigod, only to discover his human imperfections, Lélia is left with a sense of anguished disillusionment. In despair because she no longer has the ability to love, she is drawn toward an ascetic existence.

Lélia has a long-lost sister named Pulchérie (for "pulchritude," physical beauty). During the years of their separation Pulchérie has become a courtesan. The unexpected meeting between Lélia and Pulchérie can be read as a symbolic dialogue between two parts of the divided self.

Lélia is unwilling to accept the concept of love between the sexes in any form other than the most angelic and the most enduring. Pulchérie asks only for physical satisfaction. Yet neither the romantic nor the hedonist is a fully satisfying ideal. While professing to despise Pulchérie's demeaned condition, Lélia nonetheless craves her sister's experience of sexual pleasure.

That neither sister represents for the author a complete person becomes evident in the weird episode when the poet Sténio is tricked into making love to Pulchérie, whom he mistakes for his beloved Lélia. The description of Pulchérie and Lélia leading the faithful Sténio into an underground grotto is a masterpiece of *dédoublement* (division into two) designed to confuse both the reader and Sténio as to the true identity of the woman he embraces. Just as Raymon in *Indiana* confounds Noun and her mistress, so Sténio swears that he has never loved Lélia as much as when he holds Pulchérie in his arms under the mistaken belief that she is someone else.

Despite Sténio's subsequent rejection of Pulchérie when he discovers the dupery, the implications of his experience are clear: his adoration of Lélia is less than perfect without physical consummation. Lélia and Pulchérie, mind and body, spirit and flesh, must be merged to create a fully endowed person. Apart, they are incomplete, unsatisfying to themselves and to a potential mate.

It can be argued that *Lélia* represents the epitome of romanticism. Set in a fantastic convent containing grottos, marble fountains, rare birds, and dazzling flowers, Lélia's sexual and spiritual adventures read like a hallucinatory fairy tale. The exotic setting is in harmony with the characters' overwrought emotions, and this is exactly what Sand and Musset wanted for their own passion. What better place for a real-life idyll than Venice?

Sand convinced Casimir that Italy would be good for her rheumatism. She also assured Musset's mother that her son would be looked after with devoted maternal care. What about her own children? Solange, who had been staying with Sand in Paris, was sent back to Nohant, while Maurice remained in boarding school. Sand's new "child" took preference over everyone else.

The couple's flight to Venice has been narrated so often in biographies, novels, plays, and films that Musset and Sand, like Abélard and Héloïse, have become superstars in the history of French love. It is daunting to summarize what others have recounted at length, so let me just stick to the facts and, whenever possible, defer to the lovers' own words.

In her autobiography, Sand recalled how Venice, the city of her dreams, had greatly exceeded her expectations. She and Musset settled into the Hotel Danieli (still a favorite for lovers) on January 1, 1834. However, she had been sick during the Italian part of their long journey and soon succumbed to a violent fever. When she was barely back on her feet, Musset came down with typhoid fever, which brought him within "two fingers of death." Sand anxiously nursed him for seventeen days "with no more than one hour of rest each day."

This was not how Musset had tended Sand during her illness. From sources other than Sand's autobiography, including Musset himself, we know that he had used her sickness as an occasion to explore the city and, in particular, its prostitutes. The Sand-Musset fabled love affair was already showing its cracks. During Musset's illness, he was "in a state of agitation and delirium," according to Sand's February 4 letter to her editor, Buloz. She had already seen instances of his mental instability, most notably when he had experienced a ghoulish nighttime hallucination during their stay at Fontainebleau, and she was now terrified. Even the most devoted nurse could not cope alone with Musset's physical and mental deterioration.

Enter Dr. Pietro Pagello, a twenty-seven-year-old Venetian who comes to Sand's aid in caring for Musset and who manages to replace him as her lover. Musset begins to suspect their involvement and, in his delirium, strikes back. He calls her a strumpet (*une catin*), becomes furiously jealous, and destroys whatever vestiges of love Sand still feels for him, at least for now. Nonetheless, when Musset begins to recover, he and Sand leave the Danieli for a less expensive apartment, where she is able to write. After all, there are debts to be paid, and her writing has become their main source of income. After three months in Venice, Musset is well enough to make his way back to Paris on his own.

Sand stays on with Pagello till the summer. After the storms of winter, life becomes milder, enabling her to finish the first of her *Lettres d'un voyageur* (*Letters from a Voyager*), which helps improve her finances. Musset, repentant, writes on April 4: "I still love you. . . . I know you are with a man you love, and yet I am tranquil." Sand softens, but with no desire to give up Pagello. She writes Musset on June 2: "Oh, why can't I live between the two of you and make you happy without belonging to one or the other." The fantasy of the ménage à trois lives on.

Perhaps that was what she had in mind when she returned to Paris in August, with Pagello in tow. She was happy to retrieve Maurice and bring him to Nohant, where Solange and Casimir were impatiently waiting. Surrounded by family and friends, she went so far as to invite Pagello to visit, but he had the good sense to decline. Then, sensing her dwindling interest, he said good-bye to Paris and went home.

When Sand returned to Paris in October, she was greeted by a chastened Musset, eager to revive their earlier relations. He had written her impassioned letters during their separation and now swore that his only occupation would be to love her, "like Romeo and Juliet, like Héloïse and Abélard." Their joint names would go down in history: "One will never speak of one without the other." Musset's concern to be remembered as a duo with Sand speaks for his grandiosity as well as his renewed devotion to her.

Within a fortnight, he had another fit of jealousy, this one occasioned by the indiscreet revelations of a mutual friend, who convinced Musset that Sand had lied to him. Somehow she had managed to make him believe that the affair with Pagello had not been consummated until after Musset had left Venice. This was not the case. Sand had indeed been sleeping with Pagello while Musset was on his sick bed. Unable to control his rage, Musset bombarded Sand with bitter reproaches.

In her *Intimate Journal* written during the month of November 1834, Sand bares her anguished soul, though it is difficult to know for whom. For herself as a form of therapy? For Musset to bring him back? For God? For posterity? The forty pages that have survived bring us as close as we may ever come to the obsessive thoughts of a sane woman tortured by love. They recall Julie de Lespinasse's feverish letters, without the tragedy of death hovering in the wings.

To Musset Sand cries out: "You are leaving me at the most beautiful moment of my life, on the truest, most passionate, cruelest day of my love. Is it nothing to have tamed the pride of a woman, and to have thrown her at your feet?"[6]

To God she confesses: "Ah! the other night I dreamed he was next to me, that he was kissing me in a swoon of pleasure. What a rude awakening, dear God . . . that dark room where he will no longer place his feet, that bed where he will no longer sleep."

And to herself: "I'm thirty years old, I'm still beautiful, at least I would be in a fortnight, if I could stop crying."

She implores God: "Give me back the fierce vigor I had in Venice. Give me back that raw love of life which took hold of me like an outburst of anger in the midst of the most dreadful despair, let me love again. . . . I want to love, I want to be rejuvenated, I want to live." In true romantic fashion, she equates loving and living. Only by loving will she be able to regain her vital force.

She begs for God's mercy. "Let your mercy begin by granting oblivion and rest to this heart devoured by grief. . . . Ah, give me back my lover, and I shall be devout and my knees will wear themselves out on church paving stones."

Then she asks Musset for his pardon and future friendship. "I shall go, my love, to ask you to shake my hand. . . . I know that when one no longer loves, one no longer loves. But your friendship, I must have it to bear the love in my heart, and to prevent it from killing me."

To God again: "No, Lord God, do not let me become wild and destroy myself . . . suffering from love should ennoble and not degrade." Even at the nadir of despair, she clutches idealistic shards.

The vision of her youthful lover continues to haunt her: "Oh, my blue eyes, you will never look at me again! Beautiful head, I shall not see you again! . . . My little body, supple and warm, you will not stretch out over me. . . . Good-bye my blond hair, good-bye my white shoulders, good-bye to all that I loved, all that once was mine."

Sand is inconsolable. She goes to Musset's home on November 24, without finding him there. The next day he writes to their mutual friend, Sainte-Beuve, that it is impossible for him to maintain any relationship at all with his former mistress.

Sand accepts defeat. "You do not love me any longer, it's easy to see."

She acknowledges: "I behaved worse than you in Venice . . . at present I am very guilty in your eyes. But I am guilty in the past. The present is still beautiful and good. I love you, I would submit to all kinds of torture to be loved by you, and you are leaving me."

She entreats Musset one last time: "Love this poor woman. . . . What are you afraid of? She will not be demanding, that poor soul. The one who loves less is the one who suffers less. Now is the moment to love or never."

Sand's willingness to be the one who loves more and consequently to suffer more had no effect on Musset. The moment passed without reconciliation. Sand shared her sorrows with friends like the writer Sainte-Beuve, the musician Liszt, the painter Delacroix, in the hope that their combined offensive might bring Musset around. All to no avail. In December, she returned to Nohant and put on a mask of happiness for her family. But the agonizing love story was not yet over.

In January 1835, Musset and Sand would become lovers again in Paris, and once again they would begin to torture each other. This time it was Sand who could take it no longer. She would write him after two months: "I loved you like my son, with the love of a mother, I'm still bleeding from it. . . . I forgive you everything, but we must part."

MUSSET WROTE HIS VERSION OF THEIR AFFAIR in a semiautobiographical novel titled *La confession d'un enfant du siècle (The Confession of a Child of the Century).*[7] The idea was already in his head in a letter sent to Venice in April 1835, after his return to Paris. "I've a good mind to write our story: it seems that would cure me and do my heart good. I want to elevate an altar to you . . . but I shall wait for your permission."

Sand consented: "Dear angel, do what you like, novels, sonnets, poems, speak of me according to your desire; I give myself to you, blindfolded." Not for a moment did either of them forget they were writers.

Musset started the novel during the summer of 1835, after he had rushed through several other literary assignments, and it would be published in February 1836. This says something about his prolific ability to create poems, plays, and novels one after the other, as well as the rapidity of publication in France. Like Balzac, Hugo, Sand, and other romantics, Musset had prodigious inventive powers and great productivity, despite his dissolute ways. With literacy rising in France to over 80 percent for men and slightly less for women, there was a growing market of readers clamoring for emotionalistic literature.

When Musset's *Confession* appeared, it was indeed a kind of altar erected to the memory of Sand, though it was not erected exclusively to her. The first part of the novel corresponds to a period in Musset's life before he met Sand. His literary surrogate, the young hero Octave, is caught up in a meaningless bohemian existence. He is "a child of the century," one who has memories of Napoleonic glory that can no longer be realized. His sense of frustration with the political moment links him to Julien Sorel in *The Red and the Black*, but this is all the two heroes have in common since Julien lacks Octave's upper-class birth and Octave lacks Julien's steel will. Octave becomes the victim of a frivolous mistress, who betrays him with his best friend. Henceforth Octave will be ruled by alternating fits of cynicism and jealousy.

In an attempt to cure him of despair, Octave's friend, Desgenais, offers a brutal critique of love. His anti-romantic tract at the beginning of the book reaches back to eighteenth-century libertines (Versac in *The Wayward Head and Heart*, Valmont in *Dangerous Liaisons*) and coincides with the pessimistic worldview of the philosopher Schopenhauer. Desgenais chides Octave for believing in love "such as novelists and poets represent it." To search for perfect love in real life is folly. One must accept love as it is, whether it comes in the form of an unfaithful courtesan or a faithful *bourgeoise*. If you are loved, "what does the rest matter?" For a time, Octave tries to follow this policy, but ultimately it leaves him more disheartened than ever.

It is at this point that the widowed Brigitte Pierson—Sand's lit-erary surrogate—comes into his life. Unsurprisingly, Octave finds her in the country far from the depravities of Paris. Who among the romantics is not one of Rousseau's descendants? Octave is twenty, Madame Pierson is thirty. Sound familiar? We are once again in the domain of the young man in love with an older ma-ternal woman, all the more meaningful because Octave has been motherless since childhood and has just lost his father. Despite her prolonged resistance, Brigitte eventually succumbs to Octave's en-treaties, and they experience a period of sublime happiness.

> Eternal angel of happy nights, who will convey your silence? O kiss! Mysterious draught which lips pour into each other like thirsty wine-cups. Drunkenness of the senses, oh voluptuous-ness! . . . Love, oh, principle of the world! Precious flame which all of nature, like an anxious vestal virgin, incessantly watches over in the temple of God!

Musset offers Sand a love gift in this rapturous hymn and es-pecially in Octave's words that extol the benefits of remembered passion: "He can die without complaining: he has possessed the woman he loved."

Unfortunately, Octave has the same character flaw as Musset: he is prone to jealousy, even when there is no cause. Much of the book describes his jealous bouts based on nothing more than his imagination, which has become permanently darkened by the memory of his earlier false mistress. Musset knew all too well how an overly suspicious nature can undermine love.

As an author wanting to elevate an altar to Sand, he gave her fictive counterpart more moral perfection than Sand actually possessed. And that's just the trouble with Brigitte Pierson: she is too perfect, too idealized. She sacrifices herself over and over again to Octave's frenzied moods and feverish imagination. Musset did not spare himself in the portrait of his alter ego: in Octave we see the workings of a mentally unstable man, riven by jealousy, whose life becomes an ongoing nightmare for himself and for the woman who loves him.

Eventually Brigitte is forced to concede: "You are no longer the man I loved." His constant suspicion, moodiness, and rages have worn her out. Though she has done her best to give him the maternal attentions he needed, she can no longer endure the quarreling and suffering. "Yes, when you make me suffer, I no longer see my lover in you. You are nothing more than a sick child." These might have been Sand's very words to Musset.

SAND'S LOVE LIFE DID NOT END WITH Musset. Thanks to the efforts of the lawyer Michel de Bourges, who succeeded Musset in her bed, she was able to obtain a legal separation from her husband after thirteen years of marriage. Separation of bed and board was the only recourse open to an unhappily married man or woman, since divorce was prohibited. If truth be told, Casimir was no worse than most husbands and had even proved himself remarkably accommodating in accepting his wife's independent lifestyle. Never mind, the court granted Sand the separation she had requested, as well as sole possession of Nohant, with the stipulation that she pay her husband an annual stipend of 3,800 francs. As for the children, she assumed responsibility for their support, while granting their father visiting rights. Had she not been so famous and had the lawyer Michel de Bourges not been in her camp, it is unlikely that the trial would have ended so favorably for Sand. In January 1836, the court's decision included the judges' expression of contempt for a husband who "permits his wife to live alone," implying that a man who abandons his marital authority deserves what he gets.[8]

In 1838, Sand began her world-famous affair with Chopin, which lasted till 1847. In 1850, she entered into an even longer relationship with her son's friend, the engraver Alexandre Manceau, who became her secretary and live-in companion until his death in 1865. From the time she regained sole possession of Nohant, she was constantly surrounded by a bevy of remarkable friends, including Chopin, Delacroix, Liszt, his volatile mistress Marie d'Agoult, the singer Pauline Viardot, and her beloved Flaubert. She died in 1876 at the age of seventy-two. I can think of no other Frenchwoman who was more productive as a writer, nor more fully realized in her personal life. Though her marriage was not a success, she was a mother and grandmother devoted to her offspring—especially during the second half of her life when she was less prone to travel.

Sand acquired countless fans in France and abroad. In England she was admired by many of the Victorians, including William Thackeray, John Stuart Mill, Charlotte Brontë, George Eliot, Matthew Arnold, and Elizabeth Barrett Browning, who paid her two visits in Paris and honored her in a sonnet as a "large-brained woman and a large-hearted man." In Russia, she was read by everyone who could read. Along with Hugo, she was the predominant French influence on an entire generation of Russian writers, including Dostoevsky, who idolized her; Turgenev, who became one of her intimate friends; and Herzen, who cited her in his diary with the prediction that in the future "the wife will be freed from slavery." In the United States, she found allies in the transcendental writer Margaret Fuller, whose life ended dramatically when she drowned with her baby after her return from Europe; Walt Whitman, who published a newspaper article about Sand; and Harriet Beecher Stowe, for whom Sand wrote an admiring essay.

I won't enter into the causes of Sand's decline in popularity during the first half of the twentieth century; they are too numerous and too complex to be considered here. But Sand's fans in France never completely disappeared. Consider the case of Georges Lubin, whose devotion to her lasted the better part of his lifetime. Around the age of forty, he retired from his work as a banker and dedicated himself exclusively to Sand scholarship. His wife was wont to say that they lived together in a ménage à trois with George Sand. Certainly their apartment, filled with various Sand mementoes, attested to her presence. What intrigued me the most when I visited them in the early 1980s was the large file cabinet with a card for every day in Sand's life. If I remember correctly, they were white for Paris, green for Nohant, pink for her time away with a lover, and yellow when unknown. I may be wrong about the colors, but I am certain that Lubin knew more about George Sand's life and work than anyone other than Sand herself. His card catalog was essential for the huge projects he undertook as editor of her two-volume autobiography and her twenty-six-volume correspondence. And all the while, he found time to help others with the new Sand scholarship that was sparked by the centennial of her death in 1976.

Let me close with a memory of Georges Lubin amid a lively group of Sand scholars in a Paris restaurant, probably Le Procope. We knew each other from a series of conferences organized by

Hofstra College in New York and from special sessions on Sand at the Modern Language Association meetings. Sitting next to me was a Japanese professor who had come to know Sand through his admiration for Chopin. He was fascinated by the woman who had taken care of her "little" Chopin like a protective mother and was of the opinion that their relationship had been chaste. Lubin, sitting on the other side of me, gently disagreed. Chopin and Sand had been lovers in every sense of the word, at least in the beginning. Our Japanese colleague became heated, as if it were an affair of honor. Lubin, with old-school courtesy, commended the man for defending Sand's virtue. The Japanese man looked puzzled. Then, with ritual solemnity, he slowly uttered these words in French: "Ah, non. Pas Sand. Chopin. Je défends Chopin." He was defending Chopin, not Sand. Then it was Lubin's turn to become indignant on Sand's behalf, as if her honor had been besmirched. I found myself in the peculiar situation of having to intervene. "Messieurs, les duels sont interdits depuis cent ans. Veuillez terminer vos repas et laissez les morts en paix." (Gentlemen, duels have been forbidden for a hundred years. Be so good as to finish your meal and leave the dead in peace.)

Think of what Sand or Balzac could have done with such a scene!

CHAPTER NINE

Romantic Love Deflated

Madame Bovary

THE MATERIAL OF HER RIDING HABIT CAUGHT ON
HIS VELVET COAT. SHE TIPPED BACK HER HEAD,
HER WHITE THROAT SWELLED WITH A SIGH; AND
WEAKENED, BATHED IN TEARS, HIDING HER FACE, WITH
A LONG TREMOR SHE GAVE HERSELF UP TO HIM.

Gustave Flaubert, *Madame Bovary,* 1857

IN THE 1850S, WHEN FLAUBERT WAS WRITING *Madame Bovary,*
he corresponded regularly with his Parisian mistress, the poet
Louise Colet. From the house that he shared with his mother at
Croisset in Normandy, he expressed the torments of a writer dedicated to the religion of art. Sometimes he barely eked out a line a
day, and often Emma Bovary literally made him sick. Why would
anyone want to write a novel about an overly romantic woman
who marries a feckless country doctor, has two affairs and mounting debts, and ultimately commits suicide? Flaubert had his reasons. As he noted in his letter of April 12, 1854, to Colet: "A terrible

reaction is taking place in the modern conscience against what we call love. . . . Our century looks through a magnifying glass and dissects on its operating table the little flower of Sentiment, which smelled so good in the past!"[1]

Times had changed since romantics exalted all-consuming love. Realists like Flaubert were determined to deflate the romantic ideal, which he attributed to the banality of everyday existence. His commitment to portraying people "objectively," with all their defects and base cravings, contributed substantially to the French de-romanticization of love. It even left him vulnerable to the charge of indecency. A government trial against *Madame Bovary* was instituted on the grounds that it was "an outrage to public and religious morality," but fortunately for Flaubert, who was at risk for imprisonment and a heavy fine, he was acquitted on February 6, 1857. (Just as I was writing this chapter, National Public Radio reminded its listeners that it was the 154th anniversary of Flaubert's acquittal. How about that!) The prosecution had the expected results of making Flaubert better known and increasing book sales. With the notoriety surrounding *Madame Bovary*, the chic French view of love shifted from illusion to disillusion.

Flaubert and his fellow realists—Guy de Maupassant, the Goncourt brothers, Émile Zola—were out to prove that love was nothing more than a trick the mind plays on itself. As Stendhal had observed a generation earlier in *De l'amour* (*On Love*, 1822), when we fall in love, we embellish the beloved person with all the good qualities we want that person to have. Stendhal's word for that process was *cristallisation*, a term he derived from the formation of diamondlike crystals on a tree branch when it is left in a salt mine for two or three months.[2] In *Madame Bovary*, Flaubert set out to show

how *cristallisation* worked within the psyche of a young woman, successively infatuated with two men who were not her husband.

But it would be wrong to think of Flaubert solely as a realist—a term he himself repudiated later in life. Though *Madame Bovary* does indeed puncture and destroy Emma Bovary's romantic illusions, we can never forget Flaubert's assertion that he and Madame Bovary were, at some level, the same person. "Madame Bovary, c'est moi," he declared. How else could he have created that pathetic creature with whom so many readers have empathized and so many women have identified?

Let me confess at the onset, I was one of those teenage girls who identified completely with Emma Bovary. It seemed inconceivable to me that such a beautiful young woman with a fertile imagination should be asked to settle for a mediocre country doctor lacking all distinction. She who had dreamed of refinements above her station as a farmer's daughter was understandably disappointed by her humdrum marriage and driven to look elsewhere for romance. I can't say that I admired her as I did the morally upright characters in British novels, like Charlotte Brontë's Jane Eyre and Jane Austen's Elizabeth Bennet, but I did sympathize with her and bemoan her fate.

Several years later, when I was a graduate student at Harvard, I took a course on Flaubert with the then-famous Professor René Jasinski and read *Madame Bovary* again. This time I was pregnant with my first child and had trouble staying awake in Jasinski's after-lunch class. (I learned later that the medication I was taking had the side effect of making me drowsy.) Nonetheless, I struggled through the course and wrote a paper on Emma Bovary that expressed how much she had descended in my esteem. Emma's romantic reveries were no longer ones I could identify with, and Emma herself just seemed misguided and shallow. Two months after the course had ended, the birth of my daughter compelled me to dislike Emma even more. There I was with a delicious baby girl, and Emma did not have the slightest affection for her own daughter. Bad wife! Bad mother! How could I have loved the book so much when I was fifteen?

Still later, in graduate school at Johns Hopkins, I read *Madame Bovary* for a third time with insights provided by the now-famous Professor René Girard, then my dissertation director and presently a member of the Académie Française. I came to see Emma Bovary in the light of what Girard called "mimetic desire"—that is, she desired what she had learned to desire through a third party. The romantic novels she had read were, as she remembered, "all about love, lovers, sweethearts . . . gentlemen brave as lions, gentle as lambs, virtuous as no one ever was, always well dressed, and weeping like fountains." Words like "passion" and "felicity," "which had appeared so beautiful in books," had given her a false notion of what love could be. Girard's theory of mimetic desire made sense to me because I knew how books, movies, and movie magazines had affected my girlfriends and me in the formation of our romantic desires. (Of course, at Johns Hopkins, you were supposed to avoid movies, unless it was one of Ingmar Bergman's.)

This third reading of *Madame Bovary*, which was not to be my last, opened my mind to the multiple layers of meaning within the book. I began to see how romanticism and realism, illusion and disillusion, comedy and tragedy, sociology and psychology, lyricism and materialism, pathos and irony, all formed a web of interconnected threads fostering different interpretations. As a fifteen-year-old, I had been drawn into Emma's romantic fantasies. As a young wife and mother, I rejected them and adopted a down-to-earth stance toward love and marriage. As a more sophisticated reader, I could appreciate the true greatness of *Madame Bovary* as a consummate work of art. Flaubert had insisted that his prose be as rigorous as poetry: every word must count, every sentence must ring true. The total work must be so rich and tightly constructed that we never doubt its credibility, that we become captivated by its characters and plot and take away feelings and thoughts that linger long after we have read the last page. For our purposes, *Madame Bovary* represents not only a rebirth of the cynical seduction theme that had been present in France for centuries, but also as a touchstone for a new anti-romantic vision of love.

MADAME BOVARY BEGINS AND ENDS NOT WITH the heroine herself but with the story of Charles Bovary, Emma's future husband. This neat framing device situates her within the confines of marriage to a man who is physically unattractive and congenitally unimaginative. As a schoolboy, he wears a bizarre cap, "one of those sorry objects, whose mute ugliness has depths of expression, like the face of an imbecile."[3] Whew! Charles is an ugly duckling who will always remain an ugly duckling. As a newly minted *officier de santé*—a health officer or second-class doctor—he is married off by his parents to a financially comfortable widow twice his age and is destined for a mundane life until he meets Emma. Seeing her for the first time at her family's farm, where Charles has come to set her father's fractured leg, he is struck by "the whiteness of her fingernails" and "her full lips, which she had a habit of biting in her moments of silence." These expressions of refinement and sensuality, clues to her character, draw Charles back to the farm after his first wife's death and inspire him to ask for Emma's hand.

Charles and Emma's two-day country wedding begins with a realistic picture of guests arriving in carriages, one-horse chaises, two-wheeled cars, open gigs, vans, wagons, and carts, followed by a description of farming people in their best attire— women with bonnets, fichus, and gold watch chains; men with frock coats, tailcoats, and long jackets. Then a lyrical portrayal of the procession, "united like a single colorful scarf, undulating over the countryside," zeroes in on the fiddler with his be-ribboned violin leading the married couple, relatives, friends, and children to the town hall. After the ceremony, food was laid out under the cart shed, and the guests ate copiously until night. The pièce de résistance was a wedding cake in the form of a temple with a small Cupid balanced in a chocolate swing. Emma would have preferred a midnight wedding with torches, but such romantic ideas had been dismissed in favor of an old-fashioned celebration suitable for country folk. After the couple had retired for the night, they were not spared some of the usual wedding tricks: a fishmonger squirted water through the key-hole of their bedroom. The next day, Charles looked elated, whereas the bride gave nothing away.

This wedding scene, like a painting by Flaubert's contemporary Courbet, aimed at representing life as one saw it with one's eyes and heard it with one's ears. Of course, Flaubert, like Courbet and any other major artist, shaped external reality according to an inner vision. Forget grottos and mountains where lovers experience romantic transports. Instead, the author gave us an irreverent picture of love and marriage that often bordered on satire.

It is only after Emma settles into her new home that we begin to know her from the inside. We learn that she had attended a convent school, where she had enjoyed the sensual aspects of the church service: "the perfumes of the altar, the coolness of the fonts, and the glow of the candles." She had developed a cult for the beheaded Scottish queen, Mary Stuart, and other famous women like Joan of Arc, Héloïse, and Agnès Sorel, the mistress of Charles VII. Some role models! She read the French poetry of Lamartine and the English novels of Walter Scott, which ill prepared her for her future role as the wife of a modest country doctor. Little wonder that she expected more of life than her husband's coarse manners and tiresome conversation, "flat as a sidewalk." Before long Emma was asking herself: "Oh, dear God! Why did I ever marry?"

Subsequently her romantic imagination became increasingly insistent. Disillusioned by marriage and her domestic surroundings, Emma sought consolation by conjuring up what might have been. She tried to imagine events that could have led to a different husband and a different life. Emma's dissatisfaction with her present situation and her melancholy yearning for unknown romantic fulfillment have come to be called "bovarism."

At this point in the novel, an extraordinary event occurs: Emma and Charles are invited to a ball by a local marquis! The ball at Vaubyessard introduces Emma to the aristocratic luxury she had dreamed of. This is what she wants. Everything in the château where they spend the night seems designed to produce a fairy-tale romance, where superior men and women with porcelain skin and fine clothes move about in an aura of satiated pleasure. Emma takes delight in every elegant detail—the flowers and furniture, food and wines, and especially the cotillion that begins at three in the morning. Though she does not know how to waltz, she finds herself in the arms of a knowledgeable viscount, who whirls her around the ballroom at an ecstatic pace.

The aristocratic ball preceded by the farm wedding and followed later in the book by an agricultural fair offer a panoramic view of nineteenth-century provincial society. The town of Yonville-l'Abbaye, where most of the action takes place, resembles villages Flaubert knew personally in the region around his family home near Rouen. Whereas Emma's roots are among the peasant farmers and *petits bourgeois* who gather together for her wedding and the agricultural fair, her romantic head is filled with images of the local nobility. Love, as she fashions it, must come with the luxuries found in a class above her own. These material cravings are part and parcel of her adulterous liaisons and will trigger her eventual downfall.

As we might expect, adultery is the highway running through this novel. We are never far from it in French literature, be it in the twelfth century or the nineteenth. *Madame Bovary* will become synonymous with the adulteress in France, on a par with *Anna Karenina* a generation later in Russia. But what a poor, sad adulteress Emma becomes in the hands of Flaubert. Look how he mocks her in her first conversation with the notary's clerk, Léon Depuis.

"I think there is nothing as wonderful as a sunset," she said, "especially at the seaside."

"Oh, I love the sea!" said Monsieur Léon.

"And doesn't it seem to you," replied Madame Bovary, "that one's spirit roams more freely over that limitless expanse, and

that contemplating it elevates the soul and gives one glimpses
of the infinite, and the ideal?"

"It is the same with mountainous scenery," Léon said.

Here we see the cherished ideals of the romantics reduced to
banal clichés. Flaubert spares no one, not the would-be lovers, not
the village priest, not the local pharmacist.

The notary's assistant and the doctor's wife are both too shy
and too inexperienced to carry their longings beyond a stage of
platonic attraction, at least in the first part of the novel. Such is
not the case for Rodolphe Boulanger, a practiced seducer, wealthy
and handsome, with an estate on the outskirts of town. Rodolphe
sees immediately that Emma is bored by her husband and that she
yearns for romance. He says to himself: "She's gasping for love
like a carp for water on a kitchen table. With three pretty compliments, that one would adore me, I'm sure of it! It would be lovely!
Charming! . . . Yes, but how to get rid of the woman afterward?"
Those sentences sum up Rodolphe's part of the story: he is successful in seducing her with little more than flowery compliments and
expert wiles. The affair is lovely, charming, and delicious while it
lasts. And he ultimately gets rid of her with the same cynical ease
he had enjoyed when wooing her in the first place.

Emma's part of the story runs deeper. Here at last is the man
she had dreamed of, here at last is the man who will save her from
a life of monotonous despair. What could be more romantic than
the personality he invents expressly for her? He styles himself as
an advocate of passion and an enemy of conventional duty. "Our
duty is to feel what is great, to cherish what is beautiful." He and
she were obviously preordained for each other. "Why did we meet?

What chance decreed it? It must be that, like two rivers flowing across the intervening distance and converging, our particular inclinations impelled us toward each other." If this were a romantic novel, such fatal affinities might seem plausible. Instead, because the reader has been clued in to Rodolphe's intentions, there is no way we can believe he is sincere. The only person duped by his parody of the romantic hero is Emma Bovary.

After she has succumbed to Rodolphe's advances, she says to herself again and again: "I have a lover! A lover!" She recognizes herself among the "lyrical throng of adulterous women" who were the heroines of the books she had read. Those women, once the instigators of Emma's romantic fantasies, now welcome her into their fold with sisterly voices.

Emma's love affair with Rodolphe is played out against the everydayness of provincial life, with its petty triumphs and minor tragedies. The village priest, the secular pharmacist, the greedy merchant enter into Emma's story as necessary foils for her romantic sensibility. One of these secondary characters, the merchant Lheureux, will contribute substantially to her ultimate demise by abetting her appetite for luxury and drawing her into catastrophic debt.

Emma and Rodolphe make the most of their two-year affair. It comes with all the pleasures of the flesh, all the conventional expressions of love, and all the convoluted deceit that adultery requires. Charles, the consecrated cuckold, makes his daily rounds like a horse with blinders. He sees nothing beyond his good fortune in having a beautiful wife and an adorable daughter.

This "idyllic" period comes to an end when Emma, emotionally exhausted by her duplicitous life, persuades Rodolphe to run off with her. Though he pretends to acquiesce to her plan, in the end he reneges and writes her a letter that begins: "Be brave, Emma! Be brave! I don't want to ruin your life." When Emma receives his farewell letter hidden in the bottom of a basket of apricots and then sees Rodolphe's carriage leaving for Rouen without her, she falls into a delirious state that lasts for forty-three days. Ever-faithful Charles abandons his work to be constantly at her bedside, and after several months, she begins to recuperate. Will Emma have learned her lesson? Of course not.

CHARLES TAKES EMMA TO THE OPERA IN Rouen in the belief that a diversion will do her good. Settled into her box, she gives herself over to *Lucie de Lammermoor* sung by the famous tenor Lagardy. Her recollection of the novel by Walter Scott, on which the opera is based, makes it easier for her to follow the libretto, and soon she is bathed once more in the vapors of romantic love. If only she had found a man like Lagardy!

> With him she would have traveled through all the kingdoms of Europe, from capital to capital, sharing his troubles and his triumphs . . . she wanted to run into his arms, take refuge in his strength, cry out to him: "Lift me up, take me away, let us go away! All my passion and all my dreams are yours, yours alone."

Do women think like this anymore in the twenty-first century? Did they ever think like this? We are tempted to attribute Emma's absurd longings to Flaubert's masculinist view of what women want, but is that fair? Haven't we seen from Julie de Lespinasse that some women did indeed derive their entire self-worth from possessing a man's love, and some women probably still do.

What's more, Flaubert could draw upon aspects of his mistress, Louise Colet, a dyed-in-the-wool romantic endowed with the tempestuous fervor of her species. Senior to Flaubert by eleven years, she was clearly the one who loved more in their relationship. Some details in *Madame Bovary* can be traced directly to Colet, such as the cigar case with the motto *Amor nel cor* that she gave Flaubert at the beginning of their liaison and which Emma offers Rodolphe in the novel.

Like her contemporary George Sand, Colet had many lovers, including some of the choice men of her era—the philosopher Victor Cousin, the poet Alfred de Vigny, and even Sand's castoff, Alfred de Musset. And like Sand, she was a prolific writer who worked tirelessly to provide for herself and her daughter, with only a nominal husband and a stingy ex-lover (Victor Cousin) to help with her expenses. Flaubert, reclusively writing away at Croisset, loved Colet in his fashion—that is, he saw her rarely, made love avidly, wrote her regularly, criticized her work extensively, described his own literary process, and ended his relationship with Colet twice over an eight-year period, the second time for good. His remarkable letters to her contain treasured information about Flaubert as author and lover, and a vivid picture of Colet through his eyes.

Louise Colet was not the original source for Emma Bovary. That distinction belonged to a woman named Delphine Delamare, the wife of a country doctor from the Norman town of Ry and the mother of one child, a daughter. She, too, had acquired debts resulting from adulterous affairs and had committed suicide before the age of thirty. Flaubert knew about her only from the local newspapers. He took from Delamare, as he did from Colet and several other women, the raw materials he needed to create his hapless heroine.

IT WAS AT THE OPERA THAT EMMA Bovary was reunited with Léon Dupuis. Working for a notary practice in Rouen, he had gained considerable experience since his mute love for Emma several years earlier and was now in a position to make her his mistress. The scene in which their desires are consummated is one of the stylistic glories of all literature. First, they spend two hours touring the cathedral of Rouen under the guidance of an officious verger. Then, when Léon can stand it no longer, he sends for a cab and sequesters Emma for the longest city ride in Rouen's history. The entire seduction scene is seen from outside the cab with its curtains drawn.

It went down the rue Grand-Pont, crossed the place des Arts, the quai Napoléon, and the Pont Neuf, and stopped short in front of the statue of Pierre Corneille.

"'Keep going!'" said a voice issuing from the interior.

The carriage set off again and, gathering speed on the downward slope from the Carrefour La Fayette, came up to the railway station at a fast gallop.

"No! Straight on!" cried the same voice.

Three pages and five hours later, Emma emerged from the carriage, with her veil lowered over her face. This second affair, with a man less wealthy and less worldly than Rodolphe, may have been something of a comedown for Emma, but at least Léon was sincere in his love for her. They managed to meet every Thursday in Rouen under the pretense that she was taking music lessons.

Emma became bolder. In her hotel room with Léon, "She laughed, wept, sang, danced, sent for sorbets, insisted on smoking cigarettes, seemed to him extravagant, but adorable, splendid." Now it was the woman taking the lead, rather than the man. "He did not know what reaction was driving her to plunge deeper and deeper, with her whole being, into the pursuit of pleasure. She was becoming irritable, greedy, and voluptuous." Over time, Emma and Léon became disenchanted with one another. She saw him as "weak, ordinary, softer than a woman." He became frightened at her excesses and tried to rebel against her dominance. She realized that "she was not happy and never had been."

In addition to the disintegration of her love affair, the overnight trips to Rouen added to Emma's indebtedness to Lheureux. The net of doom began its inexorable descent. However foolish she had been, however much we try to distance ourselves from Emma, it is impossible not to get caught up in her final tragedy. Flaubert himself suffered agonies when he described her suicide by arsenic.

With *Madame Bovary*, French love had traveled a long way from chivalric romance. Instead of the idealized passion shared by a knight and his lady, Flaubert offers a debasing bourgeois melodrama. Instead of the noble renunciation suffered by the Princess de Clèves, we are asked to witness the degradation of a lustful provincial. Instead of the airborne romanticism of Sand and Musset, we feel the sharp edge of Flaubert's cutting knife. Who would ever believe in romantic love again?

The 1870 military victory of Prussia over France did not help the French recover their sense of identity as lovers. Indeed, until the last decade of the century, pessimistic portrayals of love dominated French thought. Flaubert's disciple Guy de Maupassant offered glimpses into bizarre behavior hidden under a veneer of normalcy. In his short stories, which were to acquire a worldwide readership, love is never more than a sensual hunger seeking satisfaction. Men and women of various social strata—gentlemen and ladies, peasants, shopkeepers, government workers—war against each other with an elegance of style that belies their underlying primitive needs. Love affairs prove disastrous, and marriage offers no relief, since husbands turn out to be either naïve cuckolds or brutal tyrants.

Even worse, Émile Zola's novels between the 1860s and 1880s presented characters from the lowest levels of society—miners, factory workers, prostitutes, criminals—resembling animals in their mating habits. What Zola called "naturalism" was a pseudoscientific approach to society, part Darwinian, part Marxist, which saw hereditary degeneration everywhere. Love was subsumed into a kind of fertility cult—after all, the French (like the Germans) were obsessed with their declining birthrate. The best one could do was reproduce as frequently as possible. And yet, romantic love, like bulbs buried underground in the winter, was only waiting for the proper atmosphere to flower again.

Taverne Olympia

Restaurant
OUVERT TOUTE LA NUIT

ORCHESTRE
DE DAMES

MONTAGNES RUSSES

28. Bould des Capucines & 6. Rue Caumartin

CHAPTER TEN

Love in the Gay Nineties

Cyrano de Bergerac

I LOVE YOU, I'M CRAZY, I CAN'T GO ON ANY LONGER,
YOUR NAME RINGS IN MY HEART LIKE A BELL.
Edmond Rostand, *Cyrano de Bergerac*, 1897

T HE GAY NINETIES IS THE TERM WE English speakers use for
what the French call *la belle époque*. In both English and
French, these terms evoke images of the Eiffel Tower, the bicycle craze, the posters of Toulouse-Lautrec, Renoir's paintings
and Rodin's statues, music halls, cabarets, operas and operettas,
boulevard plays, art nouveau, the New Woman, courtesans, actresses, high fashion, high spending, and a host of other upbeat
associations.

It is also possible to think of the gay nineties as a time when
romantic love made a comeback. After Flaubert's depressing realism and Zola's heavy-handed naturalism, after the demoralizing
defeat of the French by the Prussians in 1870, the Third Republic

was ready to prove to the world that it was still the home of fashion, food, art, literature, and love.

To be sure, love could no longer be packaged in its earlier nineteenth-century forms. It had to be remodeled for a new age, one that had learned the lessons of its forebears and would neither wallow in the excesses of romanticism nor explore the moldy corners of the soul unearthed by Flaubert. Among the newly enriched café crowd, love was as effervescent and ephemeral as champagne bubbles. A man might lose a fortune on a celebrated courtesan, but he didn't die for love—unless he was killed in a duel. Even though they were officially prohibited, duels proliferated around affairs of honor, which often meant around a woman. But even these could be lighthearted. Frequently, as soon as blood was shed from even a minor wound, the two men walked off the field arm in arm.

Love took on the theatrical aspect that was characteristic of everything else during the gay nineties. It was staged in ritualized settings, such as drawing rooms, hotel rooms, and the private dining rooms of fashionable restaurants. Those dining rooms were frequented by well-heeled men who wanted to entertain their ladies in private—that is, with the help of a knowledgeable maître d'hôtel and accommodating waiters. You can get an idea of what these private spaces were like from visiting the restaurant Lapérouse on the quai des Grands Augustins, opened in 1766 and still a perennial favorite among the affluent.

Men paraded with their mistresses or wives in horse-drawn carriages up and down the tree-lined Champs-Élysées or in the Bois de Boulogne. The women's elaborate dresses, their plumed hats and boas, were designed to showcase hourglass figures propped up by serious whalebone corsets. The men in frock coats, monocles, and high silk hats proudly displayed their trophy women to the multitudes. As Pierre Darblay baldly stated in his 1889 *Physiologie de l'amour*: "A man gets respect depending on the mistress he has."[1]

Lovers were no longer interested in communing with nature, unless it was at one of the chic coastal resorts like Trouville, Dieppe, or Deauville, where the attractions of the beach included the sight of women and men in full-body bathing suits. Marcel Proust, soon to become the greatest French novelist of the twentieth century, wrote nostalgically of his childhood trips with his mother to the Grand Hôtel at Cabourg (fictionalized under the name of Balbec) and rhapsodized about "the young girls in flower" who sprung up each year on the beach. Even when my husband and I stayed at the Grand Hôtel in the 1980s, it had the formal aura of bygone days, and the beach featured women displaying their charms. My husband, who had never seen a "topless" beach before, expressed keen appreciation for the female descendants of Proust's delectable young women.

Fontainebleau, too, was a choice retreat for the moneyed class. Close enough to Paris for an overnight excursion, it was an ideal site for lovers who—like George Sand and Alfred de Musset in the 1830s—wanted to avoid publicity. Certain hotels became known for their discretion. To this day, high-placed government officials choose Fontainebleau for their trysts.

Still, no place rivaled Paris as the city of love. It had become, once again, a vast stage for all the enterprises that give piquancy to urban life—most notably, commerce, the arts, politics, and romance. The center of the city on both sides of the Seine possessed innumerable restaurants, cafés, hotels, shops, theaters, churches, public buildings, and parks where men and women of every social class could meet and fall in love. A letter in the mail, delivered the same day it was posted, could set up a rendezvous at the magnificent new Garnier Opera House. A few words across the counter with a pretty shop girl might result in a meeting later that night at a Montmartre cabaret. A working-class couple who had already set aside sufficient funds might go hand in hand to look over the restaurant where their wedding supper was to take place. Catholic fiancés on the verge of marriage met with their parish priests for the obligatory lessons on how to live in harmony with religious precepts. (How well I remember visiting the oldest church in Tours with a Catholic boyfriend, Pat McGrady, when we were both members of the Sweet Briar Junior Year in France, and a friendly priest took us for two sweethearts seeking premarital counsel!) Despite the extramarital freedom that many men and women enjoyed, most people did indeed marry. Bourgeois couples, tender and kitschy, looked forward to lifetime unions with the hope of domestic bliss. For, as Roger Shattuck succinctly remarked in his remarkable book *The Banquet Years*: "Love cannot last, but marriage must."[2]

THE SENSE OF PARIS AS THE CITY of love was most explicit at the theater. There the staging of relations between the sexes pretended to mirror contemporary life, especially among the wellborn and the rich. Many of these plays revolved around what my French friend Philippe Martial (formerly the head librarian of the Senate), calls the great obsessive theme of the French: will they sleep together or not? Many others made light of the machinations employed by men and women intent on deceiving their spouses. The hilarious farces of Georges Feydeau were almost always triangular, with wives suspecting their husbands of infidelities and chastened husbands returning to their clever wives. Plots were stuffed with mistaken identities, improbable coincidences, lost fortunes, and happy endings. What saved these plays from soap opera tedium was the witty language and lively acting—qualities that still inspirit Parisian boulevard theater.

Some plays, especially those imported from Scandinavia, were more serious. Ibsen and Strindberg were among the naturalistic playwrights whose works appeared at the avant-garde Théâtre Libre directed by André Antoine. In these plays, Parisians got a whiff of the cold air from the north, with its penetrating chill. Not surprisingly, they were less likely to support Antoine's innovative productions featuring weighty subjects like the emancipation of women or hereditary syphilis, when they could be entertained elsewhere by frothy love affairs.

In December 1897, a new play called *Cyrano de Bergerac* opened at the Théâtre de la Porte Saint-Martin and made its author, Edmond Rostand, famous overnight. In comparison with the pseudorealistic fare to which Parisian theatergoers had become accustomed, Rostand's heroic comedy was an anomaly. Who could have anticipated that this play, based on a grotesquely ugly real-life seventeenth-century character forgotten by history, would inspire the accolades usually reserved for handsome heroes? And who could have foreseen that a tale of neoromantic love would surpass in popularity the multitude of plays devoted to sweetly cynical romance? How and why did this happen?

Between 1890 and 1897, Rostand had already created a book of verse, a farce-comedy, a play of youthful love titled *Les romanesques* (*Romantics*), a play with a medieval love theme titled *La princesse lointaine* (*The Princess of Far Away*), and a play with a New Testament theme titled *La samaritaine* (*The Woman of Samaria*). These last two plays had featured no less a star than Sarah Bernhardt, the most celebrated French actress in history. Still, Rostand at twenty-nine was totally unprepared for the sensational success of *Cyrano de Bergerac*, comparable only to the triumphant opening night of Victor Hugo's *Hernani* in 1830. *Cyrano* catapulted Rostand into instant glory and would eventually become, throughout the world, the most frequently performed French play of all time.

Here was a character who incarnated many of the attributes that the French liked to claim as their own. He was articulate and witty—far too witty for his critics—with a dazzling vocabulary that taxes nonnative and even native French speakers. Arcane words like *sarbacane* (a long wood or metal pipe), *rivesalte* (a sort of muscatel wine), *triolet* (a poem of eight verses with a specific rhyming scheme); references to little-known historical figures like d'Assoucy (a seventeenth-century burlesque poet); fashionable colors like *baise-moi-ma-mignonne* (kiss-me-my-darling) and *Espagnol malade* (sickly Spanish); and a scattering of clever puns continue to surprise the ear and challenge the mind. (I still find it useful to consult the edition of *Cyrano de Bergerac*, with notes at the bottom of each page and a French-English vocabulary at the back, that was given to me by my French teacher when I graduated from high school.[3]) Cyrano is brave, heroic, generous, loyal, and independent, and, as he asserts in the last word of the play, he has *panache*—which literally means a plume on a helmet, but also dash, flair, assertiveness, and so much more that we use it in English just as it is written in French. It is true that his exceptionally long nose deforms his appearance and subjects him to ridicule, but without that nose, there would be no story. Cyrano reminds us that love attacks the heart of even the seriously ugly and asks that we look beyond physical appearance to the soul for a person's true worth.

The real Cyrano de Bergerac was a writer and a military man, who fought at the battle of Arras during the Thirty Years War, as in the play. In 1640, he retired from the military and thrust himself onto the Parisian literary scene, where he soon became known for his independent spirit and flamboyant temperament. His published works included poems, dramas, narratives, and essays. Many of the traits and incidents attributed to Cyrano in the play, such as his skill with the sword and his fantastic reflections on reaching the moon, were based on the real Cyrano and his writings. What is not linked to the historical Cyrano is the love story, invented to serve the interests of the play. For who at the turn of the century could imagine a successfully produced comedy or tragedy without a romantic core?

The novelty of Cyrano's love for Roxane is that he is willing to sacrifice himself for Christian, the good-looking new member of Cyrano's own Cadets, a company of volunteers from the noble families of Gascony. Christian becomes the physical vessel for Cyrano's soul, and Cyrano becomes the animating spirit for Christian's body. Roxane, whom they both adore, loves both of them without knowing that Cyrano is the secret half of her beloved Christian.

Christian and Roxane fall in love with each other on the exclusive basis of their looks. He does not approach her verbally, because, as he admits in his first conversation with Cyrano, he does not know how to speak of love. Since Roxane is a known *précieuse* and would expect witty speech from a suitor, he is sure he would disillusion her. Cyrano proposes himself as an "interpreter." He will invent the language that Christian will learn by heart and recite to Roxane. He will mastermind "a hero of a novel" by combining his eloquence with Christian's physical appeal.

With letters and speeches authored by Cyrano, Christian succeeds in winning Roxane, but the minute he becomes tired of borrowed words and abandons the prepared script, he falls into disgrace.

Consider act 3, scene 5, with Roxane and Christian in the garden.

ROXANE: Let us sit down. Speak. I'm listening.

CHRISTIAN: I love you.

ROXANE: Yes, speak to me of love.

CHRISTIAN: I love you.

ROXANE: That's the theme. Embroider it.

CHRISTIAN: I . . . you . . .

ROXANE: Embroider!

CHRISTIAN: I love you so much!

ROXANE: Undoubtedly, and then?

CHRISTIAN: I would be so happy
If you loved me! Tell me, Roxane, that you love me!

ROXANE: You offer me broth when I was hoping for cream.
Tell me a little how you love me.

CHRISTIAN: But . . . a lot.

ROXANE: Oh! Explore the labyrinth of your feelings.

CHRISTIAN: Your neck!
I would like to kiss it!

ROXANE: Christian!

CHRISTIAN: I love you.

ROXANE: Again!

CHRISTIAN: No! I don't love you!

ROXANE: That's better.

CHRISTIAN: I adore you!

ROXANE: Oh!

CHRISTIAN: Now I'm becoming stupid.

ROXANE: And that displeases me.

Just as it would displease me if you became ugly.

CHRISTIAN: But . . .

ROXANE: Go and collect your lost eloquence.

CHRISTIAN: I . . .

ROXANE: You love me, I know. Adieu.

After this failure, Christian begs Cyrano for help, and together they create the famous balcony scene. Cyrano stands in the shadows and whispers words to Christian, which he repeats to Roxane leaning on the balcony above. When the words become too garbled, Cyrano takes over, and it is his voice she hears without seeing him.

ROXANE: Your words are hesitating. Why?

CYRANO: That's because it's night.

In this shadow, they grope to reach your ear.

ROXANE: Mine don't have the same difficulty.

CYRANO: They find their way with ease. Of course.

Because I receive them in my heart.

And I, I have a large heart, while you have a small ear.

And on and on in rhyming couplets that invigorate the dialogue. At the end Roxane admits: "Yes, I'm trembling, and crying, and I love you, and am yours." Christian, who has stood aside during this heady display of love talk, now comes forward and asks Cyrano to procure for him a kiss. "Since she is so stirred, I must profit from it." Then Christian climbs up the trellis against the wall and embraces Roxane, while Cyrano comforts himself below with this thought: "She kisses the words that I just pronounced." It's almost a sacrilege to paraphrase this delicious scene in English, especially in prose. Unfortunately, there is no rhymed translation I know of that truly captures its nimble word play.

From this high point at the center of the play, the action moves very fast. Roxane and Chistian succeed in being wed that very night, but he is immediately sent off to war along with the other cadets, including Cyrano. At the front, Cyrano risks his life every day by going across enemy lines to post letters to Roxane, which are ostensibly from Christian. These letters are so compelling that Roxane finds her way to the front in an extraordinary pumpkin-like carriage filled with victuals for the soldiers. Cyrano is obliged to tell Christian that he has sent more letters than Christian was aware of—in fact, two a day. When Roxane reveals to Christian that she now loves him more than before based on the power of his letters, and that she no longer loves him for his beauty but for his soul, he is devastated. He confronts Cyrano, saying: "She doesn't love me. . . . It's you whom she loves . . . and you love her too!"

CYRANO: Me?
CHRISTIAN: I know it.
CYRANO: It's true.
CHRISTIAN: You love her like a crazy man.
CYRANO: More.

Christian urges Cyrano to declare his love to Roxane so that she can choose between them, but before Cyrano can fully explain the situation to her, the first enemy shot puts an end to Christian's life. Cyrano barely has time to ease Christian's death with a lie: "It's you she still loves." Henceforth Cyrano's lips will be forever sealed.

Well, not exactly forever. Fifteen years later, Cyrano comes for his weekly visit to Roxane at the convent where she has lived as a widow since Christian's death. In the fifth act, with Cyrano himself on the verge of dying, he gives himself away. Roxane finally discovers his earlier subterfuge.

ROXANE: Those dear crazy words,
It was you all the time!
CYRANO: No!
ROXANE: The voice in the night, it was you!
CYRANO: I swear it was not!
ROXANE: The soul, it was yours.
CYRANO: I never loved you.
ROXANE: You loved me.
CYRANO: It was he, Christian.
ROXANE: You loved me!
CYRANO: No!
ROXANE: Already your protests grow weaker.
CYRANO: No, no, my dear love, I never loved you!

As he is dying from a head wound inflicted by one of his enemies, Cyrano credits Roxane for his unique love experience: "Thanks to you, a dress has passed through my life." And she, her eyes finally opened, realizes: "I loved only one person and have lost him two times."

It may seem from this brief summary that *Cyrano de Bergerac* is too sentimental and melodramatic, and hardly great literature. Granted that it may be all of those things, and yet it continues to enchant spectators worldwide. Anyone who has seen it well staged or in the French film version starring Gérard Depardieu knows how miraculously it works as a theater piece. One laughs, one cries, and, despite two onstage deaths, one comes away uplifted. At heart, we are all romantics. In the best tradition of noble heroes, Cyrano holds onto his love for Roxane without destroying her feelings for Christian. And in the end, the recognition scene satisfies everyone. It doesn't matter that Cyrano never becomes Roxane's lover; what matters is that he has never stopped adoring her and that she, at last, can love him too.

I think of Cyrano, with his panache, viewed from afar, leading a charge of amorists against all the enemies who conspire to destroy romantic love. For the French of the 1890s, these would have included cynics and debunkers, people interested only in fleeting affairs and physical enjoyment, and those willing to compromise love for other goals, such as money, social position, or political glory. And today's enemies? In both France and the United States, the ideal of only one true love is under attack. We live in a disposable society that mandates change and replacement. You don't have the latest apps on your cell phone? Throw it out and get a new one. You are tired of your partner and want someone younger or sexier or more exciting? Throw her out and get a new one. Your husband has put on twenty pounds and lost his job? Throw him out and get a new one. My God! Cyrano is infectious! He's got me saying things I would not normally say for fear of appearing tacky.

A French general once admitted to me that he had trouble holding back the tears when he reread the letters he had sent his wife from Vietnam. He re-experienced exactly the same emotions that had overwhelmed him thirty years earlier in the midst of the French-Vietnamese hostilities. He wanted to destroy the letters so that no one other than his wife would know how deeply he loved her. I suggested he leave them to a historical archive where they could inspire future generations.

If Cyrano can still move our hearts today, a century after he first appeared onstage, perhaps there is still hope for romantic love. Perhaps we will continue to believe that enduring love is worth striving for, even if we fail to achieve it.

CHAPTER ELEVEN

Love Between Men

Verlaine, Rimbaud, Wilde, and Gide

HE SAYS: "I DO NOT LIKE WOMEN. LOVE MUST BE REINVENTED."
Arthur Rimbaud, *A Season in Hell,* **1873**

WITH THE PASSAGE OF TIME, THE TERM "gay nineties" has taken on another meaning. "Gay," as we now use the term, can be applied retrospectively to the late 1890s in connection with the trials of the British playwright Oscar Wilde, which dragged homosexuality into the limelight, not only in England but also in France.

The first trial was instituted by Wilde himself in 1895 against the Marquess of Queensberry, the father of Wilde's young lover, Lord Alfred Douglas. Wilde claimed that Queensberry had libeled him by saying that he was posing as a "sodomite," but then went on to incriminate himself as a practicing homosexual during the course of the trial. Once Queensberry had been acquitted, the law went after Wilde and charged him with committing "acts against nature between men." His friends advised flight to France, but Wilde refused. While he was awaiting trial in the Old Bailey, hundreds of homosexual and bisexual Englishmen fled the country for the Continent, most of them to France.[1]

Since the second trial ended equivocally, with the jury agreeing on only one of the four charges leveled against Wilde, a third trial was ordered. Though he might have jumped bail and fled to France, he stayed put in England. After six days of court deliberations, he was judged guilty on all counts and sentenced to two years of hard labor. Wilde would emerge from the prison experience a broken man. Now a pariah in England, where he had once been the toast of society, he crossed the Channel and settled in France, first in Normandy and then in Paris. He spent his last three years in modest hotels in the rue des Beaux-Arts, openly gay and increasingly destitute. His former lover, Alfred Douglas, known to his friends as Bosie, remained in his life, but so did a string of "rent boys" until Wilde's death in 1900 at the age of forty-six. His remains were moved to the Père-Lachaise Cemetery in 1909 and still attract a throng of visitors.

Wilde's story demonstrates the contrast between the British and the French legal treatment of homosexuality. In England, homosexuality between men was made illegal by the Labouchere Amendment of 1885, whereas France, in 1791, had become the first European country to annul its antisodomy laws. With the Napoleonic Code of 1804 and the Penal Law of 1810, the decriminalization of homosexual acts was written into law. This does not mean that homosexuality was socially accepted in France, or that homosexuals were not persecuted, sometimes under other charges, but between the late nineteenth century and World War II, it was probably safer to be a practicing homo-sexual in France than in England.

The recorded history of homosexuality in France can be traced back to the twelfth century. Remember Conon de Béthune's story about the chevalier who spurns the love of an aging lady and is then accused by that lady of preferring "the hugs and kisses of a beautiful young boy" to those of women. Writing this some time after the marriage of King Philippe Auguste in 1180, Conon would have been sensitive to the condemnation of homosexual acts by the ecumenical church council of 1179, known as Lateran III. One didn't take lightly the punishment of burning or beheading.

Throughout the Middle Ages, gays were persecuted by the church, sometimes in conjunction with other crimes, such as em-bezzlement or misappropriation of funds. A good way to get rid of an enemy or a rival was to accuse him of sodomy. But from the sixteenth century onward, the French generally tolerated same-sex activities by men, especially if the men were aristocrats. After all, some prominent members of the royal family were known to be bisexual or homosexual. For example, it was no secret that Henri II had his male favorites, and that Louis XIV's younger brother, Philippe d'Orléans, was patently gay.

A few French writers presented male friendship, homoerotic or not, as superior to the love of women. In the sixteenth century, Michel de Montaigne's attachment to Étienne de La Boétie, immortalized in Montaigne's essay "On Friendship," became the prototype for what the French call *une amitié amoureuse*—a loving friendship. Montaigne contrasted heterosexual passion, described as "active, sharp and keen" but also as "fickle, fluctuating and variable," to the love between male friends, which he saw as constant, temperate, and smooth.

In the friendship which I am talking about, souls are mingled and confounded in so universal a blending that they efface the seam which joins them together so that it cannot be found. If you press me to say why I loved him, I feel that it cannot be expressed: Because it was him, because it was me.[2]

In the lexicon of love, "Parce que c'était lui, parce que c'était moi" ("Because it was he, because it was me") can stand proudly beside the medieval formula "Ni vous sans moi, ni moi sans vous" ("Neither you without me, neither I without you"). Both expressions emphasize the uniqueness of the individuals and posit the belief that he and she, or he and he, are the *only* persons suitable for one another. Such lovers or friends were, in current lingo, made for each other. In Montaigne's age, the idea of the "one true love" or the "one true friend" still had credence.

Montaigne, who lost La Boétie when the latter was only thirty-seven, continued to extol their loving friendship above all his other attachments, including his marriage, long after La Boétie's death. Given Montaigne's masculinist bias, it didn't occur to him that women could share the same bonds of friendship as male friends.

A century later, the original Cyrano de Bergerac (1619–1655) made no secret of his homosexuality. A much vaunted soldier and minor writer, he was also an atheist and a libertine, which should have gotten him into trouble with the church, but during the relatively permissive reign of Louis XIII—also suspected of homosexuality—he got away with his heretical beliefs and practices. He was even bold enough to write admiringly of an imaginary planet where men openly pair off with men. When read today, his novel,

Histoire comique des états et empires du soleil (*Comical History of the States and Empires of the Sun*), first published in 1662, comes across as science fiction way ahead of its time.

By the early eighteenth century, a community of male homosexuals from all social classes had emerged in Paris.[3] Men with similar tastes knew how to find each other in specific cabarets, bars, and taverns or in outdoor areas like the banks of the Seine, the Tuileries, the gardens of the Palais-Royal or the Luxembourg. They had to avoid the attention of the police, who continued to arrest homosexuals when they were caught cruising or in flagrante delicto, though most got off with light sentences. That was not true of two unfortunate homosexuals, burned alive at the Place de Grève on July 5, 1750. Their executions were recorded in the *Encyclopédie* of 1765, and in an observer's diary, which noted: "The execution was carried out in order to make an example, all the more because it is said that this crime is becoming very common."[4] It seems to have been the last execution for homosexuality in Paris.

Eighteenth-century philosophers, like Voltaire and Diderot (both heterosexuals), were generally on the side of homosexuals as members of a marginalized group harassed by religious authorities. But they also accused the clergy of practicing sodomy among themselves, a practice they attributed to the absence of women in their lives. Was sodomy, they asked, any more unnatural than chastity?

Rousseau, in book 2 of his *Confessions* (1770), recounted a personal incident during his conversion to Catholicism, when he was propositioned by a Moor. Disgusted by the offer, Rousseau turned to one of the priests and was surprised to find tolerance of the practice rather than censure. With a wink to his readers, he concluded that "such things were no doubt general practice in the world."[5]

• • •

THE LATE NINETEENTH-CENTURY FRENCH POETS PAUL VERLAINE
and Arthur Rimbaud became iconic figures in the history of same-
sex love. No educated French person today would be unfamiliar
with their poetry or with their short, passionate affair. By all accounts, Rimbaud had a demonic character hidden under an angelic
face. His precocious poetry had brought him to Paris from the Ar-
dennes in 1870 when he was only sixteen. Disheveled and dissolute,
he proceeded to wreak havoc in the lives of all who tried to protect
him, most notably Verlaine, a married man ten years his senior, a
new father, a respected poet, and a habitual drunk. Rimbaud insisted, as he would write in his prose poem *Une Saison en Enfer* (*A
Season in Hell*), that "love has to be reinvented." With help from
alcohol and hashish, he hoped to arrive at "a disordering of all the
senses" that would lead to some kind of mystical union. Instead,
Verlaine and Rimbaud ended up in mutual violence.

In 1873, when they were traveling together in Belgium, Verlaine was arrested for having shot Rimbaud in the wrist after one
of their violent quarrels. The police report noted that Verlaine carried "marks of active and passive pederasty"—whatever that might
mean. Like Wilde, Verlaine had considerable time in prison to reflect upon his unfortunate love affair.

Later, when he returned to Paris, Verlaine lived on pitifully as a
drunk dependent on the goodwill of his many admirers. He would
continue to write poetry, much of it frankly pornographic, until his
death in 1896. His sometime lover, Rimbaud, wrenching himself
from poetry and from France, went off to establish his legend as an
adventurer in Ethiopa. He would die from bone cancer at the age
of thirty-seven.

But despite the well-known relationship of this *drôle de ménage* (Rimbaud's term meaning "a weird couple"), it was the Englishman Wilde who proved to be more crucial for bringing homosexuals out of the closet in France. His trial and imprisonment inspired sympathetic defenders, as well as outraged detractors, on both sides of the Channel. Wilde's notorious history opened the gates for a steady stream of French books dealing with gay themes—for example, Pierre Louÿs' *Aphrodite* (1896); André Gide's *Les nourritures terrestres* (*The Fruits of the Earth*, 1897), and *L'immoraliste* (*The Immoralist*, 1902); Colette's *Claudine à l'école* (*Claudine at School*, 1900), *Claudine à Paris* (*Claudine in Paris*, 1901), and *Claudine en ménage* (*Claudine Married*, 1902); Natalie Barney's *Quelques Portraits-Sonnets de Femmes* (*Some Portrait-Sonnets of Women*, 1900); Liane de Pougy's *Idylle Saphique* (*Sapphic Idyll*, 1901); and Jean Lorrain's *La Maison Philibert* (*The House of Philibert*, 1904). In 1908, Proust would begin his obsessive portrayal of homosexual characters for his multivolume masterpiece *À la recherche du temps perdu* (*Remembrance of Things Past*), and in 1911, Gide would privately circulate *Corydon*, his treatise on homosexuality.

Allthough most of these works dealt with men, this does not mean that homosexuality among women was unknown. During the incendiary revolutionary period, Marie-Antoinette was accused not only of having male lovers, but also of lesbian activities with her female favorites. She was also accused of incest with her eight-year-old son—a charge so preposterous that even her accusers abandoned it at her trial. Fifty years later, George Sand was mocked as a lesbian because she often wore male trousers, smoked, and was more successful as a writer than all her contemporaries, save Victor Hugo. While she had many male lovers, there is some reason to believe that she was, for a time, sexually intimate with the actress Marie Dorval. Certainly the Sand-Dorval correspondence can be used as evidence of a deep love between them, whether or not it was acted on sexually. Of the Frenchwomen who began to write about female homosexuality around 1900, the one destined to become the most famous was Colette, whom we shall consider in chapter 13 with other lesbian and bisexual women.

IN THE EARLY TWENTIETH CENTURY, TWO GAY writers, André Gide and Marcel Proust, put male homosexuality on the French literary map as never before. No, they were not lovers. They were distinguished authors who knew each other and understood that what they were doing was revolutionary. Gide's books were the most important apologies for love between men since the time of Plato. His influence in addressing this subject openly and in identifying himself as a pederast cannot be overestimated. On the other hand, Proust—who will be discussed separately in the following chapter—never used the first person in writing about homosexuality. Instead, he presented a variety of homosexual characters, both male and female, in *Remembrance of Things Past*. It is no accident that these two men, Gide and Proust, produced their remarkable texts when Wilde's tragic history was still fresh and rankling.

To begin with, consider the direct connections between Gide and Wilde. Gide's first encounters with Wilde took place in fashionable Parisian circles at the end of 1891. Wilde was thirty-seven and enjoying the scandal surrounding his recently published novel, *The Picture of Dorian Gray*. His play, *Lady Windermere's Fan*, was being rehearsed in London and would become the first of several theatrical successes (including my favorite, *The Importance of Being Earnest*).

His Irish genes may have contributed to his deft use of the English language and to his remarkable command of French, which he spoke with a strong accent. Moreover, he was tall, good-looking, rich, witty, deliberately provocative, and entirely immoral. Gide was barely twenty-two and carried with him the austere Protestant baggage of his provincial upbringing in Normandy under the tutelage of a protective mother. He was overwhelmed by Wilde's personality and hedonistic doctrine. Gide wrote to the poet Paul Valéry on December 4: "Wilde is religiously contriving to kill what is left of my soul." And again on December 24: "Please excuse my silence: since Wilde, I hardly exist any more."[6] Gide later denied that he knew of Wilde's sexual orientation at this time, but what can't be denied is the intellectual and aesthetic influence the older writer had upon him. From this point on, Gide began to turn away from the strict Christian morality of his youth and surrendered himself, fitfully, to a sensualist lifestyle.

Gide met Wilde again, with his lover Alfred Douglas, in Florence in 1894, and then again in North Africa in January 1895. The January meeting would prove decisive in Gide's homosexual history, for it was Wilde who took him to a café in Blida, Algeria, and acted as a procurer for a young Arab boy. As recounted in Gide's memoir, *Si le grain ne meurt* (*If It Die*, 1926), Wilde asked: "Dear, do you want the little musician?" and Gide, in a choked voice, answered yes. Gide's experience with the boy called Mohammed left an indelible memory of sheer jubilation, the template for future encounters with boys in the days and years to come.

Wilde is the source for the character named Menalcas, who appears in Gide's *Fruits of the Earth* and again in his breakthrough novel, *The Immoralist*. Menalcas is a subversive mentor teaching freedom, sensuous delight, satisfaction of desire, amoral pleasure. He offers the ethic of the "new man," released from constraining conventions and free to follow his own nature. Rereading *Fruits of the Earth*, I felt echoes of Rimbaud, Nietzsche, Wilde, and Sartre (though the latter was not yet born) in this terribly earnest tract. I put it down with disappointment. But *The Immoralist*, which treats the same theme as a fully developed piece of fiction, held my interest to the end, even though I knew the plot by heart.[7]

Between 1895, when Wilde had procured for Gide his first homosexual encounter in North Africa, and 1897, when Gide published *Fruits of the Earth*, Wilde served out his harrowing prison term. Immediately after his release, he went to France and settled in the town of Berneval-sur-Mer near Dieppe. Gide was one of the rare writers who went to visit him there. He was shocked to find Wilde *affaibli, défait*—weakened and undone—a shadow of the man he had once been. Both of their situations had changed dramatically: Wilde had undergone a religious conversion and Gide had married. Yes, despite Gide's discovery of his homosexual nature, in 1895 he married his slightly older cousin, Madeleine Rondeaux, whom he had loved tenderly for seven years. Theirs was what the French call *un marriage blanc*—an unconsummated marriage. By most standards it was a strange union, filled with unspoken tensions, but it also represented for Gide continuity with his Norman childhood and a deep emotional attachment.

Gide's marriage to Madeleine and his homosexual longings provide the underpinnings for *The Immoralist*. Its narrator, Michel, marries Marceline *"sans amour"* to satisfy his dying father. (In life, it was Gide's mother's death that hastened his marriage.) Michel had grown up in Normandy with a rigorous religious upbringing by his Protestant mother and with an education in ancient languages and archeology from his father. At twenty-five, he had become, like his father, a respected scholar. The newly married couple's honeymoon in Italy and North Africa jolts Michel out of his cerebral existence and propels him into an intoxicating life of the senses.

What precipitates this change is Michel's near encounter with death. Weakened by his trip and the surprisingly cold North African winds, Michel starts coughing blood and is forced to recuperate for the winter in Tunisia, under the loving care of his wife. In the words of the novel: "What matters is that death had brushed me . . . with its wing. What matters is that merely being alive became quite amazing for me."

Michel's recovery coincides with his discovery of the local Arab boys, whose simplicity, physical beauty, and playfulness help bring him back to life. From the start, there are suggestions that he is sexually attracted to them: he is intrigued by their nude feet, their lovely ankles and wrists, their delicate shoulders. He wants to spend all his time with them, first with Bachir, brought to his room by Marceline, then with the group of children he finds outside in the park. Enlivened by these boys, he wills himself to get better. For the first time in his life, he takes an interest in his body. He must eat more, he must breathe the fresh air. He forces himself to forget his fatigue and take walks "in a kind of ecstasy, a silent gaiety, an exaltation of the senses and the flesh."

Moktir, one of Marceline's favorite adolescent boys, is responsible for revealing a hidden side of Michel's personality. Michel observes the boy stealing a pair of Marceline's sewing scissors and says nothing. Instead of moral indignation, he feels only amusement. Henceforth, Moktir becomes Michel's favorite. Michel is well on his way to becoming the immoralist of the book's title.

What does it mean to be an immoralist? Michel comes to believe that his only duty is to regain his health and that health is an affair of the will. Morality is reduced to a simple formula: "I must judge Good everything that was salutory for me; I must forget everything, repulse everything that did not cure me." Such will be Michel's doctrine till the end of his story, abetted by his growing fascination with boys and young men.

Gide might have allowed his surrogate self to come out of the closet entirely, but he did not. After the surprising turn of events in the second half of the novel—which I shall leave for the reader to discover—Michel admits only that he is probably drawn more to boys than to girls. While he has gotten into the habit of sleeping with an Arab girl, she claims that it is her little brother who is the real attraction. Michel concedes that "there may be some truth in what she is saying." In 1902, when *The Immoralist* was first published, that was daring enough. More explicit revelations would come later.

Michel's attraction to boys may have appeared less offensive to French readers because the boys were Arabs. During the colonial period, when both Tunisia and Algeria were under French rule, pederasty with Arab children did not incite the outrage it might have incited had the children been continental French, which says a great deal about French racist attitudes. Even today, the French don't seem to make much of a fuss about male relations with boys when they transpire outside the country. For example, there was no public outcry when President Sarkozy named Frédéric Mitterand, the nephew of former president François Mitterrand, as minister of culture, even though he had written a memoir describing in graphic detail how he had paid for sex with boys in Thailand. Certainly in the United States, no public figure would have published such a memoir, wherever the activity took place. Sexual relations between an adult and an underage male are generally considered not only reprehensible but also criminal. The legal age of sexual consent in the United States is eighteen, as contrasted to sixteen in England, and fifteen in France—statistics that speak for themselves.

The Immoralist maintains a distinction between pleasure and love that is as old as French literature. Pleasure is what Michel experiences with the Arab boys, love what he feels for Marceline. Beneath the figure of Marceline (and the figure of Alissa in his novel *La porte étroite*, translated as *Strait Is the Gate*) is the figure of Madeleine, Gide's saintly wife, whom he identified with his mother. The maternal wife remained in the permanent realm of pure love, whereas boys offered fleeting physical satisfaction.

Gide's memoir, *Et nunc manet in te* (meaning "And now she survives in you"), written after his wife's death in 1938, presents his side of their peculiar marriage, with affirmations of his lifelong love for Madeleine, as well as his admission that his sexual deviations and abandonment of Christianity had caused her great pain. Indeed they had.

When Gide fell in love with Marc Allégret, the son of a pastor in their Norman community, and took off with him for London in June 1918, it was more than Madeleine could bear. She got her revenge by burning all of Gide's letters, over twenty years of correspondence! For a man of letters like Gide, who had entrusted all his thoughts to Madeleine, this was the worst revenge she could have enacted.

In the 1924 version of his treatise, *Corydon*, Gide tried to bring love and pleasure together. Having experienced both, perhaps for the first time, with Marc Allégret, he defended the right of individuals to follow their natural inclinations, whether they conformed to conventional norms or not. Corydon, a character lifted from Virgil's *Eclogues*, is presented in dialogue with a homophobic interlocutor. They argue over the merits of same-sex love, which Corydon vigorously defends as both natural and good. One should note that he is speaking specifically about pederasty. Gide came out as a pederast and emphasized the pedagogical value of the love between a mature man and a younger male. He distinguished himself from other homosexuals, such as "sodomites," who love other mature men, or "inverts" who assume the rule of a woman—groups whom Gide considered inferior to pederasts. It's hard not to read *Corydon* today as dated and self-serving, despite Gide's courage in revealing himself. Years later, in 1946, Gide wrote that he considered *Corydon* the most important and the most useful of his books.[8]

During the first quarter of the twentieth century, when Gide's works were circulating among an intellectual elite, he helped lay the groundwork for the broader acceptance of same-sex love that would ultimately prevail in France by the year 2000. Certainly, during his lifetime, his stance was met with opposition, especially in Catholic circles. One has only to read Gide's correspondence with the poet and playwright Paul Claudel to realize what he was up against. Claudel, defender of the faith, tried unsuccessfully to convince Gide that his soul was in danger even before Gide admitted to him his "abnormality." Claudel attacked this "vice" on the grounds that it was condemned in Scripture (not by Jesus, but by Saint Paul) and that Gide could be seen as proselytizing for homosexuality. Their correspondence, and Gide's private journal, are invaluable documents in understanding how two great French writers of opposing persuasions thought about God, morality, and love. For Claudel, love was resolutely heterosexual and bound up in the sacred bonds of marriage, so much so that his passionate midlife affair, the source for his drama *Partage de Midi* (*Break of Noon*), ended in renunciation. For Gide, love was both homosexual and heterosexual, the latter reserved primarily for his wife. What did he feel for Elizabeth van Rysselberghe, who bore Gide's child in 1923? Yes, outside of marriage, Gide fathered a daughter, Catherine Gide, and he was known to have been an affectionate father and grandfather. The person who must have suffered the most from Gide's unfettered freedom was his wife Madeleine. Yet on the occasion when Claudel, in 1925, asked to see her and discuss the matter of her husband's salvation, she refused and wrote: "Those who love André Gide should pray for him. I do this every day and you do also."[9] Whether or not the prayers on his behalf helped him in the afterlife we shall never know, but the Nobel Prize in Literature, awarded in 1947, is certain testimonial to the esteem he enjoyed during his lifetime.

GIDE WAS NOT ALONE IN CARVING OUT a space for gay writers. His contemporary Marcel Proust, then Jean Cocteau, Henry de Montherlant, and Roger Peyrefitte, added their daring voices to the impressive body of literature by and about homosexuals. After World War II, Jean Genet, a former jailbird, emerged as the most original gay writer in France, especially with his plays that found favor on both sides of the Atlantic. By the time the American black author, James Baldwin, arrived in the late 1940s, Paris had become an international mecca for many foreign writers and artists who would have been uncomfortable exposing their sexual preferences in their home countries. The next two chapters will deal with other French writers, both male and female, who joined Gide in calling attention to same-sex love.

CHAPTER TWELVE

Desire and Despair

Proust's Neurotic Lovers

THERE CAN BE NO PEACE OF MIND IN LOVE, SINCE
WHAT ONE HAS OBTAINED IS NEVER ANYTHING BUT
A NEW STARTING-POINT FOR FURTHER DESIRES.

Marcel Proust, *Within a Budding Grove,* 1919

WE HAVE SEEN UNHAPPY LOVE BEFORE. FRENCH history and literature abound with stories of tormented lovers, the torment often inflicted by outside forces. Tyrannical parents. Malicious rivals. An odious husband. War. Accidents. Letters gone astray. But sometimes unhappiness is the product of one's own imagination. With Proust, we encounter a writer and characters whose romantic sorrows are mainly self-inflicted, and arise from the author's troubled psyche, from what he himself recognized as an incapacity for happiness in matters of the heart. With Proust, we enter into the domain of the neurotic lover.

Proust lays out the origins of his neurotic love at the beginning of the multivolume *Remembrance of Things Past*. There the narrator—called Marcel—traces his own adult angst to the childhood experience of waiting upstairs in his bedroom for his mother's goodnight kiss. Even worse were the evenings when there was company for dinner and Marcel was obliged to kiss his mother downstairs: "That frail and precious kiss which Mamma used normally to bestow on me when I was in bed and just going to sleep had to be transported from the dining-room to my bedroom where I must keep it inviolate all the time that it took me to undress, without letting its sweet charm be broken, without letting its volatile essence diffuse itself and evaporate."[1] In a key episode, when Marcel was sent to bed without any kiss at all, his anguish was intolerable, and he made such a scene that his mother ended up spending the night in his room. But rather than revel in this concession, Marcel saw the event as a defeat: he knew that his parents had been obliged to recognize his difference from other boys and consequently relinquish their ideal picture of him.

That bedtime kiss! The narrator admits that the anxiety surrounding that ritual has never left him. He speaks knowingly of "that anguish which later emigrates into love, and may even become permanently inseparable from it." Born from the filial love of a hypersensitive child, that angst finds its way into all of Proust's love stories.

And yet, Proust so skillfully creates the psychological reality of his characters that we enter into their skins and appropriate their desire and despair. No other writer renders the misery of love so compellingly. Reader, beware. I am a Proustian. If I were cast on a desert island with the choice of only two authors, I would ask for the works of Shakespeare and Proust. If you too are already a Proustian, you know what I'm talking about. To others, I can only say: read Proust and see if he is for you.

Proust is not for everyone. Gide (of all people!) is known to have rejected Proust's manuscript for publication by the prestigious publishing house Nouvelle Revue Française. Subsequently, in 1913, Grasset published the first volume, *Swann's Way*, at the author's expense. The second volume, *Within a Budding Grove*, had to wait until after World War I, but when it appeared in 1919, it won the prestigious Prix Goncourt for literature. Since then, Proust has had countless admirers worldwide, but also his detractors. Many find him long-winded or simply boring. Some are turned off by his endless ruminations, others by the increasing focus on homosexuality in the later volumes. There's even a button asserting MARCEL PROUST IS A YENTA. But for me, Proust has been an ongoing source of beauty and truth (pace Keats), humor, and insight, even as I recognize his twisted view of love. One recent critic has aptly titled his book *Proust, les horreurs de l'amour.*[2] Proustian love always ends badly.

Consider "Swann in Love" ("Un amour de Swann," volume 1, part 2), which constitutes Proust's most compact treatment of love. Charles Swann, a close family friend, frequently visited Marcel's father, mother, grandparents, and aunts, when they spent their Easter and summer holidays in Combray (based on the provincial town of Illiers, now renamed Illiers-Combray). As a child, the narrator was awed by this man of great wealth and impeccable taste, and he became infatuated with Swann's daughter, Gilberte, from the moment he saw her through the fence of their impressive country property.

Swann's love affair with Gilberte's mother, Odette, took place before Marcel's birth, yet the story is told as if Marcel had witnessed it himself. We watch as Swann slowly responds to Odette de Crécy's charms, even though he knows she has a shady past, is not very intelligent or cultivated, and does not correspond to the type of woman he usually desires. She has a "kind of beauty that left him indifferent . . . her profile was too sharp, her skin too delicate, her cheekbones were too prominent, her features too tightly drawn." For a long period he meets her only at night, after he has made love in his carriage to a more fleshy working-class woman. Odette does her best to arouse within Swann both physical desire and tender emotions. After one of his visits, she sends a message informing him that he has left his cigarette case behind, adding: "If only . . . you had also forgotten your heart! I should never have let you have that back."

Swann needs more than Odette's encouragement to fall in love with her. Because she is not naturally his type, he needs aesthetic associations to prompt his desire. One day he is struck by her resemblance to the biblical figure of Zipporah, Jethro's daughter, in a fresco by Botticelli in the Sistine Chapel. That association enhanced her beauty and made her more precious.

The second, even more important, association derives from a sonata played by a pianist at the home of the Verdurins, Odette's habitual dinner hosts. Though the Verdurin milieu is decidedly inferior to the one Swann usually frequents, he manages to enjoy himself, especially during the musical portion of the evening, with Odette at his side. There he discovers the sonata by Vinteuil, with its recurring "little phrase," that becomes "the national anthem of their love." The little phrase awakens in Swann a longing that prompts, and ultimately becomes identical with, his feelings for Odette. In a film, the background music would have to be Camille Saint-Saëns' Sonata no. 1 for piano and violin, opus 75, known to have been Proust's inspiration for the little phrase.

The path to loving is strange indeed. First Swann falls in love with a painting that leads him to prize Odette because of her resemblance to the painting. Then he falls in love with a musical piece that energizes his feelings for her. One last psychological experience is necessary for him to fall fully in love. Because Odette has made herself so available to him, Swann has not prized her sufficiently. Why, he has not even tried to kiss her or sleep with her! But the night that he goes to the Verdurins and finds that she has left without waiting for him, he becomes frantic. He searches for her in numerous after-hours locations, his distress compounded by the fear that she is with someone else. When he finally sees her coming out of a restaurant alone and takes her home, he cannot resist kissing her in the carriage and adjusting the cattleya orchids at her bosom, all of which lead to their first night in bed together. Henceforth, their private expression for making love will be "do a cattleya" (*faire cattleya*). This is the happy time of their love affair. "Ah! in those earliest days of love, how naturally the kisses spring into life! So closely, in their profusion, do they crowd together that lovers would find it as hard to count the kisses exchanged in an hour as to count the flowers in a meadow in May."

This happy period is short-lived. Swann, who begins giving Odette money to help her over difficult periods, slowly realizes that the rumors about her being a "kept woman" are indeed true. Still, this doesn't worry him as much as the jealousy he feels toward her past lovers and those who may still be lurking in the shadows. Jealousy becomes the sine qua non of Proustian love. Without it, Proust's heroes do not know that they are in love. Without the fear of being supplanted by another, they cannot experience love's cataclysmic upheavals. Proust seems to concur with the medieval view—remember Marie de Champagne and Capellanus—that jealousy is intrinsic to romantic love.

The more jealous Swann becomes, the more indifferently Odette behaves toward him. It's the oldest rule of love: the one who loves more suffers more. Swann takes no comfort in being wealthy, fashionable, and connected to the "best people," like the Prince of Wales and the president of the republic—people he never mentions to Odette and her circle, who pretend to find high society boring and secretly envy anyone within it. Swann is so eaten up by his jealousy for Odette that he devotes his whole life to being at her side, or spying on her, or thinking about her. Love becomes a malady, a sickness "so much a part of him, that one could not extract it without destroying him; as surgeons say, his love was no longer operable."

Love-as-sickness is more dangerous than lovesickness. The lovesick person languishes from the absence or indifference of the loved one, but usually gets over it, either by winning the beloved or by moving on to another love. As opposed to lovesickness, love-as-sickness implies that the lover is beyond hope. He or she will always suffer while in love and never reach a "healthy" state of loving, which would demand, minimally, some concern for the other person's well-being. Proust's characters are too immersed in their own internal misery to be able to care for another in any mature fashion.

Swann's experiences are the prototype for other love affairs in the novel, such as the narrator's later jealous torments concerning Albertine and the Baron de Charlus's relations with the young violinist Morel. No other piece of French literature contains such neurotic lovers—not even Alceste in *Le Misanthrope* or Des Grieux in *Manon Lescaut*. In describing his characters, Proust doesn't shy away from expressions like neuropath (*névropathe*), neurasthenic (*neurasthénique*), neurotic (*névrosé*), nervous, abnormal, lunatic, hysterical, and pathological, reminding us that he was writing at a time when Charcot and Freud's vocabulary was making its way into the popular discourse. His own father, Dr. Adrien Proust, was fully aware of the mental component of physical disorders. But Proust had to look no further than his own history of sexual jealousy, beginning with his teenage crushes on fellow students and his early love affair with the composer Reynaldo Hahn, to conjure up the green-eyed monster. Still, however personal or neurotic in origin, Proustian jealousy gives voice to the potential jealousy in everyone who has ever loved.

ANOTHER IMPORTANT ASPECT OF PROUSTIAN LOVE IS its relation to the great theme of time, which girds the entire oeuvre. Swann is aware that what he feels for Odette during the period of his greatest love is not what he will feel in the future. As much as he tries to disentangle himself from the pain of loving Odette, he clings to her because he knows that when he is released from suffering, he will be another person.

When Odette ceased to be for him a creature always absent, regretted, imagined; when the feeling that he had for her was no longer the same mysterious turmoil that was wrought in him by the phrase from the sonata, but affection and gratitude, when normal relations that would put an end to his melancholy madness were established between them—then, no doubt, the actions of Odette's daily life would appear to him as being of little intrinsic interest. . . . But the truth was that in the depths of his morbid condition he feared death itself no more than such a recovery, which would in fact amount to the death of all he now was.

At some level of consciousness, all lovers know this. If you cease to care for the person you love, you will give up a vital piece of your identity. You will become someone else. You will look back on your past love with tenderness or anger or some other combination of feelings, but you will not be able to recapture the same emotions you once felt. You may even begin to miss the pain you were once capable of feeling. Love, Proust tells us, is a mysterious intoxication, all-powerful yet fleeting, and sometimes expended on the wrong person. So Swann tells himself when his love has finally worn itself out: "To think that I've wasted years of my life, that I longed to die, that I've experienced my greatest love, for a woman who didn't appeal to me and who wasn't even my type!" Epiphanies like this remain with Proust's readers long after they have put his books back on the shelf.

WE LEARN FROM *WITHIN A BUDDING GROVE* that Swann married Odette after he had ceased to love her. The reason for his marriage to his former mistress lay in the birth of their daughter, Gilberte. It was Swann's dearest hope that someday he would be able to present both his wife and his daughter to his old friend, the Princess des Laumes (who became in time the Duchesse de Guermantes), but she steadfastly refused to meet them because of Odette's past as a demi-mondaine—a kept woman. Not only did Swann's female friends refuse to receive Odette, but they also declined invitations to his conjugal residence. That meant that he went alone to many social engagements, including dinner with the narrator's family, and that even when some of his male friends dined at his home, they came without their wives. Such were the prejudices within the tight caste system that once prevailed in France.

Ever since Marcel had first seen Swann's daughter, Gilberte, at Combray, he nurtured a secret love for her, but fearing that the daughter of such a sophisticated father would find him crude and ignorant, he was filled with both "desire and despair" at the thought of getting to know her more intimately. Part of Gilberte's attraction was the proximity she enjoyed to her father's friend, the writer Bergotte, whose books Marcel had come to admire above all others. Like Swann, Marcel endowed his love object with the supplemental value acquired from an aesthetic association. Gilberte took on the prestige of Bergotte's literary works, just as Odette had assumed some of the glory of Botticelli's frescoes. Even before he knew Gilberte face-to-face, the young Marcel projected onto her all the desirable qualities he imagined she would have, like a patina acquired through time that makes a bronze statue even more beautiful.

Later, in Paris, Marcel met Gilberte in the gardens of the Champs-Élysées, where children of their class would habitually play. (A delightful one still exists today at the Rond Point des Champs-Élysées.) There they would chat side by side on a bench, or play hide-and-seek with other friends, or even engage in some physical wrestling. One memorable bout released in the teenage Marcel an unexpected pleasure.

We wrestled, locked together. I tried to pull her towards me, and she resisted . . . I held her gripped between my legs like a young tree which I was trying to climb; and, in the middle of my gymnastics, when I was already out of breath with the muscular exercise and the heat of the game, I felt, like a few drops of sweat wrung from me by the effort, my pleasure express itself in a form which I could not even pause for a moment to analyse.

Yes, Marcel has an ejaculation, though the experience is worded so preciously one has to read it twice to make sure.

Such exertions on the part of an asthmatic boy—Marcel is afflicted by the same malady as his creator, Proust—contribute to the severe illness he contracts outdoors on a very cold day. With a fever of 104 and congestion of the lungs, he is bedridden for a long time and forced to undergo a "milk diet" that eventually cures him. But before he is up and about, he receives a letter from Gilberte that adds to his recovery. Not only does she express concern for his well-being, but she invites him to one of her teas, given on Mondays and Wednesdays. Marcel, who has not yet been invited to her home, is ecstatic.

As soon as I had finished reading the letter . . . I loved it so much already that every few minutes I had to re-read it and kiss it.

Love is strewn with these miracles for which people who love can always hope.

For almost a year, Marcel enjoys a loving friendship with Gilberte. They meet regularly at her Paris home in the company of other friends, or at meals with her parents and distinguished guests—for example, Bergotte, who turns out to have a snail-like nose and generally unfavorable appearance, in contrast to his magnificent literary style. They take walks in the Bois de Boulogne and the Jardin des Plantes. Marcel has only one desire, that Gilberte should love him and that his present happiness should continue forever. Of course, in Proust's world, such happiness is always doomed.

Suddenly, out of the blue, Gilberte becomes surly. She betrays signs of impatience when Marcel arrives uninvited at her home. On one occasion, when she had planned to go to a dancing lesson, her mother makes her stay at home to entertain Marcel. Gilberte obviously resents Marcel's presence and they end up quarreling. What might have been a minor tiff gets blown up into an extended separation, largely due to Marcel's overstocked imagination. Days and weeks go by during which he writes impassioned letters that are never sent. If he stops by the Swanns', it is only when he knows Gilberte will not be there. When she finally requests his presence, through her mother, he refuses the invitation out of pride and the expectation that another will be forthcoming. Determined to break off with Gilberte, yet hopeful of reconciliation, Marcel suffers the pangs of puppy love, which are not so different from those of his mentor, Charles Swann. He moves from desire to despair and ultimately to indifference in a trajectory that recapitulates

Swann's love for Odette, with the added painful knowledge that he himself was responsible for the breakup. "It was a slow and painful suicide of that self which loved Gilberte." By dint of telling himself over and over again that he and Gilberte had had a major misunderstanding, he comes to believe that life has irretrievably changed for them, "like certain neurotics, from having at first pretended to be ill, end by becoming chronic invalids." Eventually he arrives at a state of indifference to Gilberte and is ready to fall in love again, this time with even more devastating consequences.

AT THIS POINT OF THE NOVEL, THE reader will have read about 700 pages, with about 2,500 more to follow. I repeat: Proust is not for everyone. You have to be willing to wade through pages of analysis, with the narrator commenting on everyone's experiences, including his own, in an attempt to derive general laws that pertain to the social world. Proust's commentaries, when formulated like a maxim, are always worth reflecting on. For example: "Man is a being who cannot get outside of himself, who knows others only within himself, and, if he says the opposite, lies." This bitter assessment of human relations, which Proust enacts through a cast of memorable characters, will find supporters throughout the twentieth century. Jean-Paul Sartre, for one, will make solipsism a fundamental tenet of his existentialist philosophy. In his play *No Exit*, hell consists of "the others" who refuse to confirm one's picture of oneself. But isn't love supposed to break down the barriers between self and other and, ideally, form a unit capable of mutual empathy and reciprocal pleasure? Proust is willing to concede only "intermittencies of the heart," temporary happiness followed inevitably by suffering and despair.

• • •

PROUST'S HOMOSEXUAL CHARACTERS ARE NO MORE SUCCESSFUL than his heterosexuals in warding off jealousy and suffering. In fact, because they are obliged to hide their sexual orientation from public view, they have the added burden of maintaining love relations under a cloak of secrecy, removed from the eyes of society and the criminal justice system. At the beginning of the volume titled *Cities of the Plain* (*Sodome et Gomorrhe*), Proust offers an impassioned defense of homosexuals, whose liberty lasts "only until the discovery of their crime." Proust is thinking specifically of Oscar Wilde, "the poet one day fêted in every drawing-room and applauded in every theater in London, and the next day driven from every lodging, unable to find a pillow upon which to lay his head."

From this point on, Proust gives vent to his fascination with numerous forms of homosexual behavior. Like Gide, he drew upon his personal experience, but unlike Gide, he never came publicly out of the closet. As he is reputed to have said in a conversation with Gide: "You can tell everything, provided you don't say 'I.'"[3]

Proust made no moral distinction between heterosexual and homosexual love; his frequent application of the word "vice" to homosexual behavior seems to have been a concession to prevailing attitudes.[4] Yet Proust's depiction of gay men is hardly flattering, especially in contrast to Gide's proselytizing efforts. *Cities of the Plain* introduces a wide variety of homosexual types, from men who love only men and women who love only women to bisexual men and women who switch between sexes with the apparent ease of changing clothes. By the end of *Cities of the Plain*, there's scarcely a character who hasn't incurred the suspicion of being gay or bisexual.

Consider Albertine, whom Marcel meets at the fictional beach resort of Balbec, modeled on the Norman coastal town of Cabourg. Appearing first in the volume titled *Within a Budding Grove*, Albertine is part of a group of sportive girls who enchant the nonathletic narrator with their vitality and charm. He falls in love with all of them, before singling out Albertine. By the end of the summer, he and Albertine have become friends and lovers, inaugurating a relationship they will continue sporadically in Paris. Yet by the time they return to Balbec the following season, Marcel begins to have suspicions that Albertine may also engage in lesbian activities. He is alerted to this possibility when he and his older companion, Doctor Cottard, see her dancing with a female friend, Andrée. Cottard points out that the two women's breasts are pressed against each other and adds, in his most professional manner: "It is not sufficiently known that women derive most excitement through their breasts." This peremptory remark further inflames Marcel's suspicions.

On another occasion, Marcel sees Andrée "lay her head lovingly on Albertine's shoulder and kiss her on the neck, half shutting her eyes." Convinced that Albertine and Andrée are lovers, the wounded Marcel concocts an elaborate story destined to hurt Albertine—he tells her that he is really in love with Andrée. At the same time he prods Albertine to reveal her lesbian proclivities. Albertine is completely taken in by Marcel's story; she is indeed hurt, tearful, and prepared to break off with him for good, but she swears that his suspicions about her relations with other women are not grounded in reality. "Andrée and I both loathe that sort of thing. We haven't reached our age without seeing women with cropped hair who behave like men and do the things you mean, and nothing revolts us more." In 1921, when *Cities of the Plain* was published, out-of-the-closet lesbians were famously part of the Parisian avant-garde scene, as we shall see in the following chapter.

When Albertine mentions to Marcel that she is about to leave for Trieste with a certain older woman, whom he knows to have been the lover of Mademoiselle Vinteuil, the composer's daughter (everything is interconnected in Proust's world!), he has a complete meltdown. Alone in his hotel room, separated from his mother's room by a thin wall, he falls into a neurotic fit. From this point on, Marcel is determined to sequester Albertine and keep her from meeting Mademoiselle Vinteuil's friend or any other lesbian. He persuades her to live with him in Paris so as to keep her constantly under his eye and force her to love him, but his neurotic inquisitions and her fluid sexuality result mainly in mutual torment. One twentieth-century literary critic wrote that "the only happy experience of love" in all of Proust occurs when Marcel contemplates Albertine asleep.[5] He exaggerates. One can find several other happy love experiences. Still, his observation *is* emblematic of Proustian love on the whole. The lover, devoured by jealousy, is at rest only when the loved one is asleep, encased in the prison of her motionless body. When awake and capable of following her own desires, she will become, once again, a source of anxiety.

Anxiety is intrinsic to Proustian love because the lover craves total possession of the loved one. The lover wants the impossible—to possess the beloved in every way, including her absent moments and her past. Ironically, her mystery is both an essential ingredient in love and the source of the lover's torture: "one loves only what one doesn't possess." If mystery disappears, the lover falls out of love. The paradox of Proustian love, so unsatisfying as a general model, can still be helpful to readers who do not share his particular incapacity for happiness. Like the seventeenth-century "Map of the Land of Tenderness," it indicates potential dangers that loom on the highway of love. Can one avoid falling into the bottomless pit of jealousy? Can one keep indifference at bay after a period of romantic infatuation? It raises the question of how to transform the temporary stage of "falling in love" into the more permanent stage of "standing in love." Proust's lovers never make that transition.

I CANNOT END WITHOUT SAYING A FEW words about the Baron de Charlus, probably the best-known homosexual character in all of French literature. Charlus comes from a mighty family, is the brother of the Duc de Guermantes and the Prince de Guermantes, and wears his nobility with the scornful pride of his class. He enjoys a close friendship with Swann—the only Jewish member of the exclusive Jockey Club—until the time of the heated Dreyfus Affair, when all of France was divided over whether the French Jewish officer was or was not guilty of treason. Charlus barely speaks to anyone whom he considers beneath him, which is most everyone. And yet, because of his closet homosexuality, he often pursues young men from the working class and puts himself in humiliating situations. Such is his love for the violinist Morel, whose father had been only a servant. Charlus becomes Morel's patron and lover, and Morel rewards him with contempt and indifference, without refusing his social connections and extravagant gifts. In one hilarious incident, Charlus goes so far as to invent an imaginary insult so he can fight a duel on Morel's behalf—a duel that never takes place because Morel fears it will tarnish his own reputation.

The character of Charlus was based largely on Proust's friend, the poet, critic, and man-about-town Comte Robert de Montesquiou. Two famous portraits, one by Whistler at the Frick in New York, the other by Giovanni Boldini at the Musée d'Orsay in Paris, capture the fastidious elegance of this homosexual dandy, who was known to have had a sense of grandeur and mad outbursts similar to those in the novel. There was even a real duel with another poet over a perceived slight to Montesquiou's manhood. Montesquiou patronized a gifted young pianist named Léon Delafosse, the model for Morel, without incurring the humiliations that Morel heaped upon Charlus. From his large social circle, Proust was able to extract the raw material for his characters, though for the emotion of love, he had only to look inward to remembrances of his enduring attachment to his mother and grandmother, his high school crush on Léon Daudet, his long-term affair with Reynaldo Hahn, his passion for Alfred Agostinelli (the chauffeur and pilot who provided many elements for the character of Albertine), and the numerous young men with whom he had fleeting encounters in his later years.

With the publication of *Cities of the Plain*, Proust left himself open to attacks for his obsessive portrayals of homosexuals. Gide criticized him for having made "inverts" so unattractive, hardly the model that Gide presented to his readers. ("Invert" was a common term for homosexual at that time.) Colette, on the other hand, wrote Proust a letter of praise in July 1921: "Nobody in the world has written pages like those on the Invert, no one."

By grappling with his personal demons on the written page, Proust was able to dramatize those impediments to love that were his own: jealousy, hypersensitivity, and fear of loss, along with bouts of snobbery, cruelty, and indifference. His fictive lovers bear many of these same unfortunate traits. Yet, as readers, we are able to sympathize with them and, through them, discover previously hidden truths about ourselves. How Proust "took his private, thoroughly idiosyncratic world and made us feel at home in it" still astonishes his devotees.[6]

As an adult lover, Proust remained at heart the little boy of thirteen who had written in a friend's album that his idea of unhappiness was to be separated from his mother. Around the age of twenty-one, he wrote in another album that his principal character trait was "the need to be loved" and that his preferred occupation was "to love." He added that his greatest misfortune would have been "not to have known my mother or my grandmother." Not everyone is destined to transform the love of one's mother into the love of a heterosexual partner. And not everyone is destined to produce a masterpiece.

CHAPTER THIRTEEN

Lesbian Love

Colette, Gertrude Stein, and Violette Leduc

THANKS TO MY CONVENIENT SHORT HAIR . . . MEN
AND WOMEN FIND ME EQUALLY DISTURBING.
Colette, *Claudine Married*, 1902

B ETWEEN 1900 AND WORLD WAR II, LESBIANS came out in Paris
as never before. With their cropped hair and boyish jackets,
they were immediately recognizable to each other, as well as to
tourists, in the bars, bistros, and cabarets where gay women were
known to congregate. Newspapers given to gossip made no secret
of the fact that Madame X was living with her latest *protégée* or
that two women riders in the Bois de Boulogne went home to
the same bed. Despite ongoing religious and societal disapproval,
lesbian and bisexual women became increasingly visible before
World War I, and their androgynous figures eventually fed into
the *garçonne* or flapper style of the 1920s. In avant-garde circles, it

was even fashionable to be gay, just as it would be during the last quarter of the twentieth century in certain American universities.

Who were these women flouting age-old conventions and loving other women, instead of men? Some were originally provincials, like the courtesan known as Liane de Pougy and the young writer Colette, open to sexual opportunities in Paris that were not available in *la France profonde*. Among the provincials coming to Paris, many were working-class women—domestic servants, factory workers, models, and prostitutes—thrown together for mutual support as they earned their keep far from their families and childhood communities. Some were foreigners, like the Americans Gertrude Stein, Alice B. Toklas, Natalie Barney, and Romaine Brooks, who came to taste the aesthetic and erotic pleasures of the vaunted French capital and never went home. A good many were Parisian-born, accustomed to big-city freedom and willing to embrace whatever was new in fashion, including Sapphic clothes and modes of loving.

"Sapphic," referring to the ancient Greek lesbian poet Sappho, took on a positive meaning when used by lesbians, as opposed to the negative meaning that most men had given it. Throughout the nineteenth century, male critics had accused women of being Sapphic if they wore trousers, smoked cigarettes, wrote fiction, or departed in any other way from socially accepted norms. At the height of her renown, Liane de Pougy was one of the first women to claim the word publicly in her 1901 novel *Idylle Saphique*, based on her exalted love affair with Natalie Clifford Barney during the summer of 1899.

Barney was the acknowledged queen of the "Amazons"—a word that refers, in French, both to a riding habit and to a lesbian.

Outrageously wealthy and equally headstrong, Barney became famous for the literary salons and amateur theatricals that drew to her home on the rue Jacob a clique of French and American writers for over sixty years. It was at one of Barney's events that Colette made her theatrical debut as a shepherd in love with a nymph. At a subsequent soirée she also played the part of the legendary shepherd, Daphnis, in a play written by Pierre Louÿs. Mythological characters were popular in homosexual circles as a form of homage to the ancient Greek world that had produced Sappho, as well as such eminent apologists for homosexuality as Socrates and Plato. Louÿs, while not a homosexual himself, was the friend of André Gide and other gays, and much appreciated for his scandalous *Chansons de Bilitis (Songs of Bilitis)*, which he claimed to have translated from one of Sappho's female contemporaries. The name "Bilitis" quickly circulated as another term for lesbian and was adopted in the United States by an early lesbian rights group called the Daughters of Bilitis.

Barney did nothing to hide her love of women, which enraged her American father before he conveniently died at the age of fifty-two and left her $2.5 million! With that kind of money, Barney could well afford to spend the rest of her life writing poetry and memoirs, traveling, and entertaining her many gay friends. She counted among her female lovers the writers Colette, Renée Vivien, and Lucie Delarue-Mardrus, as well as her longtime partner, the stunning painter Romaine Brooks. Under her aegis, an elite lesbian clan thrived in Paris, the only city—according to Barney—"where you can live and express yourself as you please."[1]

But Sapphic love, so public in Paris, had to be hidden in the provinces, where whispers and rumors could result in social ostracism and even loss of employment. This was the world Colette explored in her first novel, *Claudine at School*, set in her native Burgundy. Love, the major theme of all Colette's books, sprang from pantheistic Burgundian roots and from the shining presence of her mother, Sido.

GABRIELLE SIDONIE COLETTE WAS BORN IN 1873 in Basse-Bourgogne. She was the much loved fourth child of a twice-married mother. Brought up by a doting mother, surrounded by the bounties of Burgundy, Colette carried with her throughout life the primal memories of a lost paradise, not unlike Proust's Combray. Still, the attributes of her lost paradise did not resemble his. Proust, a member of the Parisian *haute bourgeoisie* that mingled with the aristocracy, never had to work, whereas Colette's family were petit bourgeois country folk, for whom work was a necessity, as it would be for the adult Colette. But as a child, Colette considered herself a "queen of the earth," happy in her skin and enraptured by the verdant woods and vines of her native region.

When Colette was sixteen, her parents went bankrupt and were forced to sell their home and all their belongings. Colette moved with her family to a smaller home in a neighboring town. What was she to do? For a young woman without a dowry, the best scenario was to find a husband who would take her as is. "As is" did not mean second best, for Gabri (as she was called by her family) was a very attractive young thing—slim, pretty, with a foxlike face. Her long, thick, golden brown hair tied into braids hung down below her knees. In her later writing, Colette would present her adolescent self as a mixture of brusque self-confidence, sexual curiosity, and romantic longings.

Love came her way when she was sixteen in the form of Willy Gauthiers-Villars, a man fourteen years her senior. Willy was the errant offspring of a good Catholic family, with roots in publishing. He himself had literary pretentions, and by the time he met Colette, he had published several articles, though they—and everything else he subsequently published under his name—were the creation of others. Willy was a gifted fraud. He ran a factory of ghost writers, known in French as *nègres*. To this day, the French use that unfortunate word, which can only be translated as "niggers." Some of the best-known articles published under Willy's name were on music and appeared in a series called *Lettres de l'ouvreuse* (Letters of the Usherette), which Gabrielle had read before Willy entered her life in person.

A minor Parisian celebrity and rakish ladies' man, Willy was enchanted by the budding country girl, so ready for pleasures of the flesh. He had lost his first wife, the mother of his infant son, and was ready to try marriage again, though it seems that Colette would have given herself to him without marriage. (This is at least the version she presents of herself in *Claudine in Paris*.) Married in May 1893, they honeymooned in the rugged Jura region and then settled in Paris in his bachelor apartment, which Colette found small and depressing. Willy introduced her to his lively Parisian circle, replete with famous writers and musicians like Anatole France, Marcel Schwob, Catulle Mendès, Debussy, Fauré, and Vincent d'Indy, as well as many of the ghost writers in his stable. She even met Proust during a dinner hosted by the formidable Mme Armand de Caillavet (one of the models for Proust's Madame Verdurin). But Colette did not feel comfortable in salon society: she missed the nurturing atmosphere of her Burgundian homeland and the mother earth figure incarnated in Sido.

In the winter of 1894, Colette discovered that her husband was having an affair. This would be the first of his numerous adulteries during their thirteen-year marriage. Still in love with her husband, Colette was devastated, and within the year she fell into a serious illness that kept her in bed for two months. Only the ministrations of her mother, in constant attendance, brought her back to life. As sick as she was, and throughout the years to come, Colette managed to keep her deep unhappiness hidden from her mother, Sido, who may have had her suspicions but never knew the particulars of Willy's betrayals.

Sometime after her cure, Willy suggested that Colette write down her schoolgirl recollections. For several months, ending in January 1896, she wrote the pages that would become famous as *Claudine at School*. Oddly enough, Willy did not appreciate their value when he first read them. It wasn't until 1898, while tidying up his desk, that he found the manuscript stashed away in a drawer and, upon rereading it, recognized its worth. He prodded Colette to "add a little spice" to the affectionate relations between Claudine and her schoolgirl friends, and then lost no time in finding a publisher.[2] *Claudine at School*, published under the name of Willy with no credit to his wife, became a phenomenal hit, with more editions during the first half of the twentieth century than any other French book. At the time of their divorce, Colette signed the contracts that sold the novel outright under Willy's sole authorship. Later she would write: "I shall never forgive myself for having done so."[3]

What is so special about the Claudine stories that have made them popular to this day? *Claudine at School* is written as the diary of a fifteen-year-old Burgundian girl. It exudes the vitality of a country adolescent, cheeky and indomitable in her relations with her schoolmates, teachers, and even the local inspectors. She brings into the schoolroom the feel of the Burgundian countryside with its pungent woods, meadows, farms, vineyards, and roaming animals. Imbued with a rustic strength, Claudine is sure of herself and dominates everyone around her, including her indulgent father. (There is no mother in this novel.)

On her fifteenth birthday, Claudine is obliged to drop the hem of her skirts to her ankles. It's time for her to be socialized into the manners of a young lady intended for marriage. Claudine finds her own way into adulthood, spurred on by her infatuation with the newly arrived assistant schoolteacher, Mlle Aimée, who is described as small, pretty, and talkative and possessing "one of those complexions that look so delicate but are so reliable that the cold doesn't even turn them blue!"[4]

Claudine, a clever little devil, succeeds in persuading her father that she needs English lessons in her home, to be given by Mlle Aimée for fifteen francs a month. Since the little schoolteacher earns only sixty-five francs a month, how can she refuse?

The English lessons quickly degenerate into French conversations, designed by Claudine to establish a more personal rapport. She inquires about her instructor's life under the direction of the senior teacher, Mlle Sergent. Did they sleep in the same room? They did, to Claudine's jealous dismay. Already by her second English lesson, Claudine can't control her overflowing heart.

My English mistress seemed adorable to me that night under the library lamp. Her cat's eyes shone pure gold, at once malicious and caressing . . . she seemed so utterly at ease in this warm, softly lit room that I already felt ready to love her so much, so very much, with all my irrational heart. Yes, I've known perfectly well, for a long time, that I have an irrational heart. But knowing it doesn't stop me in the least.

At school, Claudine's "irrational" love for Mlle Aimée is threatened by similar feelings coming from Mlle Sergent, as well as the attentions of two male teachers from the boys' school. Mlle Aimée is receptive to her many suitors, but in Claudine's home, her pupil takes full advantage of the exclusive situation.

How nice it was there with her in the warm library! I pulled my chair right up against hers and laid my head on her shoulder. She put her arm round me and I squeezed her supple waist.

"Darling little Mademoiselle, it's such ages since I've seen you!"

"But it's only three days . . ."

" . . . Don't talk, and kiss me!"

. . .

She kissed me and I purred. Then, suddenly, I hugged her so violently, that she gave a little shriek.

I wished my English grammar to the devil! I much preferred to lay my head on her breast while she stroked my hair or my neck and I could hear her heart beating breathless under my ear. How I loved being with her!

This happy state of affairs is short-lived, since Mlle Sergent has more to offer Mlle Aimée than Claudine. The senior teacher, "a Fury, with snakes in her red hair," gradually takes over and totally subjugates Mlle Aimée, to the amusement of all the observant schoolgirls except Claudine. Mlle Sergent and Mlle Aimée become a model lesbian couple, with the senior member assuming the traditional male role of mentoring the younger, more feminine, partner.

Claudine does not let the setback with Mlle Aimée discourage her. Aimée's younger sister, Luce, wants to take her sister's place in Claudine's heart, and though Claudine rebuffs her with gruff mockery, she gets some peevish satisfaction out of Luce's servile devotion. She also knows how to fend off the men who come on to her, including the school doctor. Claudine has a creaturely confidence in herself that becomes the hallmark of Colette's female characters. Independent at all costs, they refuse to be cowed and often act with the prerogatives of men, including their sexual freedom.

No piece of literature written by an English or American woman at the turn of the twentieth century dared to portray love between women so openly. The Anglo-Saxon world would have to wait for Radclyffe Hall's 1928 novel, *The Well of Loneliness*, which attracted publicity from the legal challenges it encountered in England and the United States, but never acquired the broad success of Colette's works. Once again, the French set in motion a wave of sexual revolution that would crest more than once during the rest of the century.

IN THE SUBSEQUENT CLAUDINE NOVELS, *CLAUDINE IN Paris* and *Claudine Married*, the young heroine discovers the joys and deceptions of marriage and finds herself pushed into a lesbian relationship by none other than her husband. The circumstances of Claudine's marriage are not unlike those of Colette in real life: she marries an older, previously married man, who has a son and who introduces her to sophisticated Parisian society. True, Claudine's marriage is more attractive than Colette's—after all, we are in a novel, where it is possible to improve upon one's material situation and endow one's partner with more appeal. Initially, Claudine is enchanted with her husband, Renaud, despite their twenty-year difference in age, and she becomes captive to his voluptuous sexuality, "made up of desire, perversity, lively curiosity and deliberate licentiousness."[5] What do all these words mean? We shall find out soon enough.

Renaud wants Claudine to choose her day in Paris, which means the day she will be at home to receive visitors. Claudine refuses: such social niceties are beyond her. She sees no need to imitate Renaud in his worldly ways. One afternoon, however, when an exotic couple visit Renaud on "his day," Claudine comes under the spell of the beautiful Rézi, a Viennese-born blonde married to a rich but odious Englishman. Claudine and Rézi promise to meet at Rézi's home on the avenue Kléber at five o'clock. This is the consecrated time that French lovers meet for sexual encounters. The set phrase *un cinq à sept*—"a five to seven"—has come to signify a love tryst.

At first Claudine is satisfied with gazing at Rézi and inhaling her perfumed presence. The sensual creature we have come to know in the two earlier novels delights in observing the minute features of another lovely woman—her hair, her skin, her eyes, her eyelashes and delicate fingers. It may very well be, as one American feminist critic has claimed, the first time since Sappho that a woman author describes the pleasure she derives from gazing at another woman, and makes no excuses for it.[6]

Claudine's own appearance is of no small concern to her and

her new friend, who gives her advice on clothes, hair style, and the art of deceiving one's husband. Claudine has already cut off her long braids (as did Colette, to the great chagrin of her mother) and looks more like the "new woman" of her generation.

> Because of my shorn mane and my coldness towards them, men say to themselves: "She only goes in for women." . . . If I don't like men I *must* be pursing women; such is the simplicity of the masculine mind.

Claudine (like Colette) is attracted to both men and women. After her conjugal initiation into heterosexual love, the mysteries of lesbian love are revealed to her by Rézi.

> . . . five oclock visit to Rézi or from Rézi; she is becoming more and more attached to me without trying to hide it. And I am becoming attached to her, God knows, but I conceal it. . . .

Claudine hides her growing infatuation as best she can, limiting herself to combing Rézi's hair and sensing the presence of Rézi's body through her clothes, sometimes daring to press up against her, accidentally. Soon she, too, longs for more intimate pleasures. Her husband Renaud encourages the relationship because he considers Rézi a suitable mentor for his provincial wife. But there is also a definite voyeuristic component in his encouragement, something that Claudine recognizes as perverse. Like many men, he is intrigued by lesbians and says as much: "You women can do anything. It's charming, and it's of no consequence whatever."

Note the typical downgrading of women's sexuality, as if love between women were not as serious as heterosexual love, or to be compared with male homosexuality, which Renaud condemns. This is a position one can trace back to the Hebrew Bible's condemnation of sex between men and its silence on sex between women. Renaud takes an especially dim view of male homosexuals because he has an outrageously gay son, Marcel, who plays a minor but piquant role in Claudine's life. This two-faced treatment of female and male homosexuality was characteristic of the French at the turn of the century. Lesbians were simply not vilified as much as gay men, especially lesbians from the upper classes. In fact, postcards showing two or three comely women caressing each other in various stages of undress were considered a turn-on for men.

Claudine suspects that if she were to take a male lover, Renaud would not be so indulgent. "For Renaud, adultery is a question of sex," meaning male penetration. Eventually it's Renaud who provides Claudine and Rézi with a bachelor apartment, where they won't be disturbed by either of their husbands. He himself holds on to the key so they have to depend upon him to open the door. Talk about perversity!

I am tempted to continue this description of Claudine's love affair with Rézi, but then I would deny you the pleasure of reading the story and experiencing its surprising ending. Suffice it to say that it offers delicious pages describing female delight, without ever becoming vulgar or pornographic.

BIOGRAPHERS SEEM TO AGREE THAT THE MODEL for Rézi was based on a real incident in Colette's life, on her affair with an American woman named Georgie Raoul-Duval. For a time during the summer of 1901, both Colette and Willy were sleeping with Georgie.

The threesome ended very badly, with recriminations on everyone's part. Then the situation was exacerbated when Georgie got wind that her former lovers were writing about her. Georgie bought up the entire first printing of *Claudine amoureuse* (*Claudine in Love*) and had it pulped, but Colette and Willy managed to resell the novel and publish it under a new title, *Claudine en ménage* (*Claudine Married*). Within a few months it had sold some seventy thousand copies.

Willy, always the promoter, knew how to eke out more profit from the Claudine series. He turned *Claudine at School* and *Claudine Married* into two plays, each with highly successful runs in Paris. He marketed "Claudine" products, such as stiff schoolgirl collars, hats, lotions, perfumes, and postcards showing pubescent Claudines in schoolgirl attire. Colette and Willy, now both Parisian celebrities, continued to live together, but their marriage was soured by Willy's incessant womanizing. Colette still wanted to have a serious love relationship, and she was to find it with a woman. Her long-term union with Missy, the Marquise de Belboeuf, lasted from 1906 to 1911, the period that coincided with Willy and Colette's lengthy divorce proceedings.

Missy was born into nobility as the daughter of Auguste de Morny, a Parisian dandy and diplomat, and the Russian princess Sophie Troubetzkoy. After her father's death and her mother's remarriage to a Spanish duke, Missy and her siblings were raised in Madrid. In 1881, Missy married the Marquis de Belboeuf. From this mixture of nationalities at the highest level, she was to emerge as one of the most individualistic women of her day. Even during her marriage, Missy refused to hide her true sexual orientation, which her husband was willing to accept, for a time. They divorced in

1903. From this point on, Missy wore her hair short and dressed as a man. Other lesbians cut their hair, but none were so openly virile as Missy.

Both Colette and Missy had had lesbian affairs before they met, but Colette was to be the great love of Missy's life, and Missy was to be the stable, loving, maternal figure Colette had longed for. She moved in with Missy in November 1906, while maintaining cordial relations with Willy, who was now living with a certain Meg Villars. The press took note. The November 26, 1906, issue of *Le Cri de Paris* published a gossip article on the foursome, Colette–Missy and Willy–Meg, to which Colette wrote an indignant response: "Do not unite in the mind of your numerous readers two couples, who have arranged their lives in the most normal manner that I know of—that is, according to their own pleasure."[7]

The one person outside the foursome who was pleased with Colette's new partner was her mother, Sido. Remarkably, she wrote to her daughter: "I am happy, my love, that you have, close to you, a female friend who cares for you so tenderly. You're so used to being spoiled that I wonder what would become of you if it ceased."[8]

Colette was beginning to perform, not only in amateur theatricals but also in professional shows, much to the dismay of Willy's family, who, like most respectable bourgeois, considered actresses only one step above prostitutes. She and Missy took pantomime lessons with the famous teacher Georges Wague, and decided to put on a show created by Missy. *Dream of Egypt* (*Rêve d'Egypte*) presented Missy in the part of a male scholar who resurrects an Egyptian mummy, played by Colette. Even before their sensational onstage kiss, the couple were bombarded by negative publicity.

Whoever heard of a female member of the aristocracy, dressed as a man, appearing onstage at the Moulin Rouge! At the premiere, the opposition led by Missy's ex-husband was so vocal and violent that their teacher, Wague, was obliged to replace Missy in subsequent performances. But Colette, with her feline Egyptian movements, was so successful that it launched her as a mime and public performer. For the next four years, she would go from success to success, traveling throughout France, Belgium, Italy, and Switzerland in various spectacles, including stage adaptations from the Claudine series and a play called *La Chair* (*The Flesh*), in which she caused a sensation by baring one of her breasts. It is to this period that we owe the many tender letters she wrote to Missy, letters that attest to their mutual devotion and to Colette's dependence on Missy for emotional and financial support.[9]

Bordeaux, late September 1908: "I love you. I miss you. I miss you more than anything. Be good, take care of yourself. My God! You have made me forget how to live alone, I who had a kind of intense, melancholy taste for solitude. I love you."

Brussels, late November 1908: "I kiss you, my sweet velvet. Kiss me fully, as in the carriage when I accompanied you to the station."

Lyon, early December 1908: "I am, to my very depths, profoundly grateful for all that you are for me, for all that you do for me. I kiss you with all my heart, my dear love."

In the spring of 1909, Colette went on tour with a theatrical adaptation of *Claudine in Paris*. Missy accompanied her as her makeup artist, dresser, and hair stylist. During a short separation, a letter from Liège dated May 14 thanks Missy for her generous help and warns Missy to be careful of her health. A day later she wrote again: "My God, without you I am practically nothing."

In early June, from Marseille, Colette wrote one of her most tender love letters.

My dear love, I have finally received a letter from you, the first one! I'm very pleased. It's grumbling, it's nice, and I find it delicious because you say that you miss your odious child. My darling, that's enough to fill me with joy, and I'm blushing, all alone, with pleasure, with a sort of loving pride. I hope this word does not shock you, my modest little Missy; there's really no word other than love that can express the complete, exclusive tenderness I feel for you.

Throughout 1909 and 1910, Colette continued her itinerant career. In addition to her frenetic theatrical work—sometimes as many as thirty-two performances in thirty-two days in thirty-two French cities—she managed to produce another novel, written in hotel rooms and trains, which was published in serial form under the title *The Vagabond*.

Renée, the protagonist of *The Vagabond*, is far removed from the girlish Claudine. Thirty-four years old, she is a mime and a dancer (like Colette) pursued by a slightly younger, somewhat fatuous admirer. He rekindles in her the flame of heterosexual desire. "Suddenly my mouth, in spite of itself, lets itself be opened, opens of itself as irresistibly as a ripe plum splits in the sun."[10] Sensual lovemaking is carried to a new level of intensity, but so is the protagonist's need for independence. She is no longer the young woman under male sway. Despite her suitor's devotion and economic ease, Renée rejects his marriage proposal in favor of freedom and continued vagabondage.

Once again, literature was rooted in lived experience, for Colette was having an affair with Auguste Hériot, youthful heir to the Grands Magasins du Louvre department store, and she made no secret of it to Missy. In the summer of 1910, Missy, as generous as always to her "child," bought an estate in Brittany and deeded it to Colette. By the next summer, Colette and Missy were no longer together.

Yet it was not Hériot and his fortune who won Colette away from Missy, but another, more formidable man: Henri de Jouvenel. Jouvenel was sufficiently rich, possessed a title, and, more important, had an intellect and character strong enough to match her own. As a political journalist and later as a politician, Jouvenel became famous enough to have a street named after him in the sixth arrondissement. Their marriage, from 1912 to 1924, produced a daughter, Colette de Jouvenel, born when Colette was almost forty.

Characteristically, Colette chose her life as a writer, actress, and sexual woman over her life as a mother. She sent her daughter off to their country estate with an English nanny and rarely saw her during her early years. Nothing could dissuade Colette from her relentless pursuit of self-realization—not marriage (Henri proved unfaithful and she followed suit), not motherhood (she neglected her daughter), not sex (she had numerous lovers, male and female), not incest (she had a scandalous affair with her stepson Bertrand de Jouvenel), not religion (her third husband, Maurice Goudeket, was Jewish), not sickness (she suffered from debilitating arthritis in her later years), not the condemnation of the Catholic Church (it ultimately refused her a Christian burial). Instead, when she died in 1954, she was given a state funeral—the first given to any Frenchwoman—and was buried in the Père-Lachaise Cemetery. She wrote around fifty novels, some of which have been made into smashing films: *Gigi* with Leslie Caron, *Chéri* with Michelle Pfeiffer. Whatever else Colette did, she incarnated for over half a century the Frenchwoman who "lives her own life" (*vit sa vie*) and she probably made it possible for many other Frenchwomen, including lesbians, to live theirs more fully.

FOR THE MOST PART, AMERICANS ARE UNFAMILIAR with the lesbian culture that thrived in Paris from 1900 to World War II. If they have heard of Colette, they associate her primarily with her later heterosexual novels and films, namely, *Chéri* and *Gigi*, and with photos of her and her trademark cats. They are even less familiar with the life and writings of Natalie Barney, even though she was American by birth. Barney has always been better known in France than in the English-speaking world. But there was one lesbian couple living in Paris during the first half of the twentieth century who have become popular icons in American culture. I am speaking, of course, of Gertrude Stein and Alice B. Toklas. As I write this in June 2011, there are two major exhibitions in San Francisco featuring Stein: the first at the Contemporary Jewish Museum deals with Stein's life in Paris; the second at the Museum of Modern Art brings together the avant-garde paintings collected in Paris by Stein and her brothers.

Stein settled in Paris with her brother Leo in the fall of 1903. Their apartment at 27, rue de Fleurus was to become the choice meeting place of modernist painters and writers until World War II. Picasso, Matisse, Hemingway—these are only the best-known of hundreds of personalities who were regulars at the Stein residence. From 1907 on, the regulars were received not only by Stein but also by the woman who became Stein's lifelong companion, Alice B. Toklas.

Like Gertrude, Alice was of German Jewish origin and had been raised in the California Bay area. Whereas Gertrude had been educated at Radcliffe College and then at the Johns Hopkins School of Medicine before coming to France, Alice had remained at home as caretaker to her widowed father, and it was only after her father's death that she was able to break free from family obligations. Alice arrived in Paris with a San Francisco friend, Harriet Levy, but soon found herself under the spell of the not-to-be-denied and oh-so-imposing Gertrude Stein. At the time of their meeting, Gertrude was thirty-four and Alice thirty-one. Gertrude was short, heavy, and mannish in appearance; Alice was even shorter, thin, and distinctly feminine. Almost immediately they fell into the roles of husband and wife, though Alice did not move in with Gertrude until 1910. Three years later, Leo moved out.

As a couple, Gertrude and Alice did not resemble the theatrical lesbians surrounding Natalie Barney. They did not hang out at lesbian bars, such as Le Monocle on the boulevard Edgar-Quinet, where the female staff dressed as men. They were a stable monogamous twosome, with each assuming the duties of the gender she had chosen. Gertrude was the "man," the writer, the intellectual, the breadwinner—well, she had money from an inheritance. Alice was the homemaker, overseeing meals and arranging their social calendar. She sewed, embroidered, and created stunning vests for her beloved "hubby." As Hemingway recalled, when guests came to visit, Alice chatted with the wives, while Hemingway and the men spoke to Gertrude.

Gertrude was not shy in telling the world that she was a genius. She saw herself as a groundbreaking writer, just as Picasso was a groundbreaking painter. She created a modernist style in her early fiction (for example, *Three Lives*, *The Making of the Americans*) that has been compared to the innovations of James Joyce and Virginia Woolf, even if she never achieved their literary greatness. Her wordplay, which privileged sound over sense, has the effect of creating an insistent present moment and avoids conventional narration. The average reader will find many of her works enigmatic, if not incomprehensible, except for her highly popular autobiography titled *The Autobiography of Alice B. Toklas*, which made her a celebrity. During her 1934 lecture tour of the United States, she was accompanied by Alice, identified as her "secretary" and the "one who makes life comfortable for me."[11] *The Autobiography* gives a guarded picture of Gertrude and Alice's domestic partnership and a fuller account of their lively social life, dominated by Gertrude's massive presence.

For a peek inside their intimate relationship, one can read their love notes, published posthumously in 1999 under the title *Baby Precious Always Shines*.[12] Here Gertrude reveals her abiding affection for Alice.

> *When all is told lovely*
> *baby precious does not*
> *mind the cold, when*
> *little hubby surrounds*
> *her warm, the cold*
> *cannot do her harm . . .*

> *Dear Mrs.*
> *I take my pen in hand to congratulate*
> *you dear Mrs. on the extremely promising*

Husband you have. He promises everything
And he means it too. . . .

My dearest wife,
This little pen which
belongs to you loves to be
written by me for you, its
never in a stew nor are
you my sweet ecstacy.

Baby precious I worked
until I got all quieted
down, and I love my baby,
and we are always happy
together and that is all
that two loving ones need
my wifey and me.

The union between Gertrude and Alice lasted almost fifty years. It survived two world wars, a decline in Stein's fortune, and major quarrels with numerous friends and relatives. Somehow Gertrude and Alice managed to love each other with exemplary devotion. It is unlikely that they could have lived together so "normally" anywhere but Paris. The French gave them a home where they could realize their American ideal of monogamous marriage long before it would have been possible in their own home country.

Parisian lesbian culture went underground during the German occupation of France. Since the Nazis fiercely persecuted homosexuals in Germany and Italy and sporadically in occupied France, gay men and women had to be extremely circumspect if they did not want to land in prison or a concentration camp. The Vichy government enacted laws that raised the age of sexual consent for homosexual activity to twenty-one, while it remained fifteen for heterosexuals. Gertrude Stein and Alice B. Toklas spent the war years in the southeastern mountain town of Bilignin, where they had a summer home. Triply threatened as Jews, lesbians, and Americans, they depended on the protection of a French friend, Bernard Faÿ, who is known to have collaborated with the Gestapo, yet used his influence to save the lives of Gertrude and Alice. Gertrude lived long enough to see the war end and to be fêted as an unlikely survivor. But cancer of the stomach ended her life in 1946, and she went to join Oscar Wilde, Proust, and Colette in the Père-Lachaise Cemetery.

ANOTHER LESBIAN WRITER SURVIVED THE WAR YEARS in Paris under very different circumstances. Violette Leduc, a poor illegitimate country girl without higher education, worked in a publisher's office where, according to her own assessment, she probably wouldn't have had a job if Paris had not been "stripped of all its really able people."[13] Three novels published after the war and especially her 1964 breakthrough work, *La Bâtarde* (the English edition kept the French title) are all forms of autofiction that highlight both her lesbian and her heterosexual experiences. No writer before Leduc—not even Colette—had ever written so graphically about lesbian sexuality.

When I first read *La Bâtarde*, I was stunned. Leduc had given voice to female sexuality such as I had never heard expressed before. She knew how to evoke the absolute delight experienced by the body through the skin, as well as through the mouth, breasts, and genitals. Freud calls this "polymorphous perversity" because he is speaking from a male point of view that privileges penetration. I thought: if Leduc is describing lesbian sex, then I'm missing something. Some of us, even committed heterosexuals like myself, will feel pleasantly aroused by Leduc's description of making love for the first time in the bed of her boarding school classmate, separated from others in the dormitory only by the curtains surrounding each bed. See for yourself.

Isabelle is kissing me I said to myself. She was tracing a circle around my mouth, . . . she laid a cool kiss in each corner two staccato notes of music on my lips, then her mouth pressed against mine once more, hibernating there. My eyes were wide with astonishment beneath their lids, the seashells at my ears were whispering too loud.

. . .

We were still hugging each other, we both wanted to be swallowed up by the other. We had stripped ourselves of our families, the rest of the world, time, and light. As Isabelle lay crushed over my gaping heart I wanted to feel her enter it. Love is a harrowing invention.

. . .

Her tongue began to press against my teeth impatient to make me warm all over. I shut myself up, I barricaded myself inside my mouth. She waited: that was how she taught me to open into flower. She was the hidden muse inside my body. Her tongue, her little flame, softened my muscles, my flesh. I responded, I attacked, I fought, I wanted to emulate her violence.

We no longer cared about the noise we made with our lips. We were relentless with each other . . .

. . .

She opened the neck of my nightgown she explored the curve of my shoulder with her cheek, with her brow. I accepted the marvels she was imagining on the curve of my shoulder. . . .

Isabelle was drawing a snail with her finger on the bare patch we have behind our earlobes. . . .

A flower opened in every pore of my skin.

Violette, the novice, thought she would be satisfied without genital stimulation, but Isabelle, the experienced one, insisted on exploring Violette in all the folds of her flesh. Even the passages describing the most intimate parts of her body are written with a kind of lyricism that manages to escape pornography. Isabelle helped Violette cope with her deeply entrenched sense of ugliness, incarnated in her large nose, and the shame she felt as the illegitimate daughter of a former domestic. Isabelle was the first of Violette's lovers—both female and male—who were drawn into her troubled life.

Among her later friends, Leduc conceived a passion for the acclaimed author Simone de Beauvoir, and though Beauvoir kept an emotional distance from "the Ugly Woman," she encouraged Leduc's literary aspirations and was generous with her time, money, and editorial advice for over two decades. Leduc's account of her one-sided love for Madame (Beauvoir) in *L'Affamée* (*Ravenous*) had a "quasi-religious tone."[14] She would submit to any form of discipline in order to become worthy of her idol. So Leduc plugged away at her writing under Beauvoir's tutelage until, in 1964, she published her masterpiece, *La Bâtarde*, for which Beauvoir wrote a supportive preface. Beauvoir had hoped that *La Bâtarde* would win a major literary prize. While it did not, it sold several hundred thousand copies in its first years and remains in print to this day.[15] Not too bad for an ugly woman.

If Beauvoir refused Leduc's overtures, it was not because of her sex, as we shall see in the next chapter.

CHAPTER FOURTEEN

Existentialists in Love

Simone de Beauvoir and Jean-Paul Sartre

MY LOVE, YOU AND I ARE ONE, AND I FEEL
THAT I AM YOU AS MUCH AS YOU ARE ME.
Simone de Beauvoir to Jean-Paul Sartre, October 8, 1939

NEVER HAVE I FELT SO FORCEFULLY THAT OUR LIVES
HAVE NO MEANING OUTSIDE OF OUR LOVE.
Jean-Paul Sartre to Simone de Beauvoir, November 15, 1939

LIKE THEIR MEDIEVAL ANCESTORS ABÉLARD AND HÉLOÏSE, Jean-Paul Sartre and Simone de Beauvoir became an iconic couple during their lifetime. They remain the most famous French couple of the twentieth century, even though they never married, were frequently separated, and engaged in numerous affairs with other men and women. This unique relationship that endured for five decades shocked many of their contemporaries and still causes fierce debate among disciples and detractors, who write their biographies, attend conferences on their work, and sound off against each other in newspapers and academic articles. How is it that Beauvoir and Sartre still inspire and infuriate so many people?

When I first went to France as a junior-year student in the fall of 1952, Sartre and Beauvoir dominated the intellectual life of the Left Bank. Sartre, at forty-seven, had already published four novels, a collection of short stories, three plays, several books of literary criticism, a biography of Baudelaire, reflections on the Jewish question, and his major existential treatise, *Being and Nothingness.* My Wellesley College 1952 summer reading list for French majors included his popular *Existentialism and Humanism.* Beauvoir had not yet made it onto the Wellesley College reading list, though she was, at forty-four, the awesome author of three novels, a treatise with the paradoxical title *The Ethics of Ambiguity,* a journalistic account of her travels in the United States, and her revolutionary two-volume study of women, *The Second Sex.* Their prodigious output dwarfed that of all their rivals. Their legendary union offered a model of commitment, without legal or religious imprimatur, designed to enrage *les bien pensants* (the self-righteous) and to inflame the imaginations of the young, such as myself. Their shared philosophy of existentialism, based on the premise that God does not exist and that we are obliged to create meaning in a world devoid of predetermined meaning, encouraged myself and others in my student group to question our homegrown religious beliefs.

We looked for Sartre and Beauvoir in the haunts around Saint Germain-des-Prés and Montparnasse, where they were known to hang out. I never saw them, though others reported sightings that made me deeply envious. Existentialism infiltrated the air I breathed as I got off the number 63 bus that carried me five times a week from the fashionable sixteenth arrondissement, where I lived, to the Latin Quarter, where I attended classes. One day I spotted from the bus the elusive Samuel Beckett, whose astonishing play *Waiting for Godot* had left us collectively bewildered. Another day I saw Sartre and Beauvoir's friend, the singer Juliette Gréco, dressed in her habitual black as she walked down the rue Bonaparte, with her long black hair dancing behind.

Even if I didn't see Sartre and Beauvoir themselves, their image worked its way deeply and permanently into my psyche. They became my ideal couple, bound together by what appeared to be unswerving mutual devotion. Although they never lived under the same roof, except in hotels, they lunched or dined together every day, worked in different sections of the same café, critiqued each other's manuscripts, traveled together, and were increasingly involved in left-wing politics.

The world would learn much more about the particulars of their relationship when Beauvoir's memoirs started to appear in 1958. In the first volume, *Memoirs of a Dutiful Daughter*, she recalled how she had been invited in 1929 to study with three male students, including Sartre, when they were all preparing their *agrégation* exam in philosophy—the exam that would permit them to teach at the lycée (secondary school) level. Twenty-six students were allowed to take the final oral exams at the Sorbonne, down from a total of seventy-six who had taken the written. In a country that has a long tradition of teaching philosophy, they were the cream of the French educational system.

The notoriously grueling orals consisted of four separate tests held publicly before a six-man jury and an audience of general spectators. You had to be prepared to explicate texts in Greek and Latin, as well as French, and to present a lecture on a subject pulled out of a hat. Of the thirteen successful candidates, Beauvoir placed second. She was twenty-one years old and only the ninth woman ever to have received the *agrégation* in philosophy. She was also beautiful and well born, though her family had fallen on hard times and she was obliged to work for a living. Sartre, two and a half years older, the brilliant star of the École Normale Supérieure, came in first, even though he had flunked the exam a year earlier. Despite his short stature, partial blindness, and homely face (Sartre was the first to acknowledge his walleyed ugliness), he had so much confidence in his intelligence and winning ways that he was not shy in courting the elegant, dark-haired Mlle de Beauvoir.

"From now on, I'm going to take you under my wing," Sartre announced when he brought her the *agrégation* results posted at the Sorbonne.[1] And, indeed, he did just that. He encouraged her to nurture what she valued the most: her love of personal freedom, her passion for life, her curiosity, and her desire to be a writer. Sartre had decided long ago that literature was his calling. Initially encouraged by his widowed mother and his maternal grandfather, he never wavered in his belief that he was a genius destined for great literary success. Neither Sartre nor Beauvoir were teachers by choice; they taught to support themselves as writers. Neither wanted to marry or have children, but once they recognized each other as soul mates, they vowed to spend their lives together.

Sartre corresponded exactly to the dream-companion I had longed for since I was fifteen: he was the double in whom I found all my burning aspiration raised to the pitch of incandescence. I should always be able to share everything with him.

When I left him at the beginning of August, I knew that he would never go out of my life again.[2]

In the second volume of her memoirs, *The Prime of Life*, Beauvoir described how they conceptualized their unconventional pact, renewable every two years. Sartre provided the terminology.

"What *we* have," he said, "is an *essential* love; but it is a good idea for us also to experience *contingent* love affairs." We were two of a kind, and our relationship would endure as long as we did: but it could not make up for the fleeting riches to be had from encounters with different people.[3]

Their pact included not only the freedom to have other lovers but also the understanding that they would never conceal anything. Theirs would be a tell-all relationship, with complete honesty about their sexual partners. They believed that such an arrangement would allow for maximum freedom and authenticity and make it possible to avoid the pettiness and jealousy they associated with conventional bourgeois marriage.

Hmm. When I read these words in the early 1960s, I was married, the mother of three children, a professor of French, and witness to a sexual revolution that was gaining momentum, especially where we lived in northern California. How did Sartre and Beauvoir manage to preserve their ideals in what Americans were beginning to call an "open marriage"? The full story of their complicated connections with third parties would not be known until after their deaths.

Beauvoir and Sartre remained lovers in the physical sense of the word for about ten years, but long after they had ceased sleeping together, in fact for the rest of their lives, they maintained their "essential" love. Together they directed *Les Temps Modernes*, a leftist existentialist journal that had enormous prestige during the postwar years. Together they traveled to distant countries—Cuba, Egypt, the Soviet Union—where they were received like celebrities of the highest order. Together they continued to write during the day and socialize at night with a select circle of friends who shared their political ideas and their whiskey. Both Sartre and Beauvoir were heavy drinkers, he augmenting his alcohol with cigarettes and pills that would eventually take a huge toll on his health.

Surrounded by other postwar intellectuals, such as Albert Camus, Maurice Merleau-Ponty, Francis Jeanson, and the black American writer Richard Wright, Sartre and Beauvoir became a media sensation. Their photos, appearing in newspapers and magazines worldwide, were as recognizable to Americans, Russians, and Japanese as they were to the French. The image they consciously cultivated was based on the reality of their mutual commitment, but it also hid the presence of their many "contingent" lovers.

Both Sartre and Beauvoir had numerous sexual relations—some serious and long-term, others just passing affairs. These would come fully to light after Sartre died in 1980, and Beauvoir in 1987. Their posthumously published correspondence revealed a dizzying network of lovers on an international scale, but at the same time an unbreakable bond between the two of them.[4] Even as they graphically recounted their involvements with third parties, they professed to love one another.

Here is Beauvoir writing to Sartre on September 16, 1939, after he had been mobilized for the war: "I've just had your long Tuesday letter. The fact that it was so long and affectionate gave me real pleasure, my love. We're as one—I feel that at every instant, I love you."

Here is Sartre writing to Beauvoir on November 12, 1939: "How I love you, little Beaver, how I wish you were here. You know I love you just as much and as poetically as though it were the beginning of an affair. . . . My love, how dear you are to me, and how much I need you."

"Beaver" (*Castor*) is the affectionate name that Sartre and his university friends had given Beauvoir ten years earlier. During those ten years and for the next four decades as well, Sartre and the "Beaver" would continue to see in each other a reflection of themselves. No matter how different they appeared physically, their bond was based on a profound sense of likeness: they shared the same ideas and lived according to the same principles. They were literally doubles for each other, two of a kind joined at the brain like Siamese twins. Their psychic union evokes one of my favorite Shakespearean lines: "Let me not to the marriage of true minds admit impediments."

Nonetheless, given their pact of complete sexual freedom, each took full advantage of "contingent" love affairs, with consequences that led to unwieldy threesomes and foursomes. The late Hazel Rowley, in her remarkable dual biography of the couple, offered a revealing portrait of their "tumultuous lives and loves."[5] Sartre, by his own admission, was less sensual than Beauvoir, yet driven by an incessant desire to seduce. He left no stone unturned in his efforts to bed Beauvoir's former lycée student Olga, and when that failed, he turned to her younger sister, Wanda, pursuing her for two years before she submitted. His obsessional womanizing never interfered with his writing, but it did occasionally upset the

Beauvoir-Sartre equilibrium. Although they believed that telling each other everything would eliminate jealousy, this "transparency" didn't always work for Beauvoir. She was painfully jealous of Sartre's attentions to Olga, Wanda, and several other women with whom he had long-term affairs.

Sartre's affair with Dolores Venetti was especially threatening to Beauvoir. He met Dolores in January 1945, when he was visiting the United States as part of a French cultural delegation. A bilingual radio journalist for Voice of America, Dolores was the perfect guide for a man who had been captivated since childhood by all things American, ranging from comic books, movies, and jazz to novels by Hemingway, Dos Passos, and Faulkner. Of Italian and Ethiopan background, with an extremely pretty face, Dolores was easily seduced by the now-famous philosopher. After two days together in New York, they went to bed with each other and commenced a long-term relationship. By the following January, Sartre was again in New York and writing to Beauvoir:

> Here life is calm and uneventful. I get up around 9 o'clock . . . and I lunch with Dolores. . . . After lunch I take a walk all alone till 6 o'clock around NY, which I know as well as Paris; I meet Dolores again here or there and we stay together at her place or in some quiet bar till 2 in the morning. . . . Friday night I'm going up to her place and I'm staying there till Sunday afternoon. . . . Incidents, none. Except that Dolores's love for me scares me.[6]

I can imagine that Beauvoir was less scared by Dolores's love for Sartre than by Sartre's love for Dolores. Still, in that same letter Sartre continued to profess his attachment to Beauvoir and to insist: "I'm at my best with you and I love you very much. Au revoir, little one, I'll be so happy to be with you again."

A year later, Beauvoir began a passionate affair with the American writer Nelson Algren. It started on February 21 in Chicago, Algren's home city, which she was visiting on a tour that would result in her book *America Day by Day*. Algren was a rising literary star, having published two novels and almost completed a third, *The Man with the Golden Arm*, which was to be his most successful. Despite his lack of French and her heavily accented English, they communicated well enough to make love twice during her thirty-six hours in Chicago and to commence a long-distance relationship that would last for several years. Beauvoir seems to have experienced a kind of uninhibited physical awakening with Algren that she had not known before, not even in the early years with Sartre when, by her own account, she had given herself fully to "feverish caresses and love-making."[7] With Algren, physical desire was so intense that she had her "first complete orgasm," as she later related to her biographer Deirdre Bair.[8] Algren gave her a silver ring, which she wore for the rest of her life. From 1947 to 1964, she wrote him a total of 350 letters.[9] He wanted to marry her, but she could never pry herself away from the primary bond she shared with Sartre.

Beauvoir's relationship with Algren became public knowledge during her lifetime, but she managed to keep hidden an earlier affair that lasted nine years with Jacques-Laurent Bost, known as "little Bost." Bost had been one of Sartre's lycée students at Le Havre, and he would eventually marry Olga Kosakiewicz, Beauvoir's former student, whom Sartre had unsuccessfully tried to

seduce. They were all part of what the Beauvoir-Sartre couple referred to as the "family." Beauvoir seems to have cared very deeply
for Bost in ways that complemented her feelings for Sartre. Eight
years younger, Bost shared her passion for nature and hiking, pleasures that left Sartre indifferent. Bost also awakened in Beauvoir
the maternal sentiments she reserved for her younger lovers. Her
journal entries from 1939 and 1940 (not published until 1990) gave
expression to her constant worries about both Bost and Sartre after
they had been mobilized. Each day she wrote faithfully to each of
them and waited anxiously for return letters. She sent them parcels
containing books, tobacco, and other hard-to-obtain items. When
Bost was injured early in the war, it caused her no end of anxiety,
shared by Sartre as well.

But the most unexpected material in Beauvoir's posthumous
publications concerned her lesbian affairs with several of her students during her years as a lycée professor, and the threesomes that
were subsequently established between Beauvoir, Sartre, and the
female students in question. To the very end of her life, Beauvoir
maintained publicly that her relations with other women, however
close, had never been sexual. This was, we now know, untrue.
Beauvoir's relations with Olga, Bianca, and Natalie were passionate affairs in every sense of the word.

True to their pact, Sartre and Beauvoir confessed everything to
each other in detailed revelations that sometimes provoked tearful
outbursts from Beauvoir, which she confided to her journal if not
to Sartre. Sartre, too, though generally immune to jealousy, was
occasionally ruffled by Beauvoir's confessions. And certainly, the
two of them were often oblivious to the callous way they sometimes treated third parties.

Take the case of Bianca Bienenfeld Lamblin, who had been one of Beauvoir's students in 1937–1938 at the Lycée Molière in Paris. She was seventeen and Beauvoir thirty when their personal relationship began. As she wrote in her memoir, *A Disgraceful Affair*, published after Beauvoir's death, Bianca had been seduced both intellectually and sexually by her lycée professor.[10] After the first year, she was then passed on to Sartre, who was apparently dispassionate in taking her virginity, though verbally passionate in his letters. As a writer, Sartre worked himself up to romantic emotions that he may not have experienced in real life.

For more than a year, the older couple and the lycée student constituted a threesome. Sartre's letters to Bianca—she is called Louise Védrine in the published edition of his and Beauvoir's correspondence—attest to a very deep affection for her, or at least the semblance of one. Then, in 1940, at the outbreak of World War II, Bianca found herself abandoned by her dual mentors and lovers. The fact that Bianca Bienenfeld was Jewish and likely to be deported by the Nazis did not seem to have worried either Sartre or Beauvoir. Their reprehensible behavior in 1940 has been a source of dismay for even their staunchest admirers.

During the war, Bianca married Bernard Lamblin, one of Sartre's former lycée students, and together they escaped to the Vercors region in southeastern France, where several hundred resistance fighters managed to survive. When the war was over, Bianca and Beauvoir rekindled their friendship, which was to last until Beauvoir's death. But the posthumous publication of Beauvoir's war years journal and her letters to Sartre—works that referred directly to Bianca in a tone of ridicule—was devastating for Bianca, and she responded by writing her own version of the affair.

It was this story that I arranged to publish in English translation for a university press. When I met Lamblin in Paris, she was still bitter about events that had occurred more than forty years earlier. She had learned the hard way that Sartre and Beauvoir's high-flown ideas about essential and contingent relationships could be noxious to the add-on lover. She attributed her periodic bouts of severe depression, which had begun in 1941, not only to the Nazi horrors but also to the manipulation she had experienced at the hands of Beauvoir and Sartre. To her credit, Beauvoir took responsibility for Lamblin's deteriorating mental condition when she wrote to Sartre in 1945: "I think it is our fault. . . . She is the only person we have really harmed."

Thirty years later, when Sartre and Beauvoir discussed their personal relationship in a 1974 interview conducted by the German filmmaker Alice Schwarzer, they admitted that their lifelong union had been paid for, in part, by the emotional and sexual contributions of third parties. Modestly, they didn't mention the fact that they themselves contributed financially to the upkeep of several lovers long after the sexual liaisons were over. To the end of his life, Sartre paid monthly allowances to Wanda, Michelle Vian (the divorced wife of writer Boris Vian), and the daughter he adopted in 1965, Arlette Elkaïm. Beauvoir, too, was extremely generous toward former lovers, friends, and her widowed mother.

Since the film focused on Beauvoir, Sartre played only a small role in it, and his speech was halting, perhaps because his health was already on the decline. Beauvoir, on the other hand, spoke quickly and decisively. At that time, she was the darling of the French women's liberation movement, a group from which Sartre felt excluded. Beauvoir was so loquacious in the film that, without much prompting, she discussed female bisexuality. She presented bisexuality as natural in women, given their initial attachment to their mothers and the sense of complicity they experience with others of their same sex and gender. That complicity was apparent in a part of the film that showed Beauvoir presiding over a lively dinner in her Left Bank apartment, surrounded by half a dozen women, including her adopted daughter, Sylvie Le Bon. Both Sartre's and Beauvoir's adopted daughters would eventually become their inheritors and literary executors.

For Sartre's seventieth birthday, in June 1975, he granted a long interview to *Le Nouvel Observateur*. He admitted that there were several women in his life, but added, "Simone de Beauvoir is the only one." His tribute to her was unequivocal:

I have been able to formulate ideas to Simone de Beauvoir before they were really concrete . . . she was the perfect person to talk to . . . we have even insulted one another. . . . That's not to say that I accepted all her criticisms, but I did accept most of them. . . . There is no point in not criticizing very severely when you have the good fortune to love the person you are criticizing.[11]

LIKE MANY OF SARTRE AND BEAUVOIR'S READERS, I have had to revise my idealized picture of them and come to terms with their failings. Initially, they gave me a philosophic vocabulary with terms such as being and nothingness, existence and essence, authenticity and bad faith, and, yes, essential and contingent love. Their model of an intellectual partnership was one I formed and lived with my psychiatrist husband. Their books—Sartre's plays and his autobiography *The Words*, and Beauvoir's *Memoirs of a Dutiful Daughter*, *A Very Easy Death*, and *The Second Sex*—were on the syllabus of college courses I taught for over thirty years. When I became involved in women's studies, I realized over and over again the extent to which *The Second Sex* had raised and sometimes answered the most important feminist questions. Beauvoir's conviction that women would remain the second sex unless they could support themselves rings as true today as when she expressed that idea in 1949. For a woman born in 1908 within a class that considered work for women demeaning, Beauvoir proved that she could earn her own keep and become the full-fledged equal of a man and more. In that respect, Beauvoir and Sartre did not disappoint, for they treated each other as economic and intellectual equals till the end.

I am not the only one to quarrel with Beauvoir's negative view of motherhood. She had her reasons, and very good reasons, for seeing motherhood as an impediment to self-realization. Even today, if a woman wants to succeed in the world of business, politics, or academia, she has more chance of success if she is childless. In this respect, as in all others, Beauvoir assumed that the male model of success is what counts. She simply had no appreciation for the emotional depth and psychological growth that can be derived from parenting. It makes no sense to judge Beauvoir and Sartre according to a nuclear family model, because this is something they consistently rejected as a stifling bourgeois construct, and God knows they hated anything that smacked of the bourgeoisie from which they had come. Oddly enough, they referred to their famous threesomes as "the family," perhaps craving—despite themselves—the biological kinship they consciously eschewed.

For a long time I have been a Beauvoir groupie. I was and still am on the editorial board of the Simone de Beauvoir Society, founded some thirty years ago by my former colleague Professor Yolanda Patterson. In addition to teaching works by Sartre and Beauvoir, I wrote about her in academic books and articles. Most recently I wrote a letter to the *New York Times* in defense of the 2010 retranslation of *The Second Sex*—Beauvoir's feminist masterpiece—by my friends Constance Borde and Sheila Malovany-Chevallier, after the entire work had been trashed in the *Times* by Francine du Plessix Gray.[12]

But my most moving association with Simone de Beauvoir concerns a 1987 conference on autobiography that I organized at Stanford University under the auspices of the Center for Research on Women (now the Clayman Institute for Gender Research). With a small stipend at my disposal, I invited Beauvoir to speak at the conference; she sent her sister Hélène instead, along with Hélène's paintings. It was at this conference in April 1987 that Hélène received word of Simone's death, and she immediately flew back to Paris accompanied by a number of professors.

Simone de Beauvoir was buried next to Jean-Paul Sartre in the Montparnasse Cemetery. A single ledger tombstone covers their adjoining plots. For anyone unfamiliar with their story, it might seem strange to come upon a double tombstone, similar to those used for married couples, and find two different surnames on it. In death, their physical remains were united, but unlike Abélard and Héloïse, they had no belief in an afterlife. As Beauvoir poignantly wrote: "His death separates us. My death will not reunite us. . . . It is splendid that we were able to live our lives in harmony for so long."[13]

What, then, is the legacy that Sartre and Beauvoir bequeathed to the history of love? I see them, first and foremost, as proponents of freedom in love, as in all other aspects of life. Without the traditional legal or religious bonds of marriage, they declared themselves free to love each other in every sense of the word. They also considered themselves free to have sexual partners outside their primary couple, with an honesty about their secondary relations that still astonishes. Though a certain French tradition going back to the Middle Ages had countenanced outside lovers for married couples, none expressed that right so unconditionally, and none incorporated it into a love pact that applied equally to the man and the woman. In this respect, Sartre and Beauvoir were pioneers in the women's movement, though they might not have recognized themselves as such. Beauvoir would not make common cause with women as a group until the movement claimed her in the 1970s.

What differentiates this love from what we in the United States call "open marriage" or even "polyamorous marriage"? More than anything, it was the commitment that Beauvoir and Sartre vowed to each other and honored to the end of their lives. In spite of everything—lovers, hangers-on, adopted daughters, and male associates who took control of Sartre when he became blind and *gâteux* (decrepit)—Beauvoir remained his primary partner. They were truly wedded to each other in ways that made others envious.

Colette Audry, one of Beauvoir's colleagues when they were both teaching at the same lycée in the early 1930s, remembered a half century later: "Theirs was a new kind of relationship, and I had never seen anything like it. I cannot describe what it was like to be present when those two were together. It was so intense that sometimes it made others who saw it sad not to have it."[14]

For all their flaws, Beauvoir and Sartre offered an egalitarian model of couplehood that would have to wait two generations to become fully fashionable. Their love for each other did not die with the end of shared sex. They confirmed each other as two halves of an entity sharing a single vision. An oft-quoted definition of love written by another existentialist, Antoine de Saint-Exupéry, whose life overlapped with that of Beauvoir and Sartre, would have provided a fitting epitaph for their tombstone: "Love does not consist in gazing at each other, but in looking together in the same direction."

CHAPTER FIFTEEN

The Dominion of Desire

Marguerite Duras

HIS HANDS ARE EXPERT, MARVELOUS PERFECT. I'M VERY
LUCKY, OBVIOUSLY, IT'S AS IF IT WERE HIS PROFESSION.
. . . HE CALLS ME A WHORE, A SLUT, HE SAYS I'M HIS ONLY
LOVE, AND THAT'S WHAT HE OUGHT TO SAY . . . ALL IS
SWEPT AWAY IN THE TORRENT, IN THE FORCE OF DESIRE.

Marguerite Duras, *The Lover,* **1984**

THE WORLD OF MARGUERITE DURAS IS DOMINATED by love—
fierce, relentless passion that bursts into creaturely happiness
mingled with heartache. Duras's men and women experience ecstasy, tenderness, longing, jealousy, suffering, revenge. Their lives
are ravaged by love's course. In her fiction and films, you can sense
the pulse of love beating under every word.

Maria, the protagonist of Duras's novella *10:30 on a Summer
Night,* is haunted by memories of lovemaking with her husband
Pierre, now painful memories because she sees him consumed
with desire for her friend Claire. With Claire and their daughter

in tow, Maria and Pierre are traveling in Spain on their way to Madrid, but due to a violent summer storm, they stop for the night in an overflowing small-town inn, where the only place to sleep is on a hallway floor.

Maria, sensing the frustrated desire between Pierre and Claire, imagines:

> This must have been the first time they kissed. . . . She could see them fully outlined against the moving sky. While Pierre kissed her, his hands touched Claire's breasts. They were probably talking. But very softly. They must have been speaking the first words of love. Irrepressible, bursting words which came to their lips between two kisses.[1]

Maria drinks too much. She easily falls into wine-induced stupors. It becomes increasingly clear that she is a serious alcoholic. (Duras had her own problems with drink.) Pierre tries unsuccessfully to stop her. Despite Maria's stubborn alcoholism and Pierre's irresistible attraction to Claire, he still loves his wife and treats her with tender desire.

> "You remember? Verona?"
> "Yes."
> If he reached out, Pierre would touch Maria's hair. He had spoken of Verona. Of love all night, the two of them, in a bathroom in Verona. A storm too, and it was summer, and the hotel was full. "Come, Maria." He was wondering. "When, when will I have enough of you?"

There is a visceral understanding between the two of them. He knows that she knows about Claire, and yet he believes that the marital bond will somehow survive.

Interwoven within the story of Maria, Pierre, and Claire is a shocking event that has just occurred in the nameless town. That very day, a man had shot and killed his youthful, naked wife and the lover lying beside her.

"His name is Paestra. Rodrigo Paestra."

"Rodrigo Paestra."

"Yes. And the man he killed is Perez. Toni Perez."

As the police patrol the town and wait for dawn to catch the murderer, Maria obsesses over his fate. She has heard that he is hiding on the rooftops, and suddenly decides to help him escape. Without directly expressing the parallel between Paestra's situation and her own, Maria understands all too well how a spouse could be driven to murder out of jealousy. How she manages to deliver Paestra from the rooftops but not from his own despair; how she accepts the inevitable sexual union between Pierre and Claire; how Pierre and Maria unsuccessfully cling to their long-term love for one another—these are all themes that play out against each other in a haunting drama.

Much of the power of Duras's writing lies in what she does not say. We the readers, or viewers in the case of her films, are asked to fill in the spaces. We enter into her characters' thought processes, partake of their emotions, and add our own. However idiosyncratic her stories, they delve into a common pool of primitive emotions hidden in each of us.

The unsaid lurks behind her famously stylized language: sonorous word patterns and repetitious leitmotifs create a distinctly musical texture. It is no accident that one of her best-known novellas is titled *Moderato Cantabile*—a musical term meaning "moderately and melodiously." Here, too, a man had killed the woman he loved, but instead of fleeing he throws himself upon her inert body and strokes her hair.

> The crowd could see that the woman was still young, and that blood was coming from her mouth in thin trickles, and that there was blood on the man's face where he had kissed her.[2]

This crime of passion, this ultimate expression of transgressive love, works its way into the imagination of others surrounding the fatal couple. Once again the murder is interwoven into a more developed story, this time that of a man named Chauvin and his former employer's wife, Anne Desbaresdes. They meet by chance in the café where the murder had taken place and continue to meet there, though this is inappropriate territory for a bourgeois wife like Madame Desbaresdes. Their only topic of conversation is the murder, even though neither really knows anything about the parties involved. Nonetheless, they are drawn to the mystery of a love so wild it defies all rational understanding.

The murder beomes a catalyst for the mounting attraction between Anne and Chauvin, which reaches a level of erotic intensity far beyond the events themselves. A thousand other French stories are filled with similar events concerning love, adultery, and jealousy, yet Duras manages to endow these events with a unique incantatory power. Just as Racine in the seventeenth century elevated love to a level of tragic gravitas, so too Duras in the twentieth century draws her readers and spectators into the roiling underworld of all-consuming love.

MARGUERITE DURAS (1914–1996) WAS SEVENTY WHEN SHE wrote *The Lover*. At that time, she was already a much-honored author with over fifty novels, novellas, films, and plays to her credit. These included the world-famous film *Hiroshima, Mon Amour* and works of fiction such as *Moderato Cantabile*, which was often included in French and American courses on literature. *The Lover* won the 1984 Prix Goncourt and sold 750,000 copies by the end of the year. Later it was made into a much-acclaimed film.

The Lover is set in Vietnam where Duras was born and grew up. Named Marguerite Donnadieu (meaning "give to God"), she was the third child of parents who had come from France to educate indigenous Vietnamese children. As members of the French ruling class, her family lived comfortably in what was then called Indochina, but after the death of her father, their circumstances were considerably reduced. Like Duras, the unnamed girl in *The Lover* has a bitter schoolteacher mother, a brutal older brother, and a sweet second brother who dies young. She is fifteen and a half when she meets a rich Chinese man, older by a dozen years, on a ferry crossing the Mekong River. She is returning by bus and boat from her village of Sadec (now called Sa Dec) to school in Saigon. The man has come aboard the ferry with his black limousine and white-liveried chauffeur.

He looks at the girl in the man's fedora and the gold shoes. He slowly comes over to her. He's obviously nervous. He doesn't smile to begin with. To begin with he offers her a cigarette. His hand is trembling. There's the difference of race, he's not white, he has to get the better of it, that's why he's trembling. She says she doesn't smoke, no thanks.[3]

The man is surprised to see a white girl using the native transportation system. He asks about her family in Sadec and tells her that he lives in the big house with the large terrace and blue tiles bordering the river. He has just returned from Paris where he was a student. Would she allow him to drive her to her destination in Saigon?

Here begins the surprising history of a poor adolescent French girl with an older rich Chinese man. He has the traditional attributes of power—money and maturity—which she counters and subjugates with her youth, beauty, and skin color. Race is the subtext of this story. Being white gives her an incomparable advantage in that colonial French society, which looked down upon Asians, be they native Vietnamese or Chinese transplants. Her mother and brothers treat the man with contempt, and his father refuses the idea that his heir should marry "the little white whore from Sadec." But before arriving at that point in the narrative, we follow the romance of the French girl and the Chinese man, and it is unlike anything we have read before.

Every day the man comes in his chauffeur-driven car to the French high school she attends and drives her back to the state boarding school in which she sleeps. But one day after school he drives her to the Chinese section where he keeps a bachelor apartment. There he tells her that he loves her.

She says, I'd rather you didn't love me. But if you do, I'd like you to do as you usually do with women. He looks at her in horror, asks, Is that what you want. She says it is.

And so they make love at her request, and he is the one who weeps and moans, rather than she. Their lovemaking has nothing of the stereotypical.

He's torn off the dress, he throws it down. He's torn off her little white cotton panties and carries her over like that, naked, to the bed. And there he turns away and weeps. And she, slow, patient, draws him to her and starts to undress him.

. . .

She touches him. Touches the softness of his skin, caresses his goldenness, the strange novelty. He moans, weeps. In dreadful love.

After he has penetrated her, he wipes the blood away and washes her as if she were a baby. Their lovemaking alternates between scenes of tenderness and passion, during which she, too, comes to experience exquisite pleasure.

For a year and a half they make love regularly in his bachelor apartment, surrounded by the noises and smells of the Chinese quarter of Cholon. In time, her family finds out, and she is beaten by her mother and older brother. Her mother screams: she is no better than a prostitute, she will never be able to marry and find her place in society. This doesn't stop the family from taking the money that comes their way from the Chinese man. They even accept his invitation to a meal in an expensive Chinese restaurant, where they behave very badly, don't even speak to their host as they gobble up everything in sight.

The girls in her French school stop speaking to her. She doesn't care. "We go back to the apartment. We are lovers. We can't stop loving each other."

He gives her a valuable diamond ring. This curtails some of the criticism at home and at the boarding school, which looks the other way when she is absent at night from the dormitory. By now the lovers are joined in a ritualistic dance of love. He washes her body with special water set aside in large jars for that purpose. She abandons herself to his caresses, strokes his body as he strokes hers. Their silent caresses are occasionally broken by tempestuous outbursts.

> Then suddenly it's she who's imploring, she doesn't say what for, and he, he shouts to her to be quiet, that he doesn't want to have anything more to do with her . . . and now they succumb to it again amid tears, despair, and happiness.

Eventually the time comes when the girl must return to France for university education. The man is so pained at the thought of separation that he can no longer make love to her. "His body wanted nothing more to do with the body that was about to go away, to betray." On the day of her departure, she stands on the deck of the boat that will carry her to Europe and sees his big car on the dock, "long and black with the white-liveried driver in front. . . . That was him in the back, that scarcely visible shape, motionless, overcome." She starts to weep, hiding her tears from the mother and brother who will accompany her to France. Had she loved him as he had loved her? No. But she had loved him in her own way, and she will never forget him.

Years later, after he had married the Chinese woman his father chose for him, after they had produced an heir, he comes to France with his wife. By then, the girl from Vietnam is a well-known writer. She had lived through the war, marriages, children, divorces. He phones and she immediately recognizes his voice. His voice trembles, he is nervous, still afraid. "And then he told her. Told her that it was as before, that he still loved her, he could never stop loving her, that he'd love her until death."

WHY DOES THIS STORY MAKE ME CRY as I read its final pages? Is it because I want to believe that such an enduring love is still possible? Is it because Duras has created a myth of carnal love that goes beyond the physical and transcends barriers of race, class, and money? Or is it because this story evokes my own history of a love affair in France when I was twenty (with a Norwegian) and a phone call forty years later when we immediately recognized each other. Duras tells a story, and it becomes your own.

The Lover plays out the quintessentially French idea of love anchored in the flesh. The body of the other, when caressed and cared for like that of a child, can lead to supreme pleasure and diffuse happiness for both parties. For a time, the lovers were able to resist the prejudices of a colonial society that treated interracial unions as taboo. In this respect, Duras was well ahead of her time. Even if the lovers are eventually parted and each returns to the culture that birth dictated, this does not mean that their love was worthless. On the contrary, Duras suggests, in each of her works, that love, however curtailed, can provide an emotional wellspring as long as memory endures.

Duras opened up a subject that has had enormous ramifications in France: interracial love affairs resulting from the French colonial interventions in Indochina, Africa, the Near East, the Caribbean, and the Indian Ocean. Such unions unsettled traditional French notions of love. Whereas it was once unthinkable, or at least very rare, for a white French man or woman to marry someone of a different race, today such unions have become considerably more common. Men coming from the Ivory Coast or Guyana, women from Vietnam or the Antilles sometimes pair up with indigenous French and produce tea-skinned or café-au-lait children. France is becoming multiracial faster than anyone could have predicted when Duras was a girl.

Marguerite Duras's assiduous biographer, Laure Adler, tracked down the origins of *The Lover* in Vietnam.[4] She concluded that the Chinese lover had really existed. She visited his grave in the company of his nephew and saw his house, now turned into a police station. But the lover that Marguerite Duras wrote about in her famous novel, as well as in other works, was by no means identical with the man she had known at sixteen. Though he was Chinese, very rich, and her suitor for two years, he was definitely not nice-looking—in fact, he seems to have been quite ugly. Moreover, though he paid large sums of money to the Donnadieu family for Marguerite's company, he may not have slept with her until shortly before she departed for France. These differences and significant others are inscribed in notebooks, discovered after Duras's death, that are probably closer to the lived facts than the account in *The Lover*. Ultimately the lived events inspired a more aesthetic reality.

By the time Duras wrote *The Lover*, at the age of seventy, the Chinese lover had become part of her personal mythology, and she herself might not have been able to distinguish between life and literature. With his yellow-white skin and fine hands, his wealth and outsider status, he was the transgressive lover who had initiated her into sex and love. For the rest of her life, he would remain embedded in her consciousness. As a writer, Duras could repair the flaws in the original relationship. Such is the grace of memory. She could transform a somewhat sordid affair into a mutually passionate romance and project into posterity her vision of love as an irresistible force that penetrates through the skin, regardless of its color.

CHAPTER SIXTEEN

Love in the Twenty-first Century

APRIL IN PARIS IS SOMETIMES ALL IT'S SUPPOSED TO BE. With the horse chestnut trees in flower, sending their white spikes up like candles, and the yellow tulips drinking up the sun in the Luxembourg Gardens, I returned to my cultural home. Young and not-so-young lovers sitting on benches were still kissing each other avidly, oblivious to the tourists from every country gazing enviously at such unseemly behavior. Yes, indeed, the cupid-bedecked postcard I bought for one euro had reason to advertise Paris as the *capitale des amoureux*, the capital city of lovers. But what kind of French lovers does one find in the twenty-first century? That was the question at the top of my list when I returned to France in 2011.

First I attended the funeral services of a ninety-one-year-old woman whom I had known for more than forty years. And I had known her deceased husband even longer, as far back as my student days in Tours. Paul and Caroline had become lovers in a familiar French manner—that is to say, she was over thirty and married with two children when they met, while he was single and six years younger. I remember a letter from Paul describing their torrid love affair and his escape just in time from her marital bedroom. The expression "J'ai failli y laisser ma peau" (I almost left my skin there) remains inscribed on my brain. Leaving her husband and a very advantageous financial situation, Caroline moved into Paul's bachelor apartment, taking her daughter with her and sending her son to boarding school in Switzerland. They remained there until Paul died and Caroline went to live near her married daughter in the south of France. Whatever their problems—and there were many—their tender devotion to each other was evident to anyone who knew them. Caroline, in her seventies and eighties, was still a very elegant coquette and held onto all the wiles that Frenchwomen of her generation and class knew how to manipulate. Later, when Caroline lived in a nursing home, she lost much of her memory but not all her charm. At one point she asked her sister-in-law: "How many husbands did I have?" When her sister-in-law responded, "Two," Caroline was a little disconcerted. "What? Only two!"

I did not expect to find this kind of love and marriage among the younger generation, and I did not. Everything I encountered in Paris from friends, academics, plays, movies, and printed materials drew me into a whirlpool of present-day love relations, where the rules for men and women were in the process of change and where marriages of fifty years seemed more and more unlikely. And yet, love itself had not disappeared. Not at all. It was still as obsessively present in France as it had always been.

Popular plays with titles like *L'illusion conjugale* (Conjugal Illusion), *Le gai mariage* (Gay Marriage), *J'adore l'amour* (I Adore Love), *Un manège nommé désir* (A Merry-Go-Round Named Desire), *La meilleur amant que tu aies eu?* (The Best Lover You Ever Had?), *L'amour sur un plateau* (Love on a Tray), *Ma femme me prend pour un sextoy* (My Wife Takes Me for a Sex Toy), *Amour sur place ou à emporter* (Love Right Here or Carry Out), and *Mars et Vénus: La guerre des sexes* (Mars and Venus: The War of the Sexes) were attracting enthusiastic audiences throughout the city, and so were classical plays like *Le Misanthrope* and *Cyrano de Bergerac*. There was even a version of *Tristan et Yseult*, publicized as "a love of youth and adultery, passionate, enflamed, loaded with carnal desire," and ending with the question: "A myth or an ordinary tragedy?"

I attended a Sunday matinee of the award-winning *L'illusion conjugale*. The house was packed and the performance outstanding. So what if it dealt with the oldest of all French themes: the husband, the wife, and her lover? The wife was, of course, beautiful, thin, stylish, charming, and dependent on her husband for her material situation. She was the same stereotypical Frenchwoman who had appeared in any number of comedies during the gay nineties and the 1930s. In this play, the wife suggests that she and her husband tell each other the number of affairs they have had during the course of their long marriage. How many has he had? Well, he finally admits to twelve. She takes the number in stride. And she, how many has she had? Just one, *just one*? He explodes. One is worse than twelve. One means that she truly cared about someone, whereas his were just passing affairs. Once unleashed, his jealousy cannot be contained. He must know more. How long did it last? Who was it? Was it his best friend? The best friend arrives and further revelations take place that shake the entire foundations of the marriage. Yet in the end, the wife refuses to confirm her husband's suspicions. She retreats into mystery, a safe haven for Frenchwomen, and ultimately, it appears, the necessary glue for French marriages. Tell all and you destroy the conjugal illusion.

In 1948, the poet Paul Claudel had begun the preface to a new edition of his own play *Partage de midi* (*Break of Noon*), first written in 1909, with these words: "Nothing apparently more banal than the double theme on which this drama is based. . . . The first one, that of adultery: the husband, the wife and the lover. The second, that of the struggle between a religious vocation and the call of the flesh."[1] In 2011, you can forget about the struggle between a religious vocation and the demands of the flesh, but adultery still packs them in.

There were, however, different themes in theater, film, and fiction that pointed to new issues in the eternal quest for love. For example, the play *Le gai mariage* was emblematic of the remarkable openness with which the French now treat homosexuality. Why, even the mayor of Paris, Bertrand Delanoë, is openly gay. French laws established in 1999 allow for a form of civil union known as PACS (Pacte Civil de Solidarité) that provides all the financial benefits of matrimony, regardless of the partners' sex. Although PACS was set up with same-sex couples in mind, it has now been co-opted by heterosexual couples as well. At present, there are two civil unions for every one marriage performed in France. Civil unions are much easier to enter into than legal marriages and much easier to dissolve. Perhaps that is why straight couples are PACSing more and more frequently. Many young people, straight and gay, seem to be uncomfortable with the notion of lifelong marriage. With life expectancy hovering around eighty-four for French women and seventy-seven for men, the thought of spending fifty or sixty years with the same person may be too much to expect.

So, then, France, like the United States, is undergoing a romantic revolution. Premarital sex, living together with or without legal commitment, divorce, and serial unions are ousting old-fashioned lifetime marriage. The traditional format of husband and wife (with breathing space for his and her lovers) is becoming less of a norm than an ideal.

What has changed everything is that more women are now working outside the home and, as in the United States, trying to combine all the wifely virtues with the hard-nosed realities of the working place. My younger women friends—those under forty-five—still tend to their appearance, do the cooking, are attentive mothers, and now contribute to the family economy. This makes for the same kind of conflicts in time and energy that American women are facing. Of course, the French governmental support for maternity leave and day-care centers make it somewhat easier for French mothers to continue working. The French legally have fourteen weeks of paid maternity leave, which increases to twenty-six weeks for a third child, as well as fourteen days of paternity leave, but many mothers manage more. My hairdresser took six months with full and then partial pay for the birth of each of her daughters. A friend who has an important position with a European airline took off a year with each of her sons, and her husband got unpaid paternal leave for the year between their births. Many men have taken over child-care responsibilities that would have been unthinkable in the past. For example, my French publisher habitually leaves her daughter with her ex-husband or her live-in lover when she must travel.

There is no doubt that the reality of women as economic competitors with men has thrown a wild card into the game of love. Men who once knew what to expect of themselves and of the women who were economically dependent on them are confused by women who may earn as much as they do and sometimes even more, though the work world still privileges men in numerous ways. One senses a malaise in France among certain men and women who have become afraid of love. My women friends tell me that it is the men who shy away from permanent attachments, whereas the women invest greater emotional energy in maintaining their relationships. If this is true, French and American women have much in common.

THE NOTED FRENCH INTELLECTUAL PHILIPPE SOLLERS BEGINS his 2011 book by asking if we can imagine a novel with the title *Treasure of Love*. He believes readers would find such a title grotesque and open it only in secret.[2] Such is the contemporary disillusionment with romance, according to Sollers. Nonetheless, he titles his autobiographical novel *Trésor d'amour* and rhapsodizes about Minna, his love treasure.

Minna is thirty-five; Sollers, the male protagonist (who doubles for the flesh-and-blood Sollers), is at least twice her age. Minna was married for two years to an Italian banker and has a five-year-old daughter. So much for numbers. Venetian-born, Minna is Italian and a specialist of French literature, most notably Stendhal. Sollers and Minna share a love for Venice, where they meet on a regular basis two or three days a month, and a passion for Stendhal, whose life and work become the subtext of the novel.

Sollers sums up the history of French love in the following manner:

In three centuries, we have thus gone from repression and religious sublimation to libertinage, from libertinage to romantic passion, from there to exaggerated modesty, and once again from there to sexual and pornographic proliferation, before returning, via sickness and reproductive technology, to original, ordinary repression.

What kind of contemporary repression is Sollers talking about? Certainly not sexual repression since French men and women, like Americans, find bed partners more easily than ever before. What has become repressed is the possibility of giving oneself, heart and soul, to what used to be called "true love." Bombarded by *"amour-publicité, amour-cinéma, amour-chanson, amour-télé, amour-magazines, amour-people,"* the French are compelled to love according to criteria concocted by the media. But has one ever loved "naturally"? Hasn't there always been an intermediary that provides the model for lovers? René Girard's work on mediated desire has convinced us that the greatest works of Western literature, from Dante and Cervantes to Stendhal and Flaubert, present literary figures who took their romantic cues from earlier fictions.[3] How many women and men in the second half of the eighteenth century learned to love passionately and cry plentifully from the gospel of Rousseau's *Nouvelle Héloïse*? Today, movies, television, magazines, and the Internet provide models that literature can no longer compete with on a numerical level.

Sollers looks back to a time when the French, and the rest of the Western world, turned to literature for exemplary lovers. He evokes love as it was captured in Stendhal's greatest novels, *The Red and the Black* and *The Charterhouse of Parma* and in his essay *On*

Love. What we in the year 2011 have lost is Stendhal's process of *cristallisation*—the ability to imagine the loved one, to fantasize about that person, to gift him or her with the desirable attributes we admire.

What's more, since Internet dating services come up with whatever qualities we would like to find in a person, people can go straight to a site and construct a potential partner from online data. You want someone tall, short, into rough sex? Go to Match.com. Whereas Swann built Odette into an idealized woman, we now start with the ideal construct and then find the matching person. The satisfaction of physical and psychic desire, made too easy, has ruined the process of love.

Or has it? The Sollers persona has found his ideal love in Minna, in their silent entente and mutual adoration. He is sure of himself: "I love Minna, and she loves me." Encapsulated within the miracle of Venice, descended from an old Italian family, enmeshed within their shared admiration for Stendhal (who not incidentally adored Italy), Minna emerges from a process of crystallization—like the crystals that develop on the branches left in a salt mine, to use Stendhal's metaphor—with all the perfections Sollers has projected upon her: youth, beauty, intelligence, and a distinguished Italian genealogy.

Now and then we get a sense of what Minna thinks. She finds Stendhal's essay *On Love* old-fashioned. She loves his statement that "the admission of women to perfect equality would be the surest mark of civilization: it would double the intellectual force of the human species and its chance for happiness." Watch out, Sollers, there may be a feminist hidden under the skin of the ineffable Minna!

But Minna is not one of those "terrible" feminists who cause problems. She "has never thought of 'having a career' in a university or elsewhere. The idea of assuming power . . . is strange to her. . . . She likes her independent life, her daughter, her apartment in Venice." And so would I, and so would many other women, if we didn't have to support ourselves or contribute to a family economy. Come on, Sollers, what century are you living in? Sollers is but one of many writers—both men and women— uneasy with the changes wrought by and for women since the 1960s. He evinces a creeping malaise between the sexes, even as the narrator of *Trésor d'amour* lauds his perfect relationship with Minna.

One wonders how Sollers, married in 1967 to the feminist psychoanalytic writer Julia Kristeva, has felt about her international success in academic circles. And one wonders who the model or models might have been for Minna. Sollers and Kristeva, in the tradition of Sartre and Beauvoir, have long been an iconic couple whose private lives are subject to ongoing public scrutiny.

EVEN MORE PESSIMISTIC ARE THE WORKS OF the poet and novelist Michel Houellebecq. In his much-discussed novel *The Elementary Particles*, he writes for an age when "feelings such as love, tenderness and human fellowship had, for the most part, disappeared."[4] Houellebecq offers detailed descriptions of masturbation, pornography, prostitution, and sex tourism as quick fixes for the absence of love. Though I can appreciate his seriousness as a thinker, he puts me off—totally. I simply do not want to follow Houellebecq in his nihilistic portrayal of unlovely individuals unable to find human connection.

A few women writers are also mining the vein of unadulterated sex. Catherine Millet's 2001 memoir, translated as *The Sexual Life of Catherine M.*, focuses on her sexual experiences from childhood to adulthood, not skipping a beat as she goes from masturbation to group sex. Even the French, used to sexually explicit works, were taken aback by her tell-all exhibitionism and took to calling her "Madame Sex." In 2008, she published a sequel memoir, *Jour de souffrance* (*Jealousy: The Other Life of Catherine M.*), recounting her discovery that her partner, Jacques Henric, had been having affairs with several other women. Millet and Henric, founders and editors of the magazine *Art Press*, had been together for more than twenty years. That Millet could experience the torments of jealousy, after decades of a promiscuous open relationship, says something about the ability of the heart to assert its rights. Toni Bentley, reviewing this book for the *New York Times* (January 29, 2010), speaks of a "romantic tit for tat" that "may have its own kind of poetic justice."

Whereas Sollers, Houellebecq, and Millet come from a generation of older French intellectuals, Virginie Despentes is nothing if not young, working class, and blatantly subversive. Her 1999 novel *Baise-moi* (*Fuck Me*), followed by the film version, is a grisly tale of sex, gang rape, drugs, violence, robbery, murder, and every conceivable horror. Even with graphic sex scenes in both the novel and film, there is little one can call "erotic" and certainly nothing resembling love. Despentes co-opts the most extreme aspects of French pornography, ostensibly in the service of feminist rage, to show how marginalized peoples get their revenge on society. Her later book, *King Kong théorie* (2006) opens with startling prose: "I write from the house of the ugly ones, for the ugly ones, the old ones, the butch types, the frigid, the poorly fucked, the un-fuckables, the hysterical, the cretins, all the ones excluded from the love market."[5] Unfortunately, after the opening pages, the book descends into a rehash of American feminist theories from the 1980s (I ought to know) that adds nothing new to the debate, except dirty words. As for her 2010 novel, *Apocalypse bébé* (*Apocalypse Baby*), which won the prestigious Prix Renaudot, once again Despentes demonstrates an amazing command of lowlife language mustered to attack bourgeois values. It is true that this novel, written in the form of a *polar* (detective story or murder mystery) about the disappearance of an adolescent girl, will grip you till the end—that is, if you can take the moral bankruptcy of everyone in the book except perhaps "the Hyena," its lesbian savior. Sex, suspense, violence, a bit of emotion, perhaps even a whiff of tenderness suggest that Despentes, in her early forties, has the potential to grow beyond her present shock-value lure.

LET'S FACE IT, THE FRENCH NOVEL IS no longer the privileged home of love. For some time now, cinema has usurped that role and become the foremost conveyor of romance for both French and international audiences. If I tell my husband I want to see a certain French film, he knows immediately that it will be a love story. While American films excel in technological innovation, violence, explosions, mystery, animation, and science fiction, the French continue to zero in on the intimate space between lovers. Among the many great French filmmakers of the last half century, Eric Rohmer, Jean-Luc Godard, François Truffaut, and Claude Lelouch could package most of their films under the label "Lessons in Love."

What was listed in the *Pariscope* of April 6 to 12, 2011, that fit into this category? There was *Angèle et Tony*, a dramatic comedy about Angèle, who is released from prison and wants to regain possession of her son. The film begins with Angèle up against a wall being fucked by a young man in exchange for a toy for her son. She is skinny, good-looking, brutal, doesn't know how to behave in any traditional feminine sense. She meets Tony, a fisherman and owner of a small fishing company. He's something of a bumpkin, but he has a good heart. She wants him to marry her so she can persuade the local judge to grant her custody of her son. Slowly what was a manipulative ploy on her part turns into real affection. The film has a happy ending, wedding gown and all. I'd give it two stars out of four.

Potiche directed by François Ozon and starring Catherine Deneuve, Gérard Depardieu, and Fabrice Luchini, is a comedy set in the 1970s about a woman married for thirty years to a corporate executive who cheats on her regularly with his secretary and occasionally with other women as well. He had taken over her father's umbrella company and turned it into a big money-making establishment. But his workers, unhappy with his ultraconservative policies, go on strike and take him hostage. Suzanne, his wife, moves into the breach and proves that she is something more than a mindless *potiche*—a derogatory word for a trophy wife. Negotiating the release of her husband with the help of the local Communist mayor, with whom she had had a one-day affair early in her marriage, she takes control of the company while her husband recuperates from a heart attack. The wife (Deneuve) and the mayor (Depardieu) do not become lovers once again, as he would wish, though they dance together with an eroticism that belies their advanced years (especially his, encumbered by his enormous girth). For a moment, the mayor believes that he is the father of her adult son, but it turns out that the son was fathered by another one of Suzanne's short-term lovers. She speaks about her early adulterous adventures with an insouciance and lack of guilt that would be unthinkable in an American film. Suzanne goes on to run against the mayor for a seat in the National Assembly. Of course she wins, and plans to divorce her husband and move to Paris. It's an entertaining woman-friendly fable that casts a lighthearted look backward on the feminist upheavals that began to shake up French society forty years ago. I'd give it a three out of four.

Nous, Princesses de Clèves was the highpoint of my cinematic outings in Paris. On a Saturday morning at 10:00 a.m., I lined up outside a small Left Bank moviehouse with a hundred others eager to see this remarkable film inspired by Madame de La Fayette's novel. Set in a contemporary high school on the northern edge of Marseille, the film explores the ways in which the seventeenth-century masterpiece intersects with the lives of contemporary students from working-class families, many of whom are North African in origin. The filmmaker, Regis Sauder, encouraged by his wife Anne, a high school teacher, wanted to show how young people from a poor neighborhood "could appropriate a text from the seventeenth century, learn it, know it, and recognize themselves in it."[6] In opposition to President Sarkozy's denigration of *La Princesse de Clèves* as "useless," Sauder considers the novel "useful" because it helps young people understand themselves.

Sauder places the text itself at the center of the film. The students read it aloud or recite it by heart. From time to time, they comment on the words they have pronounced. Sauder remarks: "I remember a conversation about love with one of the young girls, Aurore, when she said, in reference to the novel but also to her own life, 'When one loves, there are no longer any limits.' I had the impression that I was hearing her heart beat when she said that."

The students understood *La Princesse de Clèves* as "a story of passionate love" that they could carry into their personal lives and discuss with their families and friends. As they acted in the film, they sensed how much they were emotionally and intellectually transformed by it. A seventeen-year-old named Abou recognized himself in the code of honor that reigned in the French court centuries before he was born, despite the glaring difference in social milieu.

Surprisingly, all the young people appreciated the advice of the princess's mother, Mme de Chartres, who would prefer death rather than see her daughter embark on an adulterous affair. They understood how important it was for the mother to inculcate a sense of family honor in her female progeny. The novel allowed them to talk to their own mothers about love, under the cover of *La Princesse de Clèves*.

Little by little, as a spectator, I became totally immersed in the lives of these young people with café-au-lait skins and features different from the conventional white faces one thinks of as French. I saw how they became one with a story about love born in a time and place so unlike their own. It was further proof to me, if ever I needed it, that words can continue to live long after they are written, and that love is recognizable from one generation to the next, however unfamiliar its wrappings. I would give this film four stars.

On the plane home from France, I saw two films by Claude Lelouch, *Roman de gare* (2007) and *Ces amours-là* (2011). I have been a Lelouch fan ever since I saw his breakthrough film *Un homme et une femme* (*A Man and a Woman*), which won the Palme d'Or at the 1966 Cannes Film Festival, as well as the Oscar for Best Foreign Language Film. At that time, as the mother of three small children with a fourth yet to come, I especially appreciated the familiarity that develops between the future lovers, both widowed, around their children attending the same boarding school. It was one of the first films I had ever seen that brought the lovers' children into the picture. I liked the slow disclosing of their past marital histories. I was particularly struck by the sensitive bedroom scene that shows the woman (played by Anouk Aimée) unable to continue with their lovemaking because she is still holding on to the memory of her dead husband. Usually cinematic lovemaking is presented as something that happens easily, leading to enormous female orgasms, without any suggestion that it can be problematic. The film was a winner then and still is.

Over forty years later, Claude Lelouch is still making films centered on love. *Roman de gare* (*Crossed Tracks*) is a quirky mystery story about a woman novelist (played by the inimitable Fanny Ardant), her ghostwriter (the smash-nosed Dominique Pinon), and an airhead hairdresser and sometime prostitute who drags the ghostwriter haplessly into her family drama. The plot is clever, the acting superb, the novelist gets her just deserts, and the ghostwriter ends up with the wayward woman. As in so many films, a tender kiss provides satisfying closure to the spectacle, even if one has few illusions about the future of the couple. Let's say, two and a half stars.

Lelouch's 2011 *Ces amours-là* (*What War May Bring*) rejoices in love on an epic scale. Focusing on the successive loves of just one woman named Ilva, it begins with her passionate affair with a German officer during the Occupation. On the one hand, the officer saves Ilva's father from execution as a hostage; on the other, Ilva's association with the German ultimately brings about her father's death at the hands of French partisans. When the Germans are finally forced out of Paris, she risks the fate of many publicly humiliated Frenchwomen, shorn of their hair as penance for their German lovers. Ilva is saved by two American soldiers— one white, one black. Since she can't choose between them, she goes to bed with both of them. Their spirited ménage à trois has a decidedly French amoralistic exuberance, until the plot turns tragic for one of the two men. Married to the other—I won't tell you which one—Ilva is unable to find happiness as an American bride. She returns to France for a third love experience, this time with a Frenchman who also turns out to be her savior. The plot is complicated. Are we expected to pass judgment on Ilva, who falls in love too easily and never foresees the negative consequences of her acts? Perhaps. Yet the film ends on an upbeat note. Lelouch situates it within the entire history of cinema, and particularly within his own oeuvre, from which numerous scenes flash by in the last minutes of the film. He offers us a jubilant finale created from diverse images of love *à la française*, all underscored by the vibrant strains of American popular music. Lelouch seems to be saying that whatever gruesome political realities we live through, whatever moral issues we face, passionate love will always endure. *Ces amours-là* is a frank celebration of love in an age when love itself, treasured for centuries, is now under attack. I give it three stars.

As I unpacked from another memorable French trip, I had no way of anticipating how much the French discourse on love would change during the next few months.

EPILOGUE

PHO ÇA ADAJ CA, L HO A'AOP HA IÈIA ADKOA.
THE MORE THINGS CHANGE, THE MORE THEY STAY THE SAME.

IN MAY 2011, FRANCE WAS JOLTED OUT of its age-old indulgence toward all forms of erotic behavior by the arrest of Dominique Strauss-Kahn, charged with having sexually assaulted a New York hotel housekeeper. Since Strauss-Kahn was the front-runner Socialist Party candidate for the 2012 presidential elections and considered nearly a shoo-in against the incumbent Nicolas Sarkozy, the shock that ran through France was seismic. It was one thing to have been a known womanizer, like so many French presidents, and quite another to have been arrested under suspicion of rape.

As a prominent politician, Strauss-Kahn had already been accused once before, in 2003, of swerving from gallantry to coercion, according to a young journalist's complaint that he had attacked her during an interview. At that time, she didn't press charges because her mother, a Socialist Party official, persuaded her not to. Also, during his tenure as managing director of the International Monetary Fund, he had a brief affair with a subordinate employee in 2008 and was subsequently rebuked by the IMF, though not dismissed because the affair was judged to be consensual. Through all of this, Strauss-Kahn's third wife, Anne Sinclair, stood loyally at his side.

In the wake of the 2011 New York scandal, the French began to question the conspiracy of silence surrounding the sexual indiscretions of their public figures. They had to consider the allegation that some men, especially powerful ones, not only expect erotic favors from their subordinates but sometimes use strong-arm methods to obtain their ends. Eventually the charges against Strauss-Kahn were dropped because it was discovered that his accuser had lied on several important issues, but French feminists were not about to forget this unsavory story: they seized the opportunity to make public pronouncements on the line between flirting and sexual aggression and hoped their clamor would cause men to think twice before forcing women into the bedroom.

This is obviously not the tawdry note I favor for the finale of a book on love. Coerced sex is not love. It is a form of violence against women, and sometimes against men. And yet, such is the complicated relationship between sex and love that the French have been known to conflate the two, and even to whitewash sexual acts committed through intimidation or brute force. The first reaction of a few French males to the Strauss-Kahn affair was to treat it as *une imprudence, comment dire: un troussage de domestique*—an imprudent act, like having sex with the maid.[1] Certainly there is a long history in France, as in other countries, of male employers taking advantage of female domestics. This can lead to pregnancies and bastard children, as in the case of Violette Leduc, but it rarely leads to love.

There has always been a cynical promotion of carnal pleasure in France, alongside the history of romantic love, ever since the latter was invented by twelfth-century troubadours. Consider *La clef d'amors* (*The Key to Love*), a medieval advice manual that even condones force. Here's some of its graphic counsel to men: "Once you have pressed your lips to hers / (Despite her long and loud demurs), / You must not stop at mere embrace: / Push on, pursue the rest apace." Like men in all centuries, the author condones the use of force by blithely assuming that the lady "really hopes you ignore / Her protests."[2]

This is the same mentality motivating Valmont in *Les liaisons dangereuses*. He will have his way with Madame de Tourvel regardless of the pain it will cause her. But in the end, his "victory" is also hers, for despite his denials, he falls in love with her. It is left to Madame de Merteuil to enlighten Valmont about the true nature of his feelings, and to unleash destructive justice.

For hundreds of years, sexual license in France was kept under loose control by the rules of courtly love, gallantry, and royal decree. As early as the fourteenth century, kings appointed their own official mistresses and looked the other way when members of their courts took lovers outside of marriage. Rarely did a king of France condemn the erotic adventures of his courtiers, unless that person tread upon territory the king himself coveted. Remember Henri IV, Bassompierre, and Mademoiselle de Montmorency in chapter 2. Even though the church took a different point of view and condemned any form of extramarital sex—sometimes even that of the royals—France has always been a country where sex has not only been tolerated but generally prized as part of the national character.

Love without sex is not a French invention. Leave it to the English, the Germans, and the Italians to project human love into the sphere of the angels. There is no French counterpart to Dante's divine Beatrice, Goethe's Eternal Feminine, or the British Angel in the House. Instead, sexually vibrant women in life and literature—such as Héloïse, Iseult, Guinevere, Diane de Poitiers, Julie de Lespinasse, Rousseau's Julie, Madame de Staël, George Sand, Madame Bovary, Colette, Simone de Beauvoir, and Marguerite Duras—have provided models for women in love. For men, Lancelot, Tristan, certain kings (notably François I, Henri II, Henri IV, Louis XIV, and Louis XV), Saint-Preux, Valmont, Lamartine, Julien Sorel, Musset, French movie stars and presidents have offered a conjoint set of virile models.

Yet, despite their emphasis on physical pleasure, most French have always understood love as something more than mere sexual satisfaction. Love privileges tender feelings, inspires esteem and fidelity, has the potential for uniting lovers permanently in enduring liaisons or lifelong marriage. Two such eighteenth-century unions that I haven't talked about (for lack of space) were that of Voltaire and Madame du Châtelet, an exceptionally distinguished pair who enjoyed a very long, multifaceted liaison, and that of the Comtesse de Sabran and the Chevalier de Boufflers, two lovers who surmounted huge obstacles for twenty years before they were able to marry.[3]

Loving marriages and liaisons that endured over time were probably as difficult to maintain in the past as they are today. George Sand called love a "miracle" requiring the surrender of two wills, so as to mingle and become one. She went so far as to compare love to religious faith, in that both share the ideal of eternity.

Well, eternity is a long time. Let us say that Sand held on to her idealistic vision of lasting love for the decade she spent with Chopin and then for the following fifteen years she shared with Manceau. To remain faithful to two men, successively, over a period of twenty-five years was not such a bad record for Sand.

A proper history of love in France would probably fill at least ten volumes. Most of these tomes would harbor romantic liaisons that were consummated in the flesh. But some, a small minority, would center on unconsummated loves. Consider, for example, the Princess de Clèves, who chose the ideal of love over its realistic fulfillment with the Duc de Nemours. Consider the youthful Félix de Vandenesse and the maternal Madame de Mortsauf in Balzac's *Lily of the Valley*. Consider the "white marriage" between André Gide and his wife, whom he professed to love until she died. Consider the characters in Eric Rohmer's films, such as *My Night at Maud's*, where talking about love preempts the sexual act.

For love in its infinite variety refuses to be bound by any outside notions of what it should be. It can take the form of irresistible passion and mutual ecstasy, or mental understanding and sweet harmony, or disharmonious jealousy and rage, to mention only some of its most notable forms. It can begin with silence, hesitation, double entendre, hidden desire, before finding the words that capture one's feelings. The formal declaration of love can be little more than a whispered "Je t'aime" or a drawn-out exposition designed to inspire a reciprocal declaration. When one says, "I love you," it is always in the hope that the beloved will feel the same way and repeat the magic formula.[4] The French, honoring Cyrano rather than Christian, tend to be fluent in love speech. For centuries, they have promoted love as an emotional and verbal engagement, a union of heart and mind, a passionate symphony that pulls out all the stops. Beethoven should have been French.

Mozart almost was, if you consider the fact that French culture dominated Europe during his lifetime, and that two of his most famous operas were based on French sources: *The Marriage of Figaro* and *Don Juan* captured the French amorous spirit to perfection. The first, based on Beaumarchais' play, is the consummate expression of French love as a game played between men and women, with men of power usually having the upper hand, but with clever women able to entrap them. In contrast, *Don Juan*, based on Molière's play, represents a more cynical, libertine attitude. Serial sex is all that Don Juan desires, and he enjoys it successfully for quite a while, but in the end, his quest for episodic pleasure is aborted. The gods of love condemn him, and take their revenge with his life.

TODAY, IT SEEMS, WE ARE LIVING THROUGH a period when the physical aspect of love tends to efface its emotional value. In both the United States and France, and elsewhere in the Western world, the trajectory goes something like this: first there is sex, then there is a lot of sex, then—sometimes—lovers learn to love. The French are going through a cynical period, similar to Flaubert's anti-romanticism, which is now infecting both women and men.

Still, even in this desolate environment, the ideal of love has not died. We find it most notably in cinema. There, film after film projects into the world the fundamentally French belief that love is the greatest of all endeavors, the most important thing on earth. Even unhappy love is preferable to no love at all. *La grande amoureuse*—we don't have an English word for the kind of woman who gives all to love—is admired, however catastrophic her behavior. The man who drives a thousand kilometers overnight, in Lelouch's film *A Man and a Woman*, to be with the woman he loves becomes something of a national hero. In 2010, the coastal city of Deauville celebrated that 1966 film on Valentine's Day by reenacting the beach scene in which the lovers are reunited. Journalist Elaine Scioloni was there with several hundred couples, including the mayor of Deauville and his wife, following a script that sent partners running toward each other across the beach for a voluptuous embrace. How's that for a civic event![5]

DURING THE SUMMER OF THE STRAUSS-KAHN AFFAIR, I found myself walking behind the Cathedral of Notre Dame and wondering how I could finish this book. Had love in France become little more than a myth? Were the French abandoning the ideal of "the great love" in favor of serial affairs? Had seduction won out over sentiment? And then my eye was drawn to a strange sight. I saw, attached to the grille on the Pont de l'Archevêché crossing the Seine, a forest of glittering objects, small padlocks with initials or names on them, sometimes with dates or hearts: C and K, Agnes & René, Barbara & Christian, Luni & Leo, Paul & Laura, 16–6–10. There must have been at least two or three thousand. And already, on the other side of the bridge, a few similar locks were clinging to the grille. How long before that side would also be completely covered?

I hung around, enchanted by the spectacle, and was rewarded by the sight of two youthful lovers, who came across the bridge arm in arm, affixed a lock to the grille, drank from each other's lips, and threw the key into the Seine.

ACKNOWLEDGMENTS

S OME OF THE MOST IMPORTANT PEOPLE WHO influenced this book are no longer alive. These include my high school French teacher, Mary Girard; my Wellesley College professors Andrée Bruel, Dorothy Dennis, Louis Hudon, and Edith Melchior; Professor René Jasinski at Harvard University; and Professor Nathan Edelman at Johns Hopkins University.

Others to whom I owe an immense debt of gratitude are my good French friends Philippe Martial, former head librarian of the French Senate, and Elisabeth Badinter, distinguished author and public intellectual.

At my Stanford University home base, I was able to count on the knowledge of Professors Keith Baker, Daniel Edelstein, Marisa Galvez, and Arnold Rampersad; Susan Groag Bell, Edith Gelles, and Karen Offen, senior scholars at the Clayman Institute for Gender Research; Romance Languages librarian Susan Sussman; Marie-Pierre Ulloa at the Stanford Humanities Center; mathematician Marguerite Frank; and psychiatrist Carl Greaves. Stanford undergraduate Alyssa Dougherty was the ideal research assistant.

A special thanks to Stanford professor emeritus René Girard, my doctoral dissertation director at Johns Hopkins and a source of inspiration ever since.

Writers Theresa Brown and Susan Griffin offered suggestions for the improvement of early chapters, as did medievalist Dorothy Gilbert for chapter 1. Constance Borde and Sheila Malovany-Chevallier, translators of Simone de Beauvoir's *The Second Sex*, read and critiqued the Beauvoir-Sartre chapter. The French journalist Hélène Fresnel and Stanford professor emeritus Marc Betrand pointed me in the direction of relevant French movies.

Emerita professor Kathleen Cohen of San Jose State University generously researched and provided many of the photos that appear in this book.

Larry Hatlett, my yoga instructor and friend of thirty years, provided enthusiastic support throughout the project.

My literary agent, Sandra Dijkstra, suggested that I write this book, and my editor at HarperCollins, Michael Signorelli, carefully shepherded it to completion.

My French daughter-in-law, Marie-Hélène Yalom, helped me with contemporary French colloquialisms. My son, Benjamin Yalom, added thoughtful comments on the manuscript, and my husband, Irvin Yalom, critiqued every word. Although he is challenged by the French language, he has shared my enthusiasm for French literature and appreciated the warm reception always offered us by our French friends.

ILLUSTRATIONS

Frontispiece

Two kinds of loving. Paintings by Edouard Manet and Honoré Daumier. Photograph copyright Kathleen Cohen.

Prologue

Tombstone of Abélard and Héloïse in Père-Lachaise Cemetery. Nineteenth-century engraving.

Chapter One

A lover gives his heart to his lady. Weaving, Arras, 1400–1401. Paris: Musée du Louvre. Copyright Kathleen Cohen.

Chapter Two

"Carte du Pays de Tendre" (Map of the Land of Tenderness). Mlle de Scudéry, *Clélie*, 1654.

Chapter Three

Front-page engraving of *L'école des femmes*, 1719 edition. From *Wikipedia*, "The School for Wives" entry.

Chapter Four

Jean-Honoré Fragonard, "The Happy Lovers," 1760–1765. Pasadena: Norton Simon Museum. Copyright Kathleen Cohen.

Chapter Five

Jean-Honoré Fragonard, "The Love Letter," circa 1770–1790. Copyright Kathleen Cohen.

Chapter Six

Republican couple going for a picnic. Circa 1790. Paris: Musée Carnavelet. Photograph by Hubert Josse.

Chapter Seven

Title page of Stendhal's *De l'amour* (*On Love*), 1822. Paris: Bibliothèque Nationale.

Chapter Eight

Romantic couple. Nineteenth-century color engraving. Signed M. Adolphe.

Chapter Nine

Flaubert dissecting the heart of Madame Bovary. Caricature by Achille Lemot. From *"Parodie,"* 1869. Paris: Bibliothèque Nationale.

Chapter Ten

Taverne Olympia poster, *La Revue blanche*, 1899. Copyright Kathleen Cohen.

Chapter Eleven

Verlaine and Rimbaud. Detail from *Un coin de table* by Henri Fantin-Latour, 1872. Paris: Musée d'Orsay. Copyright Kathleen Cohen.

Chapter Twelve

Painting of Marcel Proust by Jacques-Émile Blanche, 1892. Paris: Musée d'Orsay. Copyright Kathleen Cohen.

Chapter Thirteen

Colette at the Olympia, circa 1900. Photograph by Reuthinger. Paris: Musée d'Orsay. Copyright Kathleen Cohen.

Chapter Fourteen

Tombstone of Jean-Paul Sartre and Simone de Beauvoir. Montparnasse Cemetery, 2011. Author's photograph.

Chapter Fifteen

Girl on bicycle crossing a bridge in Vietnam built by Gustave Eiffel in 1904. Photograph by Reid S. Yalom, 2010.

Chapter Sixteen

Postcard: Paris Capitale des amoureux. LAPI–Roger Viollet/D/R.

Epilogue

Padlocks attached by lovers to grille on the Pont de l'Archevêché over the Seine, 2011. Author's photographs.

NOTES

Prologue

1. *The Letters of Abelard and Heloise*, trans. Betty Radice (London: Penguin Books, 1974), pp. 51–52. All citations from *The Letters* and Abélard's *Historia calamitatum* are from this translation.
2. François Villon, "Ballade des dames du temps jadis." My translation.
3. Louann Brizendine, *The Male Brain* (New York: Broadway Books, 2010).

Chapter One: Courtly Love

1. Jean-Claude Marol, *La fin'amor* (Paris: Le Seuil, 1998), p. 56. All English translations in this chapter are mine, except when otherwise indicated.
2. Ibid., p. 72.
3. Ibid., pp. 78–79.
4. Josy Marty-Dufaut, *L'amour au Moyen Age* (Marseille: Editions Autres Temps, 2002), p. 64.
5. Samuel N. Rosenberg and Hans Tischler, eds. and trans., *Chansons des trouvères*, (Paris: Le Livre de Poche, 1995), pp. 411, 403, 415.
6. Jacques Lafitte-Houssat, *Troubadours et cours d'amour* (Paris: PUF, 1979), p. 66.
7. Chrétien de Troyes, *Lancelot: The Knight of the Cart*, trans. Burton Raffel (New Haven, CT: Yale University Press, 1997).
8. Marty-Dufaut, *L'amour au Moyen Age*, pp. 20–21.
9. Rosenberg and Tischler, *Chansons des trouvères*, pp. 376–379.
10. Marie de France, "Equitan," *Lais* (Paris: Le Livre de Poche, 1990), pp. 80–81. My translation.

11. Marie de France, "Guigemar," *Lais*, pp. 28–29.

12. Emilie Amt, ed., *Women's Lives in Medieval Europe. A Sourcebook* (New York and London: Routledge, 1993), p. 83.

13. Ria Lemaire, "The Semiotics of Private and Public Matrimonial Systems and Their Discourse," in *Female Power in the Middle Ages: Proceedings from the 2d St. Gertrud Symposium*, ed. Karen Glente and Lise Winther-Jensen (Copenhagen: 1986), pp. 77–104.

14. Rosenberg and Tischler, *Chansons des trouvères*, pp. 80–81.

15. Ibid., pp. 84–87.

16. Denis de Rougemont, *Love in the Western World* (New York: Pantheon, 1956).

17. Elaine Sciolino, "Questions Raised About a Code of Silence," *New York Times*, May 17, 2011.

18. Elaine Sciolino, *La Seduction: How the French Play the Game of Life* (New York: Macmillan, 2011), pp. 229–230.

19. Elisabeth Badinter, *The Conflict: How Modern Motherhood Undermines the Status of Women* (New York: Metropolitan Books, 2012).

20. Diane Ackerman, *A Natural History of Love* (New York: Vintage Books, 1995), p. xix.

21. Michele Scheinkman, "Foreign Affairs," *Psychotherapy Networker*, July-August 2010, pp. 29–30.

22. Miriam Johnson, *Strong Mothers, Weak Wives* (Berkeley: University of California Press, 1988).

Chapter Two: Gallant Love

1. Cited by Maurice Daumas. *La tendresse amoureuse. XVIe–XVIIIe siècles* (Paris: Librairie Académique Perrin), 1996, p. 92. My translation. See also Henri IV, *Lettres d'amour et écrits politiques*, ed. Jean-Pierre Babylon (Paris: Fayard, 1988).

2. *Mémoires du Mareschal de Bassompierre*, vol. 1 (Cologne, 1663), p. 187.

3. Madame de La Fayette, *The Princess of Clèves*, trans. Terence Cave (New York: Oxford University Press, 1992), p. 14. All translations from *La Princess de Clèves* are from this work.

4. *The Princess of Cleves the Most Famous Romance: Written in French by the greatest wits of France; Rendred into English by a Person of Quality, at the Request of Some Friends* (London, 1679), cited by Cave, ibid., p. vii.

5. Pierre Darblay, *Physiologie de l'amour: étude physique, historique, et anecdotique* (Paris: Imprimerie Administrative et Commerciale, 1889), p. 74.

6. Alain Viala, *La France galante* (Paris: Presses Universitaires de France, 2008), pp. 9–10.

Chapter Three: Comic Love, Tragic Love

1. Molière, (*The School for Wives*, 1662). All translations from *Les précieuses ridicules* (*The Pretentious Young Ladies*, 1659), *L'école des maris* (*The Second School for Husbands*, 1661), and *L'école des femmes* (*The School for Wives*, 1662) are my own.

2. Molière, *The Misanthrope; and Tartuffe*, trans. Richard Wilbur (New York: Harcourt, Brace & World, 1965). Subsequent citations from *Le Misanthrope* are taken from this translation.

3. Jean Racine, *Phèdre*, trans. Timberlake Wertenbaker. Performed under the direction of Carey Perloff, American Conservatory Theater, San Francisco, 2010.

4. Jean Racine, *Phèdre*, trans. Ted Hughes (London: Faber and Faber, 1998). Subsequent citations from *Phèdre* are taken from this translation.

Chapter Four: Seduction and Sentiment

1. Gabriel Girard, "Amour," in ed. Gabriel Girard, Nicolas Beauzée, and Benoît Morin, *Dictionnaire universel des synonymes de la langue française: contenant les synonymes de Girard et ceux de Beauzée, Roubaud, Dalembert, Diderot* (Paris: Dabo, 1824), pp. 53–56.

2. Rémond de Saint-Mard, *Lettres galantes et philosophiques* (Cologne: Pierre Marteau, 1721), p. 132.

3. Edmond and Jules de Goncourt, *La femme au XVIIIe siècle* (Paris: Flammarion, 1982), p. 174. My translation.

4. Abbé Prévost, *Manon Lescaut*, trans. Angela Scholar (Oxford: Oxford University Press, 2004), p. 14. Subsequent citations from Prévost are from this translation.

5. Claude-Prosper Jolyot de Crébillon, *The Wayward Head and Heart*, trans. Barbara Bray (London: Oxford University Press, 1963), p. 5. Subsequent citations from Crébillon fils are from this translation.

6. Jean-Jacques Rousseau, *Julie, or The New Eloise*, trans. Judith H. McDowell

(University Park: Pennsylvania State University Press, 1968), part 1, XXIV, p. 68. Subsequent citations from Rousseau are from this translation.

7. Choderlos de Laclos, *Dangerous Acquaintances*, trans. Richard Aldington (New York: New Directions, 1957), p. 160.

Chapter Five: Love Letters

1. Julie de Lespinasse, *Lettres*, ed. Eugène Asse (Geneva: Slatkine Reprints, 1994), p. 91. Subsequent citations from Lespinasse, d'Alembert, and Guibert are my translations from this edition.

2. For a fuller version of her life, see Duc de Castries, *Julie de Lespinasse: le drame d'un double amour* (Paris: Albin Michel, 1985). See also Marie-Christine d'Aragon and Jean Lacouture, *Julie de Lespinasse: Mourir d'amour* (Brussels: Editions Complexe, 2006).

3. Cited by Aragon and Lacouture, pp. 128–129; from David Hume, *Private Correspondence of David Hume with Several Distinguished Persons, Between the Years 1761 and 1776* (London, Henry Colburn, 1820).

4. Cited by Aragon and Lacouture, p. 132; from Voltaire, *Correspondance générale* (Paris: Garnier, 1877).

5. Elisabeth Badinter, *Les passions intellectuelles*, vol. 2 (Paris: Fayard, 2002), pp. 17–20.

6. Cited by Aragon and Lacouture, p. 299; from d'Alembert's letter of June 29, 1776. Archives du Comte de Villeneuve-Guibert.

Chapter Six: Republican Love

1. Marilyn Yalom, *Le temps des orages: aristocrates, bourgeoises, et paysannes racontent* (Paris: Maren Sell, 1989); Marilyn Yalom, *Blood Sisters: The French Revolution in Women's Memory* (New York: Basic Books, 1993).

2. Elisabeth Duplay Le Bas, "Manuscrit de Mme Le Bas" in *Autour de Robespierre. Le conventionnel Le Bas*, ed Stéfane-Pol (Paris: Flammarion, 1901), pp. 102–150. My translation.

3. Madame Roland, *Mémoires de Madame Roland*, ed. Paul de Roux (Paris: Mercure de France, 1986). My translation.

4. Marilyn Yalom, *A History of the Breast* (New York: Knopf, 1997), chap. 4.

Chapter Seven: Yearning for the Mother

1. Benjamin Constant, *Adolphe*, trans. Margaret Mauldon (Oxford: Oxford University Press, 2001), pp. 31–39. All citations from *Adolphe* are from this editon.

2. Marilyn Yalom, "Triangles and Prisons: A Psychological Study of Stendhalian Love," *Hartford Studies in Literature* 8, no. 2 (1976).

3. Stendhal, *The Life of Henry Brulard*, trans. Jean Steward and B. C. J. G. Knight (New York: Minerva Press, 1968), p. 22.

4. Stendhal, *Le rouge et le noir* (Paris: Michel Lévy, Frères, 1866), p. 85. My translation.

5. Honoré de Balzac, *Le lys dans la vallée* (Paris: Classiques Garnier, 1966), p. 5. My translation.

6. Sylvain Mimoun and Rica Etienne, *Sexe & sentiments après 40 ans* (Paris: Albin Michel, 2009), pp. 20–24.

Chapter Eight: Love Among the Romantics

1. The translations from Lamartine's poems are my own.

2. George Sand, *Oeuvres autobiographiques*, ed. Georges Lubin (Paris: Gallimard, 1970), 2 vols. My translations. See also Sand, *Story of My Life: The Autobiography of George Sand. A Group Translation*, ed. Thelma Jurgrau (Albany, NY: SUNY Press, 1991).

3. George Sand, "Lettre à Emile Regnault, 23 Janvier, 1832," *Correspondance [de] George Sand*, vol. 2, ed. Georges Lubin (Paris: Garnier Frères, 1964–), p. 12. All subsequent references to Sand's letters are from this multivolume correspondence.

4. George Sand, *Indiana*, trans. Eleanor Hochman, preface Marilyn Yalom (New York: Signet Classic, Penguin Books, 1993). Subsequent citations are from this edition.

5. George Sand, *Lélia*. Translated by Maria Espinosa (Bloomington: Indiana University Press, 1978).

6. George Sand, *Journal intime*, in Lubin, *Oeuvres autobiographiques*, vol. 2, pp. 953–971; my translation. See also *The Intimate Journal*, trans. Marie Jenney Howe (Chicago: Cassandra Editions, 1977).

7. Alfred de Musset, *La confession d'un enfant du siècle* (Paris: Classiques Garnier, 1960). My translation.

8. E. O. Hellerstein et al., eds., *Victorian Women: A Documentary Account of Women's Lives in Nineteenth-Century England, France and the United States* (Stanford, CA: Stanford University Press, 1981), pp. 254–255.

Chapter Nine: Romantic Love Deflated

1. Gustave Flaubert, *Lettres à sa maîtresse*, vol. 3 (Rennes: La Part Commune, 2008), p. 425.
2. Stendhal, *De l'amour* (Paris: Garnier Frères, 1959), pp. 8–9.
3. Gustave Flaubert, *Madame Bovary*, trans. Lydia Davis (New York: Viking, 2010).

Chapter Ten: Love in the Gay Nineties

1. Pierre Darblay, *Physiologie de l'amour: étude physique, historique, et anecdotique* (Pau: Imprimerie Administrative et Commerciale, 1889), p. 83.
2. Roger Shattuck, *The Banquet Years: The Origins of the Avant-Garde in France, 1885 to World War I* (Garden City, NY: Anchor Books, 1961), p. 6.
3. Edmond Rostand, *Cyrano de Bergerac*, ed. Leslie Ross Méras (New York and London: Harper & Brothers, 1936). The most recent English translation is by Lowell Blair (New York: New American Library, 2003). All translations from *Cyrano* are my own.

Chapter Eleven: Love Between Men

1. Jonathan Fryer, *André & Oscar: Gide, Wilde, and the Gay Art of Living* (London: Constable, 1997), p. 144.
2. Michel de Montaigne, *The Complete Essays*, trans. M. A. Screech (London: Penguin Books, 1991), pp. 208–209, 211–212.
3. Bryant T. Ragan Jr., "The Enlightenment Confronts Homosexuality," in eds. Jeffrey Merrick and Bryant T. Ragan Jr., *Homosexuality and Modern France* (New York and Oxford: Oxford University Press, 1996), pp. 8–29.
4. Cited by Michael David Sibalis, "The Regulation of Male Homosexuality in Revolutionary and Napoleonic France, 1789–1815," in Merrick and Ragan, ibid., p. 81.
5. Cited by Jacob Stockinger, "Homosexuality and the French Enlightenment," in eds. George Stambolian and Elaine Marks, *Homosexualities in French Literature* (Ithaca, NY: Cornell University Press, 1979), p. 168.

6. Jean Delay, *The Youth of André Gide*, trans. June Guicharnaud (Chicago and London: University of Chicago Press), 1963, p. 289.

7. André Gide, *L'immoraliste* (Paris: Mercure de France, 1946). My translation. For an English version, see Gide, *The Immoralist*, trans. Richard Howard (New York: Knopf, 1970).

8. Monique Nemer, *Corydon citoyen: essai sur André Gide et l'homosexualité* (Paris: Gallimard, 2006), p. 27.

9. Cited by Wallace Fowlie in *André Gide: His Life and His Art* (New York: Macmillan, 1965), p. 168.

Chapter Twelve: Desire and Despair

1. Marcel Proust, *Remembrance of Things Past*, vol. 1, trans. C. K. Scott Montcrief, Terence Kilmartin, and Andreas Mayor (New York: Vintage Books, 1982), p. 24. All Proust translations are from this magnificent three-volume edition.

2. Nicolas Grimaldi, *Proust, les horreurs de l'amour* (Paris: Presses Universitaires de France, 2008).

3. André Gide, *Journal, 1889–1939*, vol. 1 (Paris: Gallimard, 1951), pp. 691–692.

4. I am indebted for this observation and others to William C. Carter, *Proust in Love* (New Haven, CT: Yale University Press, 2006), p. 100.

5. Gaëtan Picon, *Lecture de Proust* (Paris: Gallimard, 1995), p. 131.

6. André Aciman, ed., *The Proust Project* (New York: Farrar, Straus, and Giroux, 2004), p. x.

Chapter Thirteen: Lesbian Love

1. Quoted by Tirz True Latimer in *Women Together/Women Apart: Portraits of Lesbian Paris* (New Brunswick, NJ: Rutgers University Press, 2005), p. 42.

2. Colette, *My Apprenticeships & Music-Hall Sidelights* (Harmondsworth, UK: Penguin Books, 1967), p. 55.

3. Ibid., p. 57.

4. Colette, *Claudine at School,* trans. Antonia White (Harmondsworth, UK: Penguin Books, 1972), p. 16. Further citations are from this edition.

5. Colette, *Claudine Married*, trans. Antonia White (New York: Farrar, Straus and Cudahy, 1960), pp. 93–94. Further citations are from this translation.

6. Elaine Marks, "Lesbian Intertextuality," in George Stambolian and Elaine Marks, *Homosexualities and French Literature* (Ithaca, NY: Cornell University Press, 1979), p. 363.

7. *Le Cri de Paris*, December 2, 1906, cited in Colette, *Lettres à Missy*, ed. Samia Birdji and Frédéric Maget (Paris: Flammarion, 2009), p. 17. My translation.

8. Quoted by Judith Thurman, *Secrets of the Flesh: A Life of Colette* (New York: Knopf, 1999), p. 136. Taken from Sido, *Lettres à sa fille* (Paris: des Femmes, 1984), p. 76.

9. This and the following quotations from Colette's letters are my translations from Birdji and Maget, eds., *Lettres à Missy*.

10. *The Vagabond*, trans. Enid McLeod (New York: Farrar, Straus & Giroux, 2001), p. 126.

11. Renate Stendhal, ed., *Gertrude Stein in Words and Pictures* (Chapel Hill, NC: Algonquin Books of Chapel Hill, 1994), p. 156.

12. Gertrude Stein and Alice B. Toklas, *Baby Precious Always Shines*, ed. Kay Turner (New York: St. Martin's Press, 1999).

13. Violette Leduc, *La Bâtarde*, trans. Derek Coltman (New York: Farrar, Strauss, and Giroux, 1965), p. 348.

14. Isabelle de Courtivron, "From Bastard to Pilgrim: Rites and Writing for Madame," in Hélène Vivienne Wenzel, ed., *Simone de Beauvoir: Witness to a Century*, Yale French Studies, no. 72 (New Haven, CT: Yale University Press, 1987), p. 138.

15. Deirdre Bair, *Simone de Beauvoir. A Biography* (New York: Simon and Schuster, 1990), p. 505.

Chapter Fourteen: Existentialists in Love

1. Simone de Beauvoir, *Memoirs of a Dutiful Daughter*, trans. James Kirkup (New York: Harper & Row, 1959), p. 339.

2. Ibid., p. 345.

3. Simone de Beauvoir, *The Prime of Life*, trans. Peter Green (New York: Harper & Row, 1962), p. 24.

4. Jean-Paul Sartre, *Lettres au Castor et à quelques autres*, vols. 1–2 (Paris: Gallimard, 1983); Simone de Beauvoir, *Lettres à Sartre*, ed. Sylvie Le Bon de Beauvoir (Paris: Gallimard, 1990).

5. Hazel Rowley, *Tête-à-Tête. The Tumultuous Lives and Loves of Simone de Beauvoir and Jean-Paul Sartre* (New York: HarperCollins, 2005).

6. Jean-Paul Sartre, *Quiet Moments in a War: The Letters of Jean-Paul Sartre to Simone de Beauvoir 1940–1963* (New York: Scribner's, 1993), pp. 273–274.

7. Beauvoir, *The Prime of Life*, p. 55.

8. Deirdre Bair, *Simone de Beauvoir: A Biography* (New York: Simon and Shuster, 1990), p. 333.

9. Simone de Beauvoir, *A Transatlantic Love Affair: Letters to Nelson Algren* (New York: New Press, 1998).

10. Bianca Lamblin, *A Disgraceful Affair*, trans. Julie Plovnick (Boston: Northeastern University Press, 1996).

11. Cited by Rowley, *Tête-à-Tête*, p. 335.

12. Simone de Beauvoir, *The Second Sex*, trans. Constance Borde and Sheila Malovany-Chevallier (New York: Knopf, 2010).

13. Simone de Beauvoir, *Adieux: A Farewell to Sartre*, trans. Patrick O'Brian (London: André Deutsch/Weidenfeld & Nicolson, 1984), preface.

14. Bair, *Simone de Beauvoir*, p. 183.

Chapter Fifteen: The Dominion of Desire

1. Marguerite Duras, *10:30 on a Summer Night*, trans. Anne Borchardt, in *Four Novels by Marguerite Duras* (New York: Grove Press, 1978), p. 165. Subsequent translations of this novella are from this edition.

2. Marguerite Duras, *Moderato Cantabile*, trans. Richard Seaver, in ibid., p. 81. Subsequent translations from this novella are from this edition.

3. Marguerite Duras, *The Lover*, trans. Barbara Bray (New York: Pantheon Books, 1997), p. 32. Subsequent translations from this novel are from this edition.

4. Laure Adler, *Marguerite Duras: A Life*, trans. Anne-Marie Glasheen (London: Victor Gollancz, 1998), pp. 53–67.

Chapter Sixteen: Love in the Twenty-first Century

1. Paul Claudel, *Partage de midi* (Paris: Gallimard, 1949), p. 7.

2. Philippe Sollers, *Trésor d'amour* (Paris: Gallimard, 2011).

3. René Girard, *Deceit, Desire, and the Novel*, trans. Yvonne Freccero (Baltimore: Johns Hopkins University Press, 1965).

4. Michel Houellebecq, *The Elementary Particles*, trans. Frank Wynne (New York: Vintage, 2000), prologue.

5. Virginie Despentes, *King Kong Théorie* (Paris: Grasset, 2006), p. 9. My translation.

6. Citations from publicity distributed by *Nord/Ouest Documentaires*.

Epilogue

1. Words attributed to Jean-François Kahn, *Le Point*, May 26, 2011.

2. *The Key to Love*, in *The Comedy of Eros: Medieval French Guides to the Art of Love*, trans. Norman R. Shapiro (Urbana and Chicago: University of Illinois Press, 1997), p. 37.

3. Sue Carrell, ed., *La Comtesse de Sabran et le Chevalier de Boufflers: Correspondance*. Vol. 1, *1777–1785*; Vol. 2, *1786–1787* (Paris: Tallandier, 2009, 2010).

4. "Je t'aime: enquête sur une déclaration universelle," *Philosophie*, April 2011.

5. Elaine Sciolino, *La Seduction*, pp. 54–57.

Selected Bibliography

Primary Sources in English Translation

Abelard, Peter, and Heloise. *The Letters of Abelard and Heloise.* Translated by Betty Radice. New York : Penguin, 2003.

Balzac, Honoré de. *The Lily of the Valley.* [1835] Translated by Lucienne Hill. New York: Carroll & Graf Publishers, 1997.

Beauvoir, Simone de. *Adieux: A Farewell to Sartre.* Translated by Patrick O'Brian. London: André Deutsch/Weidenfeld & Nicolson, 1984.

_____. *All Said and Done.* Translated by Patrick O'Brian. New York: Warner Books, 1975.

_____. *Force of Circumstance.* Translated by Richard Howard. New York: Putnam's, 1964.

_____. *Letters to Sartre.* Translated by Quintin Hoare. London, Sydney, Auckland, Johannesburg: Radius, 1991.

_____. *Memoirs of a Dutiful Daughter.* Translated by James Kirkup. New York: Harper & Row, 1959.

_____. *The Prime of Life.* Translated by Peter Green. New York: Harper & Row, 1962.

_____. *The Second Sex.* Translated by Constance Borde and Sheila Malovany-Chevallier. New York: Knopf, 2010.

_____. *A Transatlantic Love Affair: Letters to Nelson Algren.* Translated by Sylvie Le Bon de Beauvoir. New York: New Press, 1998.

Béroul, *The Romance of Tristan.* Translated by Alan S. Fedrick. Harmondsworth, UK: Penguin, 1970.

Capellanus, Andreas. *The Art of Courtly Love.* Translated by John Jay Parry. New York: Columbia University Press, 1994.

Chrétien de Troyes. *Lancelot: The Knight of the Cart.* Translated by Burton Raffel. New Haven: Yale University Press, 1997.

Colette. *Claudine at School.* [1900] Translated by Antonia White. Harmondsworth, UK: Penguin Books, 1972.

_____. *Claudine in Paris.* [1901] Translated by Antonia White. Harmondsworth, UK: Penguin Books, 1972.

_____. *Claudine Married.* [1902] Translated by Antonia White. New York: Farrar, Straus and Cudahy, 1960.

_____. *My Apprenticeships and Music-Hall Sidelights.* [1936 and 1913] Translated by Helen Beauclerk and Anne-Marie Callimachi. Harmondsworth, UK: Penguin Books, 1967.

_____ *The Pure and the Impure.* [1941] Translated by Herman Briffault. New York: Farrar, Straus & Giroux, 1966.

_____ *The Vagabond.* [1910] Translated by Enid McLeod. New York: Farrar, Straus & Giroux, 2001.

Constant, Benjamin. *Adolphe.* [1816] Translated by Margaret Mauldon. Oxford: Oxford University Press, 2001.

Crébillon Fils. *The Wayward Head and Heart.* [1736 and 1738] Translated by Barbara Bray. Oxford: Oxford University Press, 1963.

Duras, Marguerite. *Four Novels by Marguerite Duras.* Includes *10:30 on a Summer Night.* Translated by Anne Borchardt. Includes *Moderato Cantabile.* Translated by Richard Seaver. New York: Grove Press, 1978.

_____. *The Lover.* Translated by Barbara Bray. New York: Pantheon Books, 1997.

Flaubert, Gustave. *Madame Bovary.* [1857] Translated by Lydia Davis. New York: Viking, 2010.

Gide, André. *Corydon.* [1924] Translated by Hugh Gibb. New York: Farrar Straus, 1950.

_____. *Fruits of the Earth.* [1897] Translated by D. Bussy. New York: Knopf, 1949.

_____. *If It Die.* [1926] Translated by D. Bussy. New York: Random House, 1935.

_____. *The Immoralist*. [1902] Translated by Richard Howard. New York: Knopf, 1970.

Houellebecq, Michel. *The Elementary Particles*. Translated by Frank Wynne. New York: Vintage, 2000.

Laclos, Choderlos de. *Dangerous Acquaintances*. [1782] Translated by Richard Aldington. New York: New Directions, 1957.

Lafayette, Madame de. *The Princess de Clèves*. [1678] Translated by Terence Cave. New York: Oxford University Press, 1992.

Lamblin, Bianca. *A Disgraceful Affair. Simone de Beauvoir, Jean-Paul Sartre, and Bianca Lamblin*. Translated by Julie Plovnick. Boston: Northeastern University Press, 1996.

La Rochefoucauld. *Maxims*. Translated by Stuart D. Warner and Stéphane Douard. Southbend, IN: St. Augustine's Press, 2001.

Leduc, Violette. *La Bâtarde*. Translated by Derek Coltman. New York: Farrar, Strauss, and Giroux, 1965.

Lespinasse, Julie de. *Love Letters of Mlle de Lespinasse to and from the Comte de Guibert*. Translated by E.H.F. Mills. New York: The Dial Press, 1929.

Marie de France. *The Lais of Marie de France*. Translated by Glyn S. Burgess and Keith Busby. Harmondsworth and New York: Penguin Classics, 1986.

Miller, Catherine. *The Sexual Life of Catherine M*. Translated by Adriana Hunter. New York: Grove Press, 2002.

_____. *Jealousy: The Other Life of Catherine M*. Translated by Helen Stevenson. London: Serpent's Tail, 2009.

Molière. *"The Misanthrope" and "Tartuffe"*. [1666 and 1664] Translated by Richard Wilbur. New York: Harcourt, Brace, & World, 1965.

Montaigne, Michel de. *The Complete Essays*. Translated by M. A. Screech. London: Penguin Books, 1991.

Musset, Alfred de. *The Confession of a Child of the Century*. [1836] Translated by Kendall Warren. Chicago: C. H. Sergel, 1892.

Prévost, Abbé. *The Story of the Chevalier des Grieux and Manon Lescaut*. [1731] Translated by Angela Scholar. Oxford: Oxford University Press, 2004.

Proust, Marcel. *Remembrance of Things Past*. [1913–1927] Translated by C. K. Scott Moncrieff, Terence Kilmartin, and Andreas Mayor. New York: Vintage Books, 1982.

Racine, Jean. *Phèdre.* [1677] Translated by Ted Hughes. London: Faber and Faber, 1998.

Rostand, Edmond. *Cyrano de Bergerac.* [1897] Translated by Lowell Blair. New York: New American Library, 2003.

Rousseau, Jean-Jacques. *Julie, or The New Eloise.* Translated by Judith H. McDowell. University Park: Pennsylvania State University Press, 1968.

Sand, George. *Indiana.* [1832] Translated by Eleanor Hochman. New York: Signet Classic, Penguin Books, 1993.

_____. *The Intimate Journal.* [1834] Translated by Marie Jenney Howe. Chicago: Cassandra Editions, 1977.

_____. *Lélia.* [1833] Translated by Maria Espinosa. Bloomington: Indiana University Press: 1978.

_____. *Story of My Life: The Autobiography of George Sand. A Group Translation.* [1854–1855] Edited by Thelma Jurgrau. Albany, NY: SUNY Press, 1991.

Sartre, Jean-Paul. *Existentialism and Humanism.* Translated by Philip Mairet. London: Methuen, 1948.

_____. *No Exit and Three Other Plays, The Flies, Dirty Hands, The Respectful Prostitute.* New York: Vintage, 1989.

_____. *Quiet Moments in a War: The Letters of Jean-Paul Sartre to Simone de Beauvoir 1940–1963.* Edited by Simone de Beauvoir and translated by Lee Fahnestock and Norman MacAfee. New York: Scribner's, 1993.

_____. *Witness to My Life: The Letters of Jean-Paul Sartre to Simone de Beauvoir 1926–1939.* Edited by Simone de Beauvoir and translated by Lee Fahnestock and Norman MacAfee. New York: Scribner's, 1992.

_____. *The Words.* Translated by Irene Clephane. London: Penguin, 1967.

Stein, Gertrude. *The Autobiography of Alice B. Toklas.* [1933] New York: Vintage Books, 1990.

_____ and Alice B. Toklas. *Baby Precious Always Shines. Selected Love Notes.* Edited by Kay Turner. New York: St. Martin's Press, 1999.

_____. *Three Lives.* [1909] Copenhagen and Los Angeles: Green Integer, 2004.

Stendhal. *The Charterhouse of Parma.* [1839] Translated by Richard Howard. New York: Modern Library, 1999.

_____. *The Life of Henry Brulard*. [1890] Translated by Jean Steward and B. C. J. G Knight. New York: Minerva Press, 1968.

_____. *On Love*. [1822] Translated by Gilbert and Suzanne Sale. New York: Penguin Books, 1975.

_____. *The Red and the Black*. [1830] Translated by Roger Gard. New York: Penguin, 2002.

SECONDARY SOURCES IN ENGLISH

Aciman, André, ed. *The Proust Project*. New York: Farrar, Straus and Giroux, 2004.

Ackerman, Diane. *A Natural History of Love*. New York: Random House, 1994.

Adler, Laure. *Marguerite Duras: A Life*. Translated by Anne-Marie Glasheen. London: Victor Gollancz, 2000.

Amt, Emilie, ed. *Women's Lives in Medieval Europe. A Sourcebook*. New York and London: Routledge, 1993.

Armstrong, John. *Conditions of Love: The Philosophy of Intimacy*. New York and London: Norton, 2002.

Badinter, Elisabeth. *The Conflict: How Motherhood Undermines the Status of Women*. New York: Metropolitan Books, 2012.

Barthes, Roland. *On Racine*. Translated by Richard Howard. New York: Hill and Wang, 1964.

Benstock, Shari. *Women of the Left Bank. Paris, 1900–1940*. Austin: University of Texas Press, 1986.

Bloch, R. Howard. *Medieval Misogyny and the Invention of Western Romantic Love*. Chicago: University of Chicago Press, 1991.

Brée, Germaine. *Gide*. New Brunswick, NJ: Rutgers University Press, 1963.

Brooke, Christopher. *The Twelfth Century Renaissance*. London: Thames and Hudson, 1969.

Campbell, John. *Questions of Interpretation in "La Princesse de Clèves."* Amsterdam and Atlanta, GA: Editions Rodopi, 1996.

Carter, William C. *Marcel Proust. A Life*. New Haven and London: Yale University Press, 2000.

_____. *Proust in Love*. New Haven and London: Yale University Press, 2006.

Chalon, Jean. *Portrait of a Seductress: The World of Natalie Barney*. Translated by Carol Barko. New York: Crown, 1979.

De Courtivron, Isabelle. *Violette Leduc*. Boston: Twayne, 1985.

Delay, Jean. *The Youth of André Gide*. Translated and abridged by June Guicharnaud. Chicago and London: University of Chicago Press, 1963.

Dickenson, Donna. *George Sand: A Brave Man, a Most Womanly Woman*. Oxford, New York, and Hamburg: Berg, 1988.

Dock, Terry Smiley. *Woman in the Encyclopédie. A Compendium*. Potomac, MD: Studia Humanitatis, 1983.

Faderman, Lillian. *Surpassing the Love of Men: Romantic Friendship and Love Between Women from the Renaissance to the Present*. New York: Morrow, 1981.

Fryer, Jonathan. *André & Oscar: Gide, Wilde, and the Gay Art of Living*. London: Constable, 1997.

Fuchs, Jeanne. *The Pursuit of Virtue: A Study of Order in La Nouvelle Héloïse*. New York: Peter Lang, 1993.

Galvez, Marisa. *Songbook: How Lyrics Became Poetry in Medieval Europe*. Chicago and London: University of Chicago Press, forthcoming.

Gifford, Paul. *Love, Desire and Transcendence in French Literature: Deciphering Eros*. Aldershot, UK, and Burlington, VT: Ashgate Publishing, 2005.

Girard, René. *Deceit, Desire, and the Novel*. Translated by Yvonne Freccero. Baltimore: Johns Hopkins University Press, 1965.

Glente, Karen, and Winther-Jensen, Lise, editors. *Female Power in the Middle Ages*. Copenhagen: St. Gertrud Symposium, 1986.

Guerard, Albert. *André Gide*. Cambridge, MA: Harvard University Press, 1951.

Herold, J. Christopher. *Mistress to an Age. A Life of Madame de Staël*. Indianapolis and New York: Charter Books, 1958.

Hill, Leslie. *Marguerite Duras. Apocalyptic Desires*. London and New York: Routledge, 1993.

Latimer, Tirza True. *Women Together/Women Apart: Portraits of Lesbian Paris*. New Brunswick, NJ: Rutgers University Press, 2005.

Lucey, Michael. *Never Say I: Sexuality and the First Person in Colette, Gide, and Proust*. Durham, NC: Duke University Press, 2006.

Martin, Joseph. *Napoleonic Friendship: Military Fraternity, Intimacy and Sexuality in Nineteenth-Century France*. Durham, NH: University of New Hampshire Press, 2011.

May, Simon. *Love: A History*. New Haven: Yale University Press, 2011.

Merrick, Jeffrey, and Bryant Ragan, Jr., eds. *Homosexuality in Modern France.* New York and Oxford: Oxford University Press, 1996.

Meyers, Jeffrey. *Homosexuality and Literature, 1890–1930.* London: Athlone Press, 1977.

Moore, John C. *Love in Twelfth-Century France.* Philadelphia: University of Pennsylvania Press, 1972.

Nehring, Cristina. *A Vindication of Love: Reclaiming Romance for the Twenty-first Century.* New York: HarperCollins, 2009.

Owen, D. D. R. *Noble Lovers.* New York: New York University Press, 1975.

Porter, Laurence M., and Eugene F. Gray, eds. *Approaches to Teaching Flaubert's "Madame Bovary."* New York: Modern Language Association of America, 1995.

Roberts, Mary Louise. *Civilization Without Sexes: Reconstructing Gender in Postwar France, 1917–1927.* Chicago and London: University of Chicago Press, 1994.

_____. *Disruptive Acts: The New Woman in Fin-de-Siècle France.* Chicago: University of Chicago Press, 2002.

Rougemont, Denis de. *Love in the Western World.* New York: Pantheon, 1956.

Rowley, Hazel. *Tête-à-Tête: The Tumultuous Lives and Loves of Simone de Beauvoir and Jean-Paul Sartre.* New York: HarperCollins, 2005.

Sarde, Michèle. *Colette: Free and Fettered.* Translated by Richard Miller. New York: William Morrow, 1980.

Seymour-Jones, Carole. *A Dangerous Liaison: A Revelatory New Biography of Simone de Beauvoir and Jean-Paul Sartre.* New York: Overlook Press/Peter Myer Publishers, 2009.

Shapiro, Norman R., editor and translator. *French Women Poets of Nine Centuries: The Distaff and the Pen.* Baltimore: John Hopkins University Press, 2008.

Shattuck, Roger. *The Banquet Years: The Origins of the Avant-Garde in France, 1885 to World War I.* New York: Harcourt Brace, 1955.

Skinner, Cornelia Otis. *Elegant Wits and Grand Horizontals.* Boston: Houghton Mifflin, 1962.

Stendhal, Renate. *Gertrude Stein in Words and Pictures.* Chapel Hill, NC: Algonquin Books of Chapel Hill, 1994.

Stambolian, George, and Elaine Marks, eds. *Homosexualities and French Literature: Cultural Contexts, Critical Texts.* Ithaca, NY: Cornell University Press, 1979.

Thurman, Judith. *Secrets of the Flesh: A Life of Colette*. New York: Knopf, 1999.

Vircondelet, Alain. *Duras: A Biography*. Translated by Thomas Buckley. Normal, IL: Dalkey Archive Press, 1994.

Wenzel, Hélène Vivienne, ed. *Simone de Beauvoir: Witness to a Century*. Yale French Studies, No. 72. New Haven, CT: Yale University Press, 1986.

Wickes, George. *The Amazon of Letters: The Life and Loves of Natalie Barney*. New York: Putnam, 1976.

Winegarten, Renée. *Germaine de Staël and Benjamin Constant*. New Haven: Yale University Press, 2008.

Yalom, Marilyn. *Birth of the Chess Queen*. New York: HarperCollins, 2004.

_____. *Blood Sisters: The French Revolution in Women's Memory*. New York: Basic Books, 1993.

_____. *A History of the Breast*. New York: Knopf, 1997.

_____. *A History of the Wife*. New York: HarperCollins, 2001.

FRENCH SOURCES THAT DO NOT EXIST IN ENGLISH

Apostolidès, Jean-Marie. *Cyrano: qui fut tout et qui ne fut rien*. Paris: Les Impressions Nouvelles, 2006.

Bruel, Andrée. *Romans français du Moyen Age*. Paris: Librairie E. Droz, 1934.

Castries, Réne. *Julie de Lespinasse: le drame d'un double amour*. Paris: Albin Michel, 1985.

Chalon, Jean. *Chère George Sand*. Paris: Flammarion, 1991.

Colette. *Lettres à Missy*. Ed. Samia Bordji and Frédéric Maget. Paris: Flammarion, 2009.

Conte-Stirling, Graciela. *Colette ou la force indestructible de la femme*. Paris: L'Harmattan, 2002.

Darblay, Pierre. *Physiologie de l'amour: étude physique, historique, et anecdotique*. Pau: Imprimerie Administrative et Commerciale, 1889.

Daumas, Maurice. *La tendresse amoureuse, XVIe–XVIIIe siècles*. Paris: Librairie Académique Perrin, 1996.

Delcourt, Thierry. *Le roi Arthur et les chevaliers de la table ronde*. Paris: Bibliothèque Nationale de France, 2009.

Flaubert, Gustave. *Lettres à sa maîtresse*, vol. 3. Rennes: La Part Commune, 2008.

Godard, Didier. *L'amour philosophique: l'homosexualité masculine au siècle des Lumières*. Bêziers: H & O editions, 2005.

Grellet, Isabelle, and Caroline Kruse. *La déclaration d'amour*. Paris: Plon, 1990.

Grimaldi, Nicolas. *Proust: les horreurs de l'amour*. Paris: Presses Universitaires de France, 2008.

Grossel, Marie-Geneviève, ed. *Chansons d'amour du Moyen Age*. Paris: Livre de Poche, 1995.

Lacouture, Jean and Marie-Christine d'Aragon. *Julie de Lespinasse: mourir d'amour*. Brussels: Editions Complexe, 2006.

Lafitte-Houssat, Jacques. *Troubadours et cours d'amour*. Paris: PUF, 1979.

Lespinasse, Julie de. *Lettres*. Ed. Eugène Asse. Geneva: Slatkine Reprints, 1994.

Lorenz, Paul. *Sapho 1900: Renée Vivien*. Paris: Julliard, 1977.

Marol, Jean-Claude. *La fin'amor: Chants de troubadours, XIIe et XIIIe siècles*. Paris: Editions du Seuil, 1998.

Marty-Dufaut, Josy. *L'amour au Moyen Age*. Marseille: Editions Autres Temps, 2002.

Mimoun, Sylvain, and Rica Etienne. *Sexe et sentiments après 40 ans*. Paris: Albin Michel, 2011.

Morin, Benoît. *Dictionnaire universel des synonymes de la langue française: contenant les synonymes de Girard et ceux de Beauzée, Roubaud, Dalembert, Diderot*. Paris: Dabo, 1824.

Nelli, René. *Troubadours et trouvères*. Paris: Hachette, 1979.

Nemer, Monique. *Corydon Citoyen: essai sur André Gide et l'homosexualité*. Paris: Gallimard, 2006.

Pougy, Liane de. *Idylle Saphique*. [1901] Paris: Editions Jean-Claude Lattès, 1979.

Richard, Guy, and Annie Richard-Le Guillou. *Histoire de l'amour, du Moyen Age à nos jours*. Toulouse: Editions Privat, 2002.

Rosenberg, Samuel N., and Hans Tischler, eds and trans. *Chansons des trouvères*. Paris: Livre de Poche, 1995.

Saint-Mard, Rémond de. *Lettres galantes et philosophiques*. Cologne: Pierre Marteau, 1721.

Sand, George. *Correspondance*. Edited by Georges Lubin. Paris: Garnier Frères, 1964–. 26 vols.

_____. *Elle et lui*. [1858] Meylan: Editions de l'Aurore, 1986.

Sollers, Philippe. *Trésor d'amour.* Paris: Gallimard, 2011.

Verdon, Jean. *Le plaisir au Moyen Age.* Paris: Librairie Académique Perrin, 1996.

Viala, Alain. *La France galante: essai historique sur une catégorie culturelle, de ses origines jusqu'à la Révolution.* Paris: Presses Universitaires de France, 2008.

Viallaneix, Paul, and Jean Ehrard. *Aimer en France, 1760–1860*, vol. 1. Clermont-Ferrand: Université de Clermont-Ferrand, 1980.

INDEX